W0114785

Advance Praise

Nistha's first-person stories make vivid the effervescence that characterizes entrepreneurship in modern India—the twists and turns, the ups and downs, the creativity and sheer exhilaration. Read and enjoy!

Tarun Khanna
Jorge Paulo Lemann Professor, Harvard Business School;
Director, Lakshmi Mittal South Asia Institute, Harvard University

Entrepreneurs rarely open up as candidly as Nistha has gotten them to. Kudos to her.

Allwin Agnel
Founder/CEO at PaGaLGuY.com

Indian start-up ecosystem needs relatable inspiration, and this book brings that. While it is fascinating to read about Jobs, Musk, Gates and Zuckerberg, our entrepreneurs can learn more from home-grown entrepreneurs whose challenges and approaches are more relevant to our business models. I was especially fascinated to read the story of Girish Mathrubootham.

Balaji Viswanathan
CEO at Invento; Most followed writer on Quora

A fascinating peep into the struggles and successes of varied start-ups that lucidly brings out the diversity of experiences and provides a nuanced introduction to entrepreneurial processes.

Rakesh Basant
Professor of Economics, IIM Ahmedabad

This is a 'must-read' for all entrepreneurs. Nistha has truly captured an authentic perspective of what it takes to build companies in India!

Prashant Mehta
Partner, Lightbox

I worked with Nistha for several years—she has a tremendous intellect and a fearless entrepreneurial spirit. This will be a fun read!

Ken Wilson
CEO, Tower Research Capital Markets

The Indian flavour of entrepreneurship is as creative, vibrant and colourful as the country itself. Part textbook and part tour guide, *No Shortcuts* captures that flavour in a way that delivers both generalizable lessons and insights into the unique character of Indian entrepreneurs in their environment.

Stuart Read
Professor, Willamette University

Entrepreneurship can be a lonely journey, and while every entrepreneur learns valuable lessons each day, not everyone's story comes out to inspire others. These stories are important for all aspiring entrepreneurs in the journey. Nistha has done a great job there. A must-read!

Ashish Tulsian
CEO at POSist

NO
SHORTCUTS

NO
SHORTCUTS

Rare Insights From
15 SUCCESSFUL
Start-up Founders

NISTHA
TRIPATHI

Los Angeles | London | New Delhi
Singapore | Washington DC | Melbourne

First published in 2018 by

SAGE Publications India Pvt Ltd
B1/I-1 Mohan Cooperative Industrial Area
Mathura Road, New Delhi 110 044, India
www.sagepub.in

SAGE Publications Inc
2455 Teller Road
Thousand Oaks, California 91320, USA

SAGE Publications Ltd
1 Oliver's Yard, 55 City Road
London EC1Y 1SP, United Kingdom

SAGE Publications Asia-Pacific Pte Ltd
3 Church Street
#10-04 Samsung Hub
Singapore 049483

Published by Vivek Mehra for SAGE Publications India Pvt Ltd, typeset in 11/14 pt Adobe Garamond by Fidus Design Pvt. Ltd, Chandigarh and printed at Chaman Enterprises, New Delhi.

Library of Congress Cataloging-in-Publication Data
Name: Tripathi, Nistha, author.
Title: No shortcuts: rare insights from 15 successful start-up founders / Nistha Tripathi.
Description: Thousand Oaks : SAGE Publications India Pvt Ltd, [2018]
Identifiers: LCCN 2018033750 (print) | LCCN 2018036273 (ebook) | ISBN 9789352808274 (E pub 2.0) | ISBN 9789352808281 (Web (PDF) | ISBN 9789352808267 (print (pb))
Subjects: LCSH: New business enterprises—Case studies. | Entrepreneurship—Case studies.
Classification: LCC HD62.5 (ebook) | LCC HD62.5 .T757 2018 (print) | DDC 658.1/1—dc23
LC record available at https://lccn.loc.gov/2018033750

ISBN: 978-93-528-0826-7 (PB)

SAGE Team: Manisha Mathews, Apoorva Mathur, Shobana Paul and Rajinder Kaur

To the entrepreneurs—for keeping it interesting
To the spouses of the above—for ~~tolerating~~ supporting them
To the investors—for adding to the chaos
To the others—for consuming what they create and populating the market
To the reader—for skipping TV to read this
To HBO—for delaying Game of Thrones and giving me time to finish the book this year

Thank you for choosing a SAGE product!
If you have any comment, observation or feedback,
I would like to personally hear from you.

Please write to me at **contactceo@sagepub.in**

Vivek Mehra, Managing Director and CEO, SAGE India.

Table of Contents

Foreword

I was happy when Nistha approached me to write this foreword—happy because for all that has been said about Indian start-ups in the media, blogs and other books, there is no concise volume of the journey of so many start-ups that budding entrepreneurs and people wanting to join can refer to and learn from.

Painstakingly compiled for over two years, here are the stories of how Girish of Freshworks builds his marketing, by using experimentation as a primary driver; or how Jaydeep of Faasos hires, by telling people a few years into their dream job, 'now that you know this is not what you thought it was, come here'; and many other gems which are worth more than the weight of this book in gold.

However, before you get into Nistha's work, let me help set some context on why now is one of the greatest times to start up.

Since the first significant wave of Indian start-ups in 2008, till 2017, one question loomed large: Will those who invest their efforts and money ever see a return? This was an important question because US$20 billion+ had been invested in these start-ups, and thousands had quit their jobs in prestigious companies to work out of cramped rooms, giving birth to their dreams. Famous old economy entrepreneurs wrote blogs and gave interviews stating that there was an element of madness to the whole thing, and that the survival of such business models was questionable. The mainstream Indian newspapers during those years screamed the likes off, 'huge cash burn at start-ups' and 'another start-up shuts down', and further supported these headlines with stories of investors fleeing the fledgling start-up ecosystem.

Flee they did. The year 2016 totalled significantly lower investments in start-ups than 2015, from US$9 to 4.5 billion. Valuations of many large and iconic start-ups came down. Fewer people left their sunny offices to embrace the missionary life of a start-up.

Even the government seemed worried and introduced taxes such as Angel Tax and E-commerce Tax, and tried to stop the functioning of many new innovative models. This gloom continued into 2017.

For those who understand it, both a start-up and investing in them are a J-curve business. The company starts and soon runs into rough weather as it attempts to grow. Its value falls and thereby its very survival is threatened (many don't make it). This is the left side of the J. It then travels at this low for some time. This is the bottom of the J. Then the passionate, talented and driven founder behind the start-up figures out how to make it work. The business thereafter moves to the right side of the J and begins to climb steadily upwards, and finally that reaches great heights.

By the middle of 2017, Indian start-ups, after their hard learnings, had moved to the right side of the J, emerging stronger and were set for a long and consistent growth. Money flow into them resumed, totalling US$13 billion of investments in 2017, and people again started leaving comfortable jobs to explore their dreams. Parallelly, the Indian IPO market started to grow, with 153 IPOs of US$11.6 billion.

In 2018, we are firmly travelling up the right side of the J-curve as a whole. Big boom events such as Walmart–Flipkart doing a US$16 billion transaction, Ola expanding aggressively overseas, and heavy funding at mid-stages into start-ups such as Pharmeasy, Sharechat and Bira are testimony to this. The market has also significantly grown, thanks to Jio, UPI, Aadhaar and the generally growing awareness. Massive inflows into mutual funds, as Indians move their savings from real estate and gold to SIPs, will likely keep the IPO market robust and listed valuations rich, allowing for strong exits.

It is in this second coming of the Indian start-up ecosystem that this book has arrived. If you are a start-up entrepreneur, wanting to start up or join a start-up, I wish you the best of luck and happy reading of this little treasure you hold in your hands.

Rehan Yar Khan
Managing Partner,
Orios Venture Partners

Introduction

You know start-ups have become a mainstream phenomenon when Indian families start looking for a son-in-law who is an entrepreneur. We have come a long way from terming it 'doing your own business' to calling it a start-up in India. For me, a 'start-up' is the ultimate expression of who the entrepreneur is and what he values. Although many institutes study the *science* behind building a successful start-up, I was curious about the *art* behind it. So I decided to understand it from those who were committed to building something irrespective of the outcome. For this, I picked 15 courageous, willing and patient founders from India. I am sharing their stories in this book.

What makes me think that I can attempt a book on such a fuzzy subject? What traits do I have to qualify as a worthy writer of such a book? Amidst these valid doubts, a tiny voice in my head speaks up. I realize that I have a very important qualification for writing this book—I tried creating three ventures that bombed. *I tried and failed*. I had read *The Lean Startup, Zero to One* and many other famous Silicon Valley books. See, I did validation by running Google ads for a fashion rental business in India, and there were people who gave me their email addresses. Then why did my venture die before finding those customers? I knew what questions to ask a successful entrepreneur precisely because I had failed many a time before finding a glimmer of success in the fourth one. I had that hunger and curiosity, and I had the courage to fail. But clearly, I did not have something that had made other people succeed. And that itself was a motivation to write this book. So here I am, my dear reader, venturing on this journey on your behalf and, of course, my own.

I did interview after interview, or rather, conversations. These founders are used to giving interviews. But I wanted the real story, so we chatted. And some gems, hidden even to their own self, fell out. I gathered those and placed them on these pages. Being well aware of the perils of the narrative bias, I refrained from tainting these conversations with my interpretations. There is another reason why I eschewed coming up with a 'how-to' framework for start-ups—these interviews show how contradictory different approaches have been.

Prasanna Sankar (LikeALittle) makes a convincing case as to why lean start-ups and growth hacking do not work, abetted by Tarun Mehta's (Ather Energy) disbelief in over-pivoting. Amit Ranjan (SlideShare) and Paras Chopra's (Wingify) success, on the contrary, shows what good pivoting can do. Varun Aggarwal (Aspiring Minds) and Girish Mathrubootham (Freshworks) lend their authority to the belief that fundraising is important, while Sameer Guglani (Madhouse) argues as to why it can be dangerous. Rather than being disappointed that I cannot find a common thread, I take delight in these apparent contradictions for that is what reality is—*messy*. In fact, this delicious messiness, lack of a framework, subjective nature of stories and individual convictions that clash with each other add to the final feeling of awe that I experienced upon finishing this book. I have every hope to transfer this feeling to the reader.

As Truman Capote said, 'Failure is the condiment that gives success its flavor'; how can this book be complete without talking about failure? So we have the nail-biting story of Prasanna from LikeALittle that did not end in a successful exit. What it shows is... well, I would rather have you read it to find out! Plus, the word 'success' is subjective. Sameer Guglani (Madhouse) considers Madhouse to be a massive success in terms of learning, albeit the financial returns were trivial.

As I started gathering the stories, it took a long time before I found Tarun Mehta (Ather Energy) for talking about hardware start-ups. In my conversation with Mr Sanjeev Malhotra, CEO of the Nasscom CoE-IOT (Center of Excellence for IOT [Internet of Things]) product accelerator, he highlights government efforts in this direction including a state-of-the-art lab for testing hardware products, discounted consultancy for how to design or manufacture your product, networking/mentors and a structured curriculum for IOT training in colleges.

Further insights came from Vikram Rastogi who runs Hacklab that provides incubation and business assistance to hardware product entrepreneurs working on solar tech, intelligent systems, sensor networks, IOT devices, etc. While some hardware founders have managed to get strategic partners such as Amruth Puttappa for his solar grid-tie inverter, there are others who are frustrated with the lack of support and investment in India. For a country that built the Mars Orbiter Mission, Mangalyaan, in just 11 per cent of the cost of NASA, one expects more. The potential is still untapped.

Another category I struggled with was a woman-led start-up. I wish that in my next book, I would have the pleasure of interviewing strong business women and that the set of choices would be significantly larger.

My search then led me to Indian founders in Silicon Valley, and I interviewed two of them—Prasanna Sankar (LikeALittle) and Ankit Gupta (Pulse). During the book research phase, I also encountered other serial entrepreneurs who had tried a couple of ventures in India with decent commercial success before deciding to head to London and Silicon Valley. I cannot help wondering why, in so many cases, does the founder discover his true passion or talent in a foreign land?

Can we improve entrepreneurship in India by fortifying our academic hallways? Can we nurture Stanford's and Harvard's entre-preneurial ecosystem in Indian universities? Professor Rakesh Basant from IIM Ahmedabad shares how the A-league consortium (including the premier business, design and technology institutes in Ahmedabad and Gandhinagar areas) is inspired by the culture of Silicon Valley schools. The idea is to facilitate multidisciplinary collaboration among students—which is what the essence of entrepreneurship is. The role of good design in the success of the Pulse app, which was developed on Stanford campus, is evident. Perhaps, by encouraging students from NID (National Institute of Design), IIMA, IIT Gandhinagar, etc., to come together and work as a team, we can take baby steps towards a similar culture in India.

All in all, this book tells stories of intellect and audacity. These stories have a lot to be read between the lines, for what is left unsaid is as critical as what is said. These entrepreneurs, so disjointed in their backgrounds, journeys and even motivations, are unsurprisingly united in their doggedness. What catches one's attention is how similar these stories are to something that you may have heard about a classmate or neighbour who nearly made it but didn't. If not for the stubborn tenacity, a few fortuitous turns of events or a flash of inspiration, many of the people featured here would remain on the reader's side.

As Paul Graham said,

'In fact I suspect if you had the sixteen-year-old Shakespeare or Einstein in school with you, they'd seem impressive, but not totally unlike your other friends. Which is an uncomfortable thought. If they were just like us, then they had to work very hard to do what they did. And that's one reason we like to believe in genius. It gives us an excuse for being lazy. If these guys were able to do what they did only because of some magic Shakespeareness or Einsteinness, then it's not our fault if we can't do something as good.'[1]

The crux is not to undermine what these individuals have been able to achieve but to feel encouraged that others can reach there too. *You can reach there too.*

During the writing of the book, I got to see the personal side of these founders for which I am grateful. It was an honour to take them down the memory lane and get them to recount what it was like in those days when they did not know what would happen with their ideas or ventures, when they were simply trying to survive and then thrive. In sharing such candid details about their ventures, they have undoubtedly shared the wealth of their hard-earned lessons. Their wisdom and perspicacity were expected to shine through, but it was their humility that made this book-writing exercise extremely gratifying for me.

---

[1] What You'll Wish You'd Known (Jan 2005). Available at http://www.paulgraham.com/hs.html, accessed on 8 August 2018.

In the end, I am an education counsellor who advises students to understand their career goals first and then chalk out a path to get there. Entrepreneurship, on the other hand, works in the reverse. As effectuation principle[2] and few seers imply, it is better to start with what you have, leverage what you know and work towards the best option. In the process, learn and keep the company of smart people. But I am not going to oversimplify it. After all, I know how hard it is, and that is why instead of some smartass advice that means only a little, I offer you this book and stories of people who got something right in their own words. What you get out of it is determined by your own state of mind. A poet seeks *sahrdaya* (having their hearts with it) in her readers. I seek *sahmanas* (having their mind with it) in the readers of this book.

May it find a place in your bookshelf for an inspiration, repeated reference and, above all, a reminder of your own possibilities. *Remember, you can reach there too!*

---

[2] See http://www.effectuation.org/sites/default/files/research_papers/what-makes-entrepreneurs-entrepreneurial-sarasvathy_0.pdf, accessed on 24 May 2018.

How to Use This Book?

This book is a collection of interviews that cover the journeys of some of the most interesting and successful founders from India. The focus is leaning a tad bit towards the early one to four years of the start-up. Founders share their thought processes and actions as they built their first business. Rather than talking in hindsight, the narrative follows the sequence of events that unfolded and decisions that were taken—what, how and why. For the reader, this can act as a compendium of the start-up advice and the cautionary tales. Not meant to be an end-to-end read, this book is best studied interview by interview in your preferred order. And then, keep it as a handy reference so that you can pick it up again when you are contemplating your own venture or for advice around a specific business problem you are facing.

Table 1 Summary of the Backgrounds of the Leading Entrepreneur Featured in Each Interview

Entrepreneur	Year of Founding	Age at the Time of Founding	Professional Background Before Starting Up	Current Status of the Start-up
Ankur Singla (Akosha)	2009	26	Lawyer	Pivoted to Helpchat in 2015 and Tapzo in 2016
Varun Aggarwal (Aspiring Minds)	2008	25	MS student at MIT	Raised US$500,000 angel and undisclosed amount in Series A till June 2017
Tarun Mehta (Ather Energy)	2013	23	Deputy manager (automobile)	Raised US$43 million till June 2017

Entrepreneur	Year of Founding	Age at the Time of Founding	Professional Background Before Starting Up	Current Status of the Start-up
Jaydeep Barman (Faasos)	2011	36	Management consultant	Raised US$50 million till June 2017
Nikhil Rasiwasia (Fashiate)	2014	31	Scientist	Acquired by Snapdeal in 2015
Girish Mathrubootham (Freshworks)	2010	35	Product manager	Raised US$149 million till June 2017
Deepak Syal (GreyB)	2007	25	Patent research associate	Bootstrapped, cash flow positive
Ankit Maheshwari (Instablogs)	2005	25	Software engineer	Sold in parts in 2012
Prasanna Sankar (LikeALittle)	2010	23	Software engineer	Pivoted away and then shut down, Prasanna left it in 2013
Sameer Guglani (Madhouse)	2004	27	Software engineer	Acquired by SeventyMM in 2007
Ankit Gupta (Pulse)	2010	23	MS student at Stanford	Acquired by LinkedIn for US$90 million in 2013
Amit Ranjan (SlideShare)	2006	32	Accounts manager (FMCG)	Acquired by LinkedIn for US$118 million in 2012
Paras Chopra (Wingify)	2009	22	Software engineer	Bootstrapped, cash flow positive
Gaurav Munjal (Unacademy)	2015	24	Software engineer	Raised US$18 million till July 2017
Nithin Kamath (Zerodha)	2010	31	Telesales executive and trader	Bootstrapped, cash flow positive

Apart from Unacademy, which is Gaurav Munjal's third start-up, all other interviews cover the first major start-up of the respective founders. This is to ensure that we get the lessons they learnt when they started from scratch.

Interviews are tagged with a set of start-up functions that the interview talks the most about, their industry and current status. For example, if you are seeking advice or context on pricing, you can read the Pulse interview first. If you are looking for a successful bootstrapped start-up, you can look at Zerodha. If you are thinking of building a food tech start-up, you can start with Faasos and so on.

Many readers will find it helpful to know what the start-up is about and how it is doing before reading the full interview. A full description is available at the beginning of each interview for this purpose. To begin with, please read those first and then pick up the one that interests you most. I have taken utmost care in covering interesting non-repetitive details so that each interview adds something new to your understanding. In other words, make sure you read them all. The takeaways in the end are not a summary of the interview but are points worth highlighting.

I have added a couple of more categorizations of interviews by industry and their current status here.

Categorization by industry:

- Analytics: Aspiring Minds and Wingify
- Automobile/Hardware: Ather Energy
- Food: Faasos
- E-commerce: Fashiate
- Business software: Freshworks
- Media-sharing platforms: Unacademy, Pulse and SlideShare
- Entertainment and content: Madhouse, Instablogs
- Social media: LikeALittle
- Fintech: Zerodha
- Internet services: Akosha and GreyB

Categorization by current status and end results:

- Venture backed and acquired

  - SlideShare: Acquired by LinkedIn for US$118 million in 2012
  - Pulse: Acquired by LinkedIn for US$90 million in 2013
  - Madhouse: Acquired by SeventyMM in 2007
  - Fashiate: Acquired by Snapdeal in 2015
  - Instablogs: Sold in parts in 2012

- Bootstrapped and cash flow positive

  - Zerodha
  - Wingify
  - GreyB

- Venture backed and still running

  - Freshworks
  - Unacademy
  - Faasos
  - Ather Energy
  - Aspiring Minds

- Venture backed and pivoted away

  - Akosha: Pivoted to Helpchat in 2015 and then Tapzo in 2016
  - LikeALittle: Pivoted to Circle app in 2012, which is no longer in existence; Prasanna Sankar left it in 2013

Disclaimer: The factual information contained in the interviews are as supplied by the founders, and the author has included the same in good faith. The author or the publisher assume no responsibility for any discrepancy. However, please report errors (if any) to the author on www.startupbookindia.com.

A Note on the Interviewees

The diversity among the founders selected for the interviews is, perhaps, a good representation of the demographics of Indian entrepreneurial founders (refer to Table 1). Most of them hail from engineering, and that too computer science backgrounds, but have gone into more varied professional streams. Majority of the founders started their ventures when they were in their early 20s. However, the founders who started later appear to have better leveraged their experiences and showcased more polished leadership and decision-making.

Having some domain experience did put the founder at an advantage as is evident in the case of Nithin who had 10+ years of trading experience before starting Zerodha, Tarun who had significant prototyping experience before starting Ather and Girish whose Zoho product management experience was pivotal in Freshwork's success. The notable exceptions here are Jaydeep who chose the food industry and has thrived in a domain in which he had no experience but endless passion to compensate with, and Sameer Guglani who was a movie lover but had no operational experience. The bottom line is that the founders chose an area which excited them and kept them inspired to keep working even when the chips were down.

Most of the founders also highlighted the greater satisfaction they felt in building the business irrespective of the financial outcome. Notably, when Prasanna saw that LikeALittle had stopped growing exponentially, his motivation flagged—an outcome of having chased the idea of success instead of something that fundamentally excited him. It is the only commercially unsuccessful story included in the book because the lessons coming out are more powerful than some of the success stories.

In the end, it is hard to discount the luck factor as almost every founder admitted how things fell in place at a certain point in his journey. When Nikhil calls himself lucky for getting acquired within four months of thinking of an idea behind Fashiate, I feel that 'timing' would be a better explanation. Instablogs could have been a bigger success if the founders had hung on to it a bit longer, and Madhouse's premature exit can be attributed to the entry of a heavily funded competitor.

Nearly everyone hailed from a middle-class family with no heavyweight business background. So it appears that the entrepreneurial drive is not a function of upbringing alone. The itch to start was mostly innate and became irrepressible when exposed to a certain kind of environment either physically (Ankit in Stanford, Tarun in IIT and Sameer in his start-up job) or through books (Prasanna, Ankur and Paras).

Finally, I cannot help noticing a heightened sense of self-awareness in all the interviewees. The founders were acutely aware of what they lacked, and found a way or partner to compensate for it. Varun knew his limited understanding of the business and sales, and had Himanshu in his team. Ankur found a tech arrangement by trial and later through Morpheus to compensate for his non-tech background. In the cases of Deepak and Sameer, they were able to learn the missing skills. So if you think that you do not have that one factor required to succeed, don't worry—you are already halfway there. You now know what you lack. Go figure out a way to overcome that and create your own unique path to success. Who knows, my next book might feature you!

PART 1

Ideation, Validation and Pivoting

We did not know that we will get venture capital or not.
We did helpdesk because that is the only thing we knew.
— Girish Mathrubootham (Freshworks)

Every moment is a trade; you are trading whatever you believe in.
Zerodha itself is a trade to me. I am playing because I believe in my odds.
—Nithin Kamath (Zerodha)

Google Website Optimizer is very complicated and I struggled using it
myself. That was a mini light-bulb moment there. If I was finding it
difficult, other marketers must be finding it even more difficult.
—Paras Chopra (Wingify)

Our novelty was not in coming up with this idea.
But I feel what we got right was the timing and
the application of the technology for the right product.
—Nikhil Rasiwasia (Fashiate)

A successful start-up needs customers and the best way to ensure that is to identify a problem which you yourself need to resolve. Putting more than 20,000 hours in the trading sector before launching Zerodha helped Nithin to come up with right product features.

Other successful ways of starting up have been in the cases where the founder possessed an advanced understanding of the audience or the domain. The case in point is Freshdesk (now Freshworks) where Girish knew exactly what and how to build based on his helpdesk software experience, and he entered the market when users were frustrated with Zendesk. Nikhil Rasiwasia's timing with Fashiate was perfect as e-commerce was booming and technology advancement in imaging techniques was just right.

Sometimes, the starting product is there, but not quite. You will find it out in the validation phase. The founder is still looking for the product market fit, and to achieve that, the idea needs to be pivoted. Paras Chopra has the perfect pivoting story as he simplified his overly complex first prototype based on the comments on the *Hacker News*[1] website, and the users flocked to it right away.

The four start-ups mentioned in this section highlight how they found the ideas which the market responded to. That is the beauty of a right idea—the market will respond to it and you simply cannot ignore it. Apart from these four, another great pivoting story is that of Ankur Singla who was struggling to figure out the correct USP (unique selling proposition) in his legal-tech start-up, Akosha. The moment he pivoted to consumer complaints, he found the perfect product market fit.

Prasanna Sankar warns against over-pivoting with his own lessons from LikeALittle. Another founder who believes that there is no glory in pivoting every six months is Tarun Mehta. For a balanced understanding, one must additionally read these contrasting viewpoints as well.

---

[1] *Hacker News* (https://news.ycombinator.com) is a social news website focusing on entrepreneurship and run by Paul Graham's investment fund and start-up incubator, Y Combinator (YC).

If you know the enemy and know yourself, you need not fear the result of a hundred battles. If you know yourself but not the enemy, for every victory gained you will also suffer a defeat. If you know neither the enemy nor yourself, you will succumb in every battle.

—Sun Tzu, *The Art of War*

1 Girish Mathrubootham: Freshworks

Breaking the myth that Indians can only build services companies, Girish built a cloud-based customer service helpdesk, Freshdesk, which today services more than 100,000 enterprises globally (including Cisco, Verizon and Warby Parker).

Customer Service Software
#product #marketing #culture #saas

Freshdesk was founded in 2010 by the former Zoho Corp executive Girish Mathrubootham and his colleague Shan Krishnasamy after a bad customer experience on account of a broken TV. In June 2017, Freshdesk was rebranded as Freshworks to create an umbrella brand, which includes Freshservice, Freshsales, Freshcaller, Freshteam, Freshchat, etc.

Starting with personal savings of US$4 million, Girish designed a helpdesk software loaded with features that he knew mattered from his years of product experience at Zoho. These features, missing from the incumbent Zendesk software, along with aggressive pricing made Freshdesk attractive from day one. When the company won US$40,000 in the Microsoft BizSpark Startup Challenge in June 2011, Girish spent all the prize money on marketing to gain quick traction. His call proved a winner as customers flocked quickly.

With one of the fastest customer growths in India, Freshworks attracted a first round of funding worth US$1 million from Accel

Partners in December 2011. Over the last five years, Freshworks has raised US$149 million from Accel, Tiger Global, CapitalG (formerly Google Capital) and Sequoia Capital India. With multiple products such as Freshservice and Freshsales as part of its product suite today, Freshworks has over 120,000 customers. It became a Unicorn (one-billion-dollar valuation) in July 2018.

When Girish graduated with a degree in electrical engineering in 1996 without a job offer in hand, there was only one way out. 'Family and friends ask you that you have finished college and you don't have a job? So MBA actually helped save me from that question,' he reminisces. 'There were 40 seats with 12 seats for OC (open category) in Madras University and I was number 13. It so happened that somebody moved out and I got in.'

Those two years saw the metamorphosis of Girish 'the engineer' to Girish 'the dreamer'.

Riding the IT Trend

'In *BusinessWorld* and *Business India*, there is a section at the end where they profile successful businessmen. I remember dreaming with my friends that someday, we will be on those pages. After MBA, I was one of the first to get placed on the campus in a shipping company that paid ₹12,000. But I declined because it involved selling silver alloys to industrial consumers. I had read that the shipping industry was going through a downturn. I knew it was important to pick a growing industry. IT was a booming industry. So I got a small job in an IT company in their Java division. The point is, I chose that 5,000-rupee job over the bigger one.'

Next, Girish got himself a big break at the HCL Cisco Offshore Development Centre by studying Java on his own. In fact, the general manager of HCL Technologies said that they didn't have an MBA in a programming role. But Girish stuck to his belief in IT and they made an exception for him.

'In hindsight, they were right, and I was not that great a programmer. I was inclined more towards non-tech roles,' Girish laughs.

Then began a series of entrepreneurial strides. First, he tried his hand in the Amway business. Soon, he started training people in Java where he was training roughly 20 students a month. Then, amidst the dot-com boom, with a name like Cisco on his resume, Girish went to the USA through a consulting company. Not enjoying consulting, he returned to India against the advice of all his friends and got back to his training company.

However, with the dot-com bust in 2001, there were no IT jobs in demand, and his training business suffered. Except for Aptech and NIIT, everybody went down. 'While I came from the USA hoping to build a successful training franchise business, I did not want to stay in the negative environment. So I quickly shut down and joined AdventNet which is today known as Zoho.'

AdventNet (Zoho) Days

AdventNet became the grooming ground for the ultimate entrepreneur in Girish.

'I joined AdventNet as a pre-sales engineer for a telecom product called WebNMS. A pre-sales engineer is a technical consultant who answers any questions that a prospective customer may have and helps with customizations. Once the customer's questions have been answered by the pre-sales engineer, the salesperson comes and closes the deal.'

For the uninitiated, WebNMS was an OEM (original equipment manufacturer) network management system used by the networking equipment manufacturing vendors selling routers, switches, etc. AdventNet was one of the only two big players who provided software that these companies could package along with their hardware.

'Amway had taught me the power of referral and selling, and my training business helped me sharpen my articulation skills. It had made me become a better pre-sales engineer because I had to talk about the merits of the product and convince the customer.'

It was not long afterwards that Girish got bored of doing the same thing again and again. So he created 40 canned pre-sales demos based on each possible case. This freed up a lot of his time. Next, he asked his manager if he could take over marketing for other parts of the world. His manager shared a key wisdom with him. He said, 'Girish, marketing is a consultative role and you are an authoritative person. That's why you are feeling this way.' But impressed nonetheless by his initiatives, Girish's manager asked him to become a product manager and build an end-user OEM software for the company.

'So I started googling "What does product management mean?",' Girish chuckles.

Learning Product Management

'When I started as a product manager, I had to build wireframes, figure out requirements and work with pricing and all. Learning was great, and I enjoyed doing all that. I was not afraid to talk to customers or visit them because I came from pre-sales training background. Our older product was designed for developers, and we did not put much efforts into design and user interface. This time, I put a lot of focus on our interface and made sure that it was loved by our customers. And that was a very refreshing change where the entire management saw that customers complimented us on this UI (user interface). I became the champion for a product manager who focuses a lot on UI and product usage.'

Amit Ranjan (SlideShare) had mentioned that product management means complete ownership of the product, including the financial accountability. Girish does not disagree.

'When I owned this product, I felt I am the owner and CEO of the product, who is responsible for the revenue also. I am constantly thinking—if I am charging US$1,300 for my product, how can I move the price to US$2,500? If you want to play with the pricing, can you move from one-time payment to annual subscription? What part of growth should come from sales channel and what part should come from features?

There are companies where product management is run as an authoritative function responsible for P&L, etc., and there are companies like Yahoo! where it is run like a consultative function. My realization is that in Zoho, I was running it like an authoritative manager. In Freshdesk, I can see that some of our product managers are coming from a world where they were consultative product managers. They will understand building specifications and requirements very well, but they don't actually own the business unit and think of the product revenues. So now, my understanding of the organization is that you either have a P&L and product person together, or you hire a general manager that looks into P&L and have a separate head of product. It is an interesting distinction to understand and it impacts your hiring strategy. Choose whatever works for you, but understand what it means. My preference is to have a product person understand the P&L role as well, and if we don't have this person, I would like to hire a P&L person who comes from the product background.'

For Girish, getting into product management at AdventNet was like a fish finding water. Even today he considers himself to be a product manager at heart.

The SaaS Attraction

While Girish continued at AdventNet, a lot was changing in the Internet space. In 2006, the company started a SaaS business, and eventually it started gaining more and more popularity. So in 2007–2008, the company changed its name to Zoho because at least a few million customers knew the brand by Zoho and no one had heard of AdventNet.

Girish was made vice president (VP) of product management and was selling the Manage Engine division (separate from Zoho).

He moved to the USA in December 2007 and spent 1.5 years there building their Austin office and focusing on marketing and product management. In 2008, economic recession hit the US market and hiring freezed. Girish's team was in India, and he was getting bored sitting with a small team in Austin.

'I did not like being away with a small team in the USA, managing people through emails and forums. I had become this manager guy who was just managing teams and doing conflict resolution, etc. because the team was on auto pilot. It was not very enjoyable to me. So I talked to my CEO and came back to Chennai in June 2009. If SaaS is going to be the future, then it means that a lot of the IT departments will no longer be very relevant. If you look at new age companies today, the entire infrastructure is on Amazon and I don't have that many servers or applications to manage. So the role of the IT was shrinking. See, in 1999, I had seen and ridden the Java wave. In 2001, I saw the falling market. Here again, I was seeing a rising opportunity in SaaS business. If SaaS is going to be the future, then what am I doing managing the IT divisions? That was the bigger picture. I felt it was a good time for someone like me to do something in SaaS.'

When Girish was relocating to India, he shipped his TV from the USA which reached India in a broken state. He tried emailing the insurance company 28 times over six months, submitting and re-submitting various documents to no avail. As a last resort, he posted his story on web forums, and within two days, the shipping company's president apologized and paid his insurance money. Girish was already building customer support solutions at AdventNet, and this was the moment he saw the power of social influence! Imagine—six months of back and forth versus two days of a complaint on a social website.

While this situation had already made its impression on Girish, he read an article on *Hacker News* (a popular forum created by Y Combinator or YC) about Zendesk raising their prices by 60–300 per cent that caused a rising wrath among their customers. The following comment from a user named 'megamark' caught his attention:

'Here's a potential customer to whosoever can get this right at the right price. It seems like there's still a huge opening in this market for someone to come in and take all of Zendesk and eSupport's customers.'

This was too much to ignore for someone who was already caught in the scene. Right then, he decided to build something in the customer support market delivered as SaaS.

The Birth of Freshdesk

'The *Hacker News* post showed that Zendesk was the only cloud-based help-desk at that time, and was not working out too well for its users. I knew that helpdesk is not a new market. It is quite a mature market. The only thing is everyone thinks of it as an email-based support. The opportunity that we were able to spot was to bring the social support as well. It was more of an idea but I am the kind of person who cannot do 10 things. When I am into something, I am into it full time. The more I thought and researched about it, the more I got excited. I went and told my boss that this is something I plan to do and, therefore, I quit towards end of 2010.'

Girish asked his colleague Shaan to join him, and he immediately agreed. They started working on the software in October 2010, but instead of starting from scratch, they bought an existing software with the basic functionality of getting an email and converting it to a ticket.

'It was called Helpkit or something, and somebody was selling it for US$400. It didn't matter that in next three months, Shaan rewrote the whole thing. It gave us a good start. Right from day one, we had something that we could see in action.'

As the popular *gyaan* goes, one should validate an idea before building something. But Girish had built four helpdesks before starting Freshdesk. He knew the market inside out.

'We did not know that we will get venture capital or not. We did helpdesk because that is the only thing we knew. So we did not seek market validation or show our prototype to others.'

Let us understand how the customer support software actually worked. Every company usually has a support@companyname.com email address. Freshdesk asked them to forward that to a unique address generated by Freshdesk. For example, if HDFC is signing up, they would get a unique address like support@hdfc.freshdesk.com. They simply had to forward their customer emails to this unique address, and Freshdesk would automatically create a ticket. HDFC support staff could just log in to the Freshdesk dashboard and see all the tickets.

Freshdesk began a round of quick hiring, and by December, they had been joined by two more people—a developer and a designer. Then, by February, another developer and a customer support person joined. Even though Girish did not have the product ready, he knew a support personnel would be useful. Till the product was ready, Girish asked him to play the role of a QA (quality auditor). After the release, he became their support and pre-sales person.

Early Customer Acquisition and Marketing Channels

Where Freshdesk stands apart from its peers is in its mind-bending growth. It acquired 100 customers in the first 100 days! A lot of it had to do with Girish's aggressive mindset. Freshdesk had won US$40,000 of prize money in the Microsoft BizSpark India Startup Challenge in June 2011. At that point, the company had a runway for 18 months because everyone was taking minimal salaries and office expenses were low. In fact, Girish and Shaan were not taking any salary. When this prize money came in, the founders had not planned for it.

'Conventional wisdom said that we should keep it for the runway. But what I knew was that our success depended on finding a scalable customer acquisition channel. So I spent all that money on different marketing experiments. We tried out all the channels. The bad news was that we lost a lot of money but the good news was that we figured out which channels were working. Google AdWords turned out to be very expensive. Instead, we found something called BuySellAds.com. It was a long tail of designer blogs which allowed us to put in US$50–100 of budget in multiple websites. Even today, I would say that those were the most efficient customers we acquired. US$20 per month would give us 40 leads, which is 50 cents per lead which is very very low.'

The Tricky Issue of SaaS Pricing

In the *Hacker News* thread, the biggest complaint that people had with Zendesk was the price point. So that was one obvious area that Freshdesk focused on. Zendesk's starting price was US$29, while Freshdesk's highest plan was US$29. Zendesk had a small starter plan for three users for US$10, but the moment you had a fourth user, you had to pay US$29 four times per month! Freshdesk introduced plans for US$9, US$19 and US$29, and offered a 30-day trial period.

'In those days, we did not even have a salesperson. We would just wait for them to contact us at the end of the trial.'

SaaS pricing has always been a tricky topic. Entrepreneurs are often not clear on how much to price their products.

'Our initial philosophy was—leave money on the table and give customers a great experience. Gradually, we introduced US$49 and US$79 plans. The idea was to add more features and then introduce higher plans. There was an interesting experiment around our freemium plans. Initially in 2012, we introduced our first freemium plan that kept the first agent free on all plans. That didn't really work because if someone has only one agent, then they can just use the email and have no need for the software. In February 2013, we revamped to say that we are giving away US$9 plan for free which had support for three agents. And we removed the "first agent free" clause from other plans. So for advanced features, businesses had to pay right from the first agent. This worked very well because we managed to separate the users—whoever wanted basic support could use the free version and we did not put too many limits. Budget-conscious customers were happy with that, and it gave us lot of adoption and visibility. What we did was that we added our branding on these free customers. In all their support emails, it said "powered by Freshdesk". And when they shared their knowledge-base article on Twitter, etc., it had the Freshdesk URL as well.'

Understanding the Target Customer and Building Features That Mattered

All the blogs that Girish found from BuySellAds.com were targeting the web designers and developers, and the small companies who provided services to other businesses. Now, since Freshdesk wanted to support B2B (business-to-business) customers, they had built some features for that kind of audience. For example, a time-tracking feature where they could bill the customer at the end of the month and so on. They also offered integration with QuickBooks which is an invoicing system. With all this, the product started attracting one set of customers initially, and Girish's team kept making it better and better for them. Their banner ads would talk about customer support software on these blogs, and those who clicked would find out that this Freshdesk software was super affordable!

When asked about conversion, Girish chuckles.

'In those days, we were not even measuring the conversions. We did not set up the complete lead tracking. One thing I can tell you is that the moment we put the first salesperson in May 2012 and told him to call everybody who had signed up, our revenue doubled.'

It might seem that Freshdesk was mainly competing on price, but that would be a premature conclusion.

'Pricing was the main complaint, but we also did our research and went to competitors' forums and saw what other features customers were requesting.

We identified the gaps in existing solutions actively and went after that. We found some key features like multi-product support and multi-brand support that were missing in those days. So the first thing we did was to build the multi-brand support. Many a time, even start-ups and small sites have two brands. They want the same team to support both those brands. We were probably the only helpdesk at that point to do that. That helped bring new customers in the initial days. At that time, we were playing catch up. People wanted an iPhone app, people wanted integration with Salesforce, etc., and we just had to keep building those.'

I saw a Quora post where someone had commented, 'The most amazing thing you'll realize about Girish is how well he knows his market.' How did he reach this point?

'I think what that post is referring to is that I have run a customer support myself for seven to eight years at Zoho. The SaaS was the new angle, but we were building a product that we were comfortable with. I already knew some of the problems and what the customer wants. For example, a customer is generally okay if you come back with the solution in 24 hours rather than going back and forth three times to find the solution. That's when the customer starts getting frustrated. So we built features in Freshdesk to address such situations. For example, we had a feature called "supervisor" whereby if any issue goes back and forth for more than three times, it gets escalated to a more knowledgeable agent. This really resonated well with our audience. When we gave demos, people would say that, "Hey, I can see that you guys clearly understand this space of customer support". That was the consistent feedback we got.'

Handling Global Sales

Freshdesk's first customer was a college in Australia. They bought the US$19 plan and had three agents. They are still with Freshdesk. Cisco was their 30,000th customer. They already had Verizon and Warby Parker accounts by then. People find it difficult to sell globally when sitting in India. How did Freshdesk manage to get so many global customers?

'So many things are difficult, right? If Uber is running in India, they face a different set of problems. When people say entrepreneurship is about taking risks, I say that it is about minimizing the number of risks that you take so that you can increase your chances of success. We chose to build a helpdesk because that is what we knew. We started working from a small office because we wanted to reduce cost and increase our runway. We knew that we can sell from Chennai and we were not talking to big enterprises, we were talking to SMBs. If you play to your strengths, you increase your chances at success. In any of these accounts, it started with somebody in one department trying us out.'

Zendesk probably did not imagine that a small start-up is going to come and pull out the rug beneath its feet. A particularly tensed moment occurred when Zendesk's CEO made aggressive comments about Freshdesk being a 'rip-off'. Girish retorted with a full article on how they compare against Zendesk features and pricing, and why Freshdesk is better.

'Well, we are competitors and there is no personal rivalry. The thing is we constantly see each other in every deal we compete for. What we have done with Zendesk story is that if someone comes to fight with us, we are more than ready to fight in the right way.'

Funding Timeline and the Need for Fundraising

Girish had a small angel round of US$50,000 from his friends and added his personal saving to the tune of ₹35–40 lakh while starting Freshdesk. On 18 March 2011, he participated in an AppSumo blog competition where one had to write a blog post on how their start-up is a lean start-up. There was US$50,000 worth of prize money. That is when he wrote that blog post on how he quit his job and how a simple comment on *Hacker News* gave rise to his start-up.[2] As soon as he posted that on *Hacker News*, it went viral. On 19 March, Freshdesk got 30,000 visitors to the website and 175 sign-ups.

'In total, we had 300 sign-ups from that post. One of the things I had done in the blog post was to thank a few people who were helpful. One such person was Naval Ravikant from Venture Hacks and he was just starting AngelList. Naval said, "Why don't you put your company profile on AngelList?" So I did that. He approved the post and till this date, I think we are the only Indian company who have raised funds successfully using AngelList. Anand Daniel who was in Accel saw that post and was the first one to reach out to us. I sent the pitch deck to him, and eventually, we put out a public beta in May. On 7 June we launched the product, got our first customer on 10th, and by 28th we had six customers from four different countries. So Accel was able to see us grow from public beta with zero customers to 70 customers in two months from all around the world. At that time, our monthly recurring revenue was only US$2,100.'

In June 2011, Freshdesk won the Microsoft BizSpark competition. Within one or two months, they received the US$1 million funding from Accel.

'Series A term sheet was actually signed on 28 August 2011 and the money came in October. We only announced it on 1 December. And Zendesk rip-off article came out on 2 December. So they thought we were small fish until we raised money, and they thought we would not matter. The moment we got the funding is when they attacked us.'

On Quora, Girish has written,

'I have first-hand experience working with Shekhar Kirani of Accel (he is on our board at Freshdesk) and he is also new to venture capital. I think Freshdesk was his first deal. Of all the VCs (venture capitalist) I have interacted with, I would rate Shekhar as one of the best.'

---

[2] See https://blog.freshdesk.com/the-freshdesk-story-how-a-simple-comment-on-h-0/, accessed on 24 May 2018.

He elaborates what attracted him towards Shekhar.

'When Accel was talking to us, another investor was giving us US$500,000 for a smaller dilution. Accel was giving us US$1 million, and a third investor offered us US$2 million but at a much higher dilution, so we did not want that. While we were debating internally as to what to do, my team made an interesting remark. They said that Girish, we think you should take money from Shekhar (Accel). I asked why. They said, "With other investors, you are talking and they are listening but Shekhar is constantly pushing you and asking tough questions. We think you also need someone to push you". So I think that was a good feedback and that's how we decided to go ahead with Accel.'

It is good to see an entrepreneur being selective and having the luxury of choosing a venture capital firm. That says as much about Freshdesk's robust business as it does about Girish's values. One wonders what kind of hard questions were asked!

'I don't remember that much right now but it was something along the lines of "Who are your initial customers?", "Where are they coming from?" and "Why is it attractive for them?" Since our product was not built for a specific segment in mind, we were acquiring customers through search queries, etc. In that, we are different from let's say Hotelogix, which is built specifically for hotels. For us, it is more of a generic support software that anybody can use. Therefore, Shekhar's questions were valid and made us think harder. On that point, I do think that it is better to let the product run on discovery mode initially, but later you want to start understanding what is working better so that you can double down on the right segments. His questions made us think more about the market.'

From bad valuation to the pressurizing board meetings, start-up streets are littered with stories of founder–VC marriages gone wrong. Girish mentions what he values in a VC.

'A lot of VCs look at projections and Excel but they don't understand the business well. Shekhar spent a lot of time understanding the business, market, exactly why the customer was buying our software and so on. This was important to me. He was someone I would go to for advice.'

Later, when Tiger Global funding happened in 2012, they commissioned a comprehensive survey of all Freshdesk customers (approximately 214 customers). Around 80–100 customers responded.

'We asked questions were like—what do you like about Freshdesk, what you don't like, features you want, etc. Pretty much, the report came out very very strongly in our favour. The only thing that people wanted was missing features like building an iPhone app and all. So Tiger realized that if this company has funding, they can build these things.'

Things like this made Freshdesk attractive to the VCs from the beginning, and the company never faced problems in fundraising.

Fundraising versus Bootstrapping

Girish hails from Zoho, which is famous for growing without ever taking venture capital money. When asked about bootstrapping, Girish has a clear opinion.

'Zoho started in 1996 as AdventNet, selling initial products to telecom vendors at price ranging from US$250,000–500,000. So it was a very different phase. The manage engine product that I managed was also an on-premise software which would sell for anywhere between US$3,000 to US$30,000. A lot of cash flow was being generated by the time the SaaS business was started. But in SaaS business, a customer pays monthly. A customer who pays me US$30 per month may cost me US$300 to acquire. He will become profitable for me only after 10 months. So if I don't have lot of money to begin with, my growth will be limited. If I have US$100,000 and I grow organically, it is a slow growth path.

Bootstrapping can work if you are in a relatively new market, where you have some monopolistic advantage with a strong defensible product. For example, one of my good friends is Ritesh of BrowserStack. He is running that kind of a business where he doesn't have a lot of competition, and there is word-of-mouth marketing and pricing power. So he can continue bootstrapping. But in my case, since Zendesk had already raised money, investors who had not invested in it were looking for its alternatives. If we had not taken money, they would have invested in one of our competitors. Each business is very different, and therefore, you need to evaluate the situation based on maturity of the market, availability of the customers, how many established players are there, etc. Once there are three to four established players, it is hard for others to get funding also. In that sense, what we did in hindsight was correct. If we had not taken money, we could not have been this successful and some other helpdesk would have been funded.'

Building a Workplace That Employees Love

The Internet is full of Freshdesk employees raving about its culture. What are the few key things that make Freshdesk a great place to work?

'I will summarize it in two words—operational freedom. We need to inspire people to work and we make sure we hire the right kind of people, and by that I don't mean IIT/IIM only. We try to find natural talent. So somebody who enjoys talking should be in sales, and somebody who is empathetic and has attention to detail should be in support; somebody creative should be in marketing and it doesn't matter what degree they have. Reality in India is that most people do BE in computer science for their parents' sake, but they might like to do other stuff. Once we identify the right talent, we put them in roles which unlock their potential. We don't believe in making them work. Our job as coaches is to help them flourish. And if it means switching to some other department, that is fine, and even if means switching to another company, so be it. We treat it very professionally.'

There was a phase when start-ups were paying ridiculous salaries. Instead of short-term poaching, Girish values building a culture that helps attract good talent in a competitive start-up landscape.

'We never paid those salaries. There is a story of our employee that I should share. One person went to Housing.com for 2.5 times the salary he was making with us. We had just identified him as a good designer from a small company, and even before he could contribute to one of our products, Housing.com offered him this salary because he had put "product designer at Freshdesk" in his LinkedIn profile. Now he is back with us.

I will tell you another story. There was another guy and there was this start-up that had raised US$20 million recently. This start-up offered him the role of talent acquisition at twice the salary he was getting from us. Not only that, as he was deciding on what to do, they kept increasing the salary. Finally, he accepted their offer but he came to meet me on his last day to say goodbye. He said, "G, I am saying goodbye but please continue to be my mentor". So I said that since you are calling me your mentor, let me share my views. I was telling him that there is quite a lot of negativity around how venture capital funds are being used in the ecosystem. The reason why Ola Cabs or Uber can charge so low on their rides is the venture capital that the independent cab driver does not have. So I told this guy that what is happening with your offer is the same thing. The reason this company is offering you so much can be that they are thinking that since you are in HR, they can access all Freshdesk people through you. He said, "I would never do that". So I said, "Think about it. As the CEO, if I have paid you so much money and I ask you to do this, what would you do? That CEO has raised US$20 million, so he is doing it". By that time, I had raised US$95 million and I could have played this game much more aggressively, but I believe that you have to compete in a fair manner. Should all the bootstrapped start-ups die because we are funded? Everyone should then start poaching but this is not how we can work. You have to be a responsible player. Anyway, long story short, the person did not end up leaving us and stayed in Freshdesk.'

Throughout the interview, Girish's gravitas clearly shows, which has come from years of toil. His dream of being featured on business magazines has already come true. And so have many other dreams. What has been the biggest challenge for him while building Freshdesk?

'I would say building the culture is the hardest thing to do. When you are just focusing on growth and revenue, building culture and caring for people can take a backseat. As a VC-funded company, we need to make sure we are growing fast but also scaling the culture at the right pace. Getting the team to work as one team as more people join is the biggest challenge.'

Fond Memories

If one had to find a movie industry parallel for Girish, it would probably be Rajnikanth (who incidentally is a personal hero of his), given the kind of adulation that he inspires in the start-up fraternity today. But he fondly remembers the days before he became the posterchild of Indian entrepreneurship.

'Between October 2010 and September 2011, six of us were living together, eating together. There was just one restaurant in that area. We went there daily, brought the meal and ate back at our office. In those days, there were long power cuts, like two hours per day. We had to choose between using the power backup for our laptops or for the fans and lights. We chose to keep the Internet and laptops running. It became unbearably hot; that's when we bought the generator. Those were the early days which were real fun. We used to take breaks together and spent time talking and dreaming about how it will pan out. But none of us thought that it would become so big.'

Girish winning Microsoft BizSpark India Startup Challenge 2011

Girish's Book Recommendations

- *First, Break All the Rules* by Curt Coffman and Marcus Buckingham

- *Every Business Is a Growth Business* by Ram Charan
- *Execution* by Lawrence Bossidy and Ram Charan

Key Takeaways

Person

- *Picking macro trends:* Girish went for what he thought is the next big wave and succeeded twice in riding those.
- *Singular focus:* Girish started Freshdesk full time with a clear conviction and dedication. His ability to start quickly and market aggressively with Microsoft BizSpark money paid dividends by getting early traction.

Product

- *Building on a clear opportunity:* Girish systematically built a product when customers were unhappy with the leading player, Zendesk.
- *Leveraging team experience:* Girish chose to build a customer care software because he had the experience of building four helpdesk software prior to Freshdesk.
- *Going to market quickly:* Buying a starting piece of software helped to reach the market more quickly.
- *Attacking the gaps in existing solution:* Using the requests from Zendesk customer forums, Girish incorporated features that were missing in existing helpdesks and that proved very useful in attracting early customers.
- *Starting and perfecting for one focus group before expanding:* Since small businesses were their early users, building more features (such as time-tracking) useful for them made the product popular among designers and freelancers. Expanding to other segments became easier after having a set stream of clients.

Marketing

- *Figuring channels that worked aggressively early on:* Putting money in figuring marketing channels in the beginning helped discover BuySellAds from which the early users came.
- *Viral branding on free users:* Designing the packages carefully helped attract both low- and high-budget users. The brand name grew fast by using 'powered by' strategy for free users.

People

- *Encouraging happiness:* Giving operational freedom instead of assigning roles based on degrees helped employees thrive in doing things they are good at.
- *Avoiding bad practices:* Freshdesk has been mindful of not getting into salary competition against other start-ups, thereby gaining more trust from its employees.

In fact, researchers have settled on what they believe is the magic number for true expertise: ten thousand hours.

—Malcolm Gladwell

2   Nithin Kamath: Zerodha

From losing ₹400,000 in personal trading to bootstrapping a hyper-growth, online trading platform, Nithin recounts the fascinating story behind building Zerodha—India's first discounted flat fee broker.

Online Trading and Investing Platform
#product #marketing #business_model #bootstrapped #fintech

Zerodha was founded in 2010 by Nithin and his brother Nikhil Kamath who had been trading for the most part of their lives. When Nithin got tired of his day trading routine, the idea was to build a low-cost but user-friendly online trading platform that he could use himself. A series of fortuitous events made it possible, including National Stock Exchange (NSE) launching its Now platform. True to its name, Zerodha lowered the barriers for traders with its first-in-India flat brokerage fee structure, and faster trading experience on NSE Now. Introducing its 'zero fee for equity delivery trades' amidst an increasing competition, it caught viral word-of-mouth popularity.

Nithin's attempt to attract tech talent and build a sophisticated in-house platform along with creative pricing has served the company well so far. More impressive is his focus on developing the ecosystem through educating people and incubating fintech start-ups. Without any paid marketing, Zerodha today serves more than 380,000 customers (adding 30,000 users per month) and generates

₹240 crore in annual revenues (growth of 100 per cent year on year [YOY]). On the way, they have been touted as the Bootstrap Champ by the Economic Times Startup Awards 2016 and received the BSE's Emerging Equity Broking House Award 2014–2015.

The best part is that Zerodha is completely bootstrapped and handsomely profitable.

Most of the articles on Zerodha refer to it as 'India's first discount broker'. 'Discount broker' is a term that was coined in one of the magazine interviews. 'When we explained that we let people trade at deep discounted prices, someone put out this term in one of the articles. It just refers to a discounted transaction/brokerage fee,' Nithin clarifies.

And before you wonder what 'zerodha' means, it stands for zero obstacles (*rodha* means barrier in Sanskrit).

'Most of the firms in trading and securities claim that they will help you make more money. I somehow did not want to put out that kind of messaging. We thought about what we are trying to achieve—and it was to break barriers for traders.'

400,000 Down the Drain

It all began when older people in his Marwari neighbourhood were making money trading stocks. A 16-year-old impressionable Nithin thought he could also make a quick buck. In 2001, when derivatives were introduced in India, Nithin jumped in on the opportunity without understanding it fully. He reflects back,

'That is when I lost around ₹4 lakh which might be equal to ₹10 lakh today. I am not from business family, so it was a lot of money. Of course, the loss did affect me, and I cried for two/three days. Soon, I joined a call centre to start earning. I was working at nights, and in the day, I would trade with whatever little money I was earning. I worked there for three years and recovered my lost capital.'

But he regained more than the money he had lost.

'Over the years, I have noticed how money is not the sole factor why I am doing this. I blew up all the money because I was trying to chase something. I have learnt what it means to be a trader now. A friend of mine shares this interesting perspective on how few things that we portray in our mythology make sense. This whole image of Goddess Lakshmi on a lotus is symbolic. If you try swimming towards the lotus or chasing it, it simply goes farther away. But if you just stand at one place and do the right thing, it will come to you. That is how my attitude has evolved about money in recent times. We are extremely lucky to have reached this stage without raising any money. I am lucky to have such great people around me. If you look at it, trading is not just limited to stocks. Every moment is a trade; you are trading whatever you believe in. Zerodha itself is a trade to me. I am playing because I believe in my odds.'

One day in 2005, Nithin met an NRI guy, Prakash, in his gym. When he asked what Nithin did for a living, Nithin showed him his trading account performance. Prakash was so impressed that he asked Nithin to manage his portfolio of ₹25 lakh. The arrangement was that Nithin would keep 20 per cent of the profits he made. That was the day Nithin quit his call centre job and never looked back.

The brokerage tools those days were dominated by ICICI Direct, India Infoline, etc. While everybody had an online platform, things were still very offline. For example, Sharekhan had 50–60 branches (including franchisee offices) in Bangalore because there was a lot of relationship management involved on the road.

Nithin managed Prakash's portfolio well, and more clients started coming through him.

'I was generating 25–40 per cent returns. Once I had 15–20 clients, it became harder to manage their accounts because you have to log in into everybody's account and then place the trades. In 2006, Reliance Money opened shop in India. I took a franchisee of them and opened an office in Bangalore. By being a broker, I could immediately get an access to a dealer terminal which lets you place the orders on behalf of multiple clients simultaneously, rather than logging in and out 100 times.'

With the dealer terminal, Nithin could now service even more clients. For the running costs of around ₹150,000–200,000 per month, he was generating a cumulative revenue of ₹500,000–600,000 per month from brokering and his own trading. His lifestyle was comfortable, but he knew that one cannot grow too big by a franchise model alone. 'Reliance Money was still like a job because if I did not go to work for 15 days, I did not earn. It was never a business. And then the 2008 recession happened. Multiple things happened which led to me thinking of Zerodha.'

Self-Doubt and the Birth of Zerodha

In 2008, when the stock market crashed, Nithin was short and made a lot of money, attracting even more clients. But early 2009 was not a good time to trade because markets were quite flat.

'Traders typically make money in a direction, and if the markets are not moving much, then traders don't make money. I used to be a long volatility trader. In stock markets, you can make money by betting on a direction or by calling on volatility. I used to make money by betting that volatility would increase irrespective of the direction. You only lose money if the market doesn't move.

In May 2009, UPA came into majority. Just the day before election results came out, I decided to square off my positions at 3:25 PM. The Indian markets close at 3:30 PM. The next day, markets opened 20 per cent higher and that happened next day as well, so the whole market had gone up by 40 per cent in two days. It had never happened in the Indian stock market before. It was one of those trades where if I had held on to my position, I would have made a shit load of money. It could have been a 1,000 per cent return. You cannot be a long volatility trader and miss a 40 per cent move in the market. It was a big frustration. In that frustration of losing that opportunity, I decided that I will stop trading. That was a key moment.'

Nithin compares active day trading to a game of T20. 'It burns you out, you cannot do it forever.' His younger brother Nikhil had joined him by then. They realized that Nikhil was an even better trader.

'He was making more money in trading than me. There was no sense in both of us sitting and trading. I was already thinking of taking a break, and as I was thinking what to do next, we looked at getting hedge fund licences, etc., too. I said why not be a brokerage service that we, as traders, never had. I had used 10–11 brokers by then and knew that what I needed as a trader was something that no one else was offering in a good way. That is when the idea for Zerodha came to us. We decided that Nikhil would keep trading. If none of this worked, he would still make money and recover our running costs. That is how everything started. I haven't put a single trade after 2009 and Nikhil has only done trading since then. He leads our prop trading desk at Zerodha.'

Nithin felt that the transaction cost mattered the most. Traditional brokers have fancy offices in Nariman Point, but why should a trader pay for those? The irony is that the cost of the trade does not increase with the size of the trade; in fact, it only drops as the size grows bigger. But in India, everybody was charging by the percentage of the size of the trade.

'If I buy one share or a million share, why should I pay a higher transaction fee? That is how we came to the concept of a flat brokerage fee. We wanted to keep it low cost. Traditional brokerage fee is somewhere around 0.75 per cent, whereas we offered a flat fee of ₹20 per transaction. Later, we introduced zero fee for equity investing. Second, a lot of brokerage houses were using energy and money into research and advisory services. As an independent trader, I did not care for that research or advice. All I needed was a platform which is stable; I did not want any fancy features. As a trader, it irritated me if someone pushed their advice on to me. I am thinking one way about a stock and if someone puts this other idea in my head and if that messes up my earlier thought, then I used to get very annoyed. Another thing is that advisory is a very thankless job. You give good advice, no one remembers. You give a bad one and everybody is after you.'

Nithin chuckles. 'We decided to get rid of that.'

Few things needed to fall in place for Zerodha to work. In 2008–2009, NSE had launched a platform called NSE Now. It was a free trading platform for the members of the stock exchange.

'Your clients could get access to it if you were a member. I happened to see that platform and immediately noted that because NSE Now was co-located in the NSE campus, the last-mile connectivity problem would not be there. So even though the interface was quite basic, it was more stable than other platforms. This appeared to me as an arbitrage opportunity. There was this platform which was faster, more stable and it was coming free of cost! Next thing to consider was that the cost of being a broker in India came out to be ₹1.5 crore as refundable deposit. Fortunately, they waived our membership fee to encourage us, as we were young and they liked our idea.'

Another key development was SEBI introducing short margin penalty in 2009. It meant that a broker could not allow a client to carry positions overnight unless the client maintained a minimum margin approved by SEBI. Before that, brokers could use their leverage to allow whatever they wanted. 'This was a big step in creating a level playing field and a big reason why we could enter the brokerage industry.'

Overall, Zerodha bet was hedged because Nithin and his team were themselves traders.

'We would be saving transaction costs, and if it doesn't work out, I would go back to trading after 1–1.5 years. We had around ₹1.6–1.7 crore in our savings at that time. So we decided to put it as deposit and get started. We already had an office, and now we had the access to a free trading platform which would have otherwise been the costliest component. I keep telling the guys at the exchange that if it wasn't for NSE Now, we would not be here. So with all those thoughts in mind, we went live in August 2010.'

Nithin was being modest. In 2009–2010, brokers were in a state of shock after the recession. They were trying to figure out other things instead of building a retail brokerage business model. It was to Nithin's credit that he stuck to his gut when the market was down.

Challenges and Customer Acquisition

It wasn't easy to establish credibility.

'It is not an e-commerce start-up; people are putting their actual money in their trading accounts. Over and above that, since we were offering discounted brokerage fee, people questioned us more because low cost is usually associated with low quality. The second challenge has always been around regulations. SEBI has done a brilliant job in India. There has never been a counter-party default on exchanges in India—ever. The whole of India went demat in four years, whereas the USA took 22 years to do that. It is an impressive feat for SEBI, but it also means that it had to face all these issues, which causes it to overly regulate at times. The third and more recent challenge is the technology infra-backbone. If it is raining in Mumbai or someone is digging the roads, they might just cut a lease line.

I have lost track of how many lease lines we have to create a backup to another backup to another backup. In our business, we stream so much data, and on the commercial side, there is no Jio. We spend tens of lakhs of rupees every month in infrastructure. If you leave these out, we are pretty frugal.'

One of the things that helped Zerodha get its first 1,000 clients was that Nithin was quite popular on many trading forums as an active trader. He could spread the message about its benefits online. Also, working in the call centre, he had done a lot of telemarketing.

'I had sold anything and everything on phone by then. I had that experience of cold calling. That is how we started and got the initial clients. In September 2011, the *Economic Times* article that popularized the term 'discount-brokerage' came out. And that journalist was the friend of a friend who was himself using Zerodha. Once that article came out, it brought a certain level of credibility as well. Before that, we were doing 100–150 accounts a month and suddenly it became 300 accounts a month.'

Zerodha's flat brokerage fee helped them grow through word of mouth.

'So we have not spent many marketing dollars. Additionally, our blog and content initiatives fuelled our search engine results. It is hard to put a number on how many customers it generated, but I would say that we are 250th most popular website in India according to Alexa. That also helps.'

In late 2012, for the first time, competition started to rise, which emphasized a similar low-cost and more functional approach towards trading.

'That is when it hit us that being low cost will not be an edge forever. It has to be technology. So I started scouting for how we can take this business forward by building a better platform. It is going to be a fight of platforms in the end. Anyone with a better trading platform and user experience will win it. That is what we are working on 24×7.'

Figuring Out the Technology Part

No one in the team was from the tech background. Also, NSE Now worked with only NSE stocks.

'What if someone wanted to trade on BSE or MCX? So we tied up with Omnesys which offered a white-labelled platform for online trading. Now we could trade on any exchange. Then, in 2013, I met Kailash Nadh who heads our technology now. He had come to India and was trying to build something in the capital markets along with a few friends. I have always tried to be around good intelligent people by investing in their businesses, etc. I was bankrolling his start-up, but they had to fold the idea because they did not get the required exchange approvals. However, we liked each other and I convinced him to join us. A big challenge until he joined was that being in brokerage or stock market is not looked up to in the Indian community and it was extremely tough to attract talent. I have been told to get a real job all my life. He is a PhD and probably the most intelligent technologist I know. So once he joined, we started building our tech team. He had built a lot of open-source projects and was well known. Our tech team then started making the platform that we had always wanted to.'

Meanwhile, Nithin also invested in another company called TradeLab, started by IIT Kharagpur students. They built a desktop platform called 'Pi'. Because of his investment, Nithin got an exclusive period to use it for two years, and that is how Zerodha's first desktop client was launched in 2014.

'Until then, we were running on white-labelled technologies which were available to everyone. Now, we had our own platform, and we could say that we are not compromising on anything anymore. In-house also, we started building smarter tools. We built our reporting and analytics platform called Q. 2015 is when we launched our Kite app. With that, we took a first-ever minimalistic approach to the trading experience. It is a web- and mobile-based platform and we lost all the buttons, jargon and made it a very simplistic UI. The problem with most of the trading platforms is that they clutter it with a ton of features just to make it seem advanced, but 99.9 per cent of the people never use those. So we let go of everything that we thought was not helpful and built this clean platform. Today, Kite probably contributes the most trading turnover on Indian exchanges. We have one to two lakh people placing orders on it every day.'

The Rationale and Trade-Off Behind Zero-Fee Business Model

Nithin observed that the active day-trading population in India is minuscule—probably 500,000–700,000 people. So it was not possible to build a scalable business model on top of that.

'Once we had Kite, we knew that the focus cannot just be on active traders anymore, we need to reach out to the investing population as well. I would say there are 60 lakh people who actively invest in India and a passive 2–3 crore who have demat accounts. We wanted to reach out to all of them. Somehow, we were getting branded as an FNO (futures and options) only broker. To get over that image was mandatory, and we felt that going zero brokerage for equity delivery trades will help.'

Zero fee was introduced in 2015. But the term is misleading—zero fee is applicable only for equity delivery trades which constituted 10 per cent of their business. They retained ₹20 per transaction on intraday and FNO trades.

'Overall, I would say that zero fee has affected 10 per cent of our revenues. But the gains have been bigger. If you think about it, the difference between ₹20 and zero is not that much anyway but "zero" is an eye candy and a talking point. We had 60,000 clients in December 2015, and by this announcement we got great word-of-mouth publicity. We now have 380,000 clients and are adding 30,000 accounts a month. Also, the new clients came in and saw that we are more than just low cost. They saw that the product is better in itself. That again helped increase our word-of-mouth publicity. We have never spent on Google Ads or any paid marketing.'

Additionally, the company makes money when it onboards clients and opens a new account. It has started distributing mutual funds and just got the NBFC (non-banking financial corporation) licence with which it can enter the lending market. There is a fee when someone trades using our application programming interface (API) or use call and trade facility, etc. Then, Nikhil heads their prop trading desk in which they trade the market themselves and that contributes to 20–25 per cent of overall revenues.

Zerodha is one of the few bootstrapped and larger profitable start-ups in India. Initially in 2010, the team met a bunch of people for funding, but it was one of the worst times to raise money or get into brokerage. After one year, they started making some money, and the only reason they would have needed money was to spend on advertising.

'But I did not believe that advertising was the way to go. After that, we just did not need money. I remember I was on my way to Cochin and the flight got delayed. I was with Prithish who handles the PR and Kailash, and we were just having a beer. I said that we have not done anything interesting for a while and that is when this idea of zero brokerage came to us. That was Friday and on Monday, we announced zero brokerage fee! Not having external investors helps in being extremely fast.'

Growing from 100 to 1,000

Zerodha was off to a solid start, but competing on low prices was tricky. Nithin soon realized that they were becoming a big fish in a small pond.

'The problem in India for anyone building a start-up in the investment tech side is that the Indian market is extremely shallow. Last year, there were around 40–50 lakh Indians who had invested at least once a year. And that number has stayed the same in last 10 years. So the only way to scale is to get new people to come into the market. And that will happen. It was in the news that the number of taxpayers in India has gone up from 4 crore to 6.26 crore in 2017. That increase of 2.5 crore people is more than the entire population of Australia. If anyone is interested in the capital markets in India, I think now is the best time.

Zerodha is a great place if someone has an intent to trade or to learn. But if you have neither, then Zerodha does not have a product for you. The key is to help grow the ecosystem itself.

We decided to start Rainmatter which is an incubator for fintech start-ups that are helping the ecosystem grow. We caught the attention of multiple start-ups in that. One was called Digio which enables e-signatures and e-KYC (know your customer), etc. They make the process of onboarding clients, which is otherwise very physical, easier and paperless using the Aadhaar layer. There is a start-up called Balance that has built an app that helps you impulsively to save. With these investments, the idea is to grow the size of the overall market. We also make a big push on educating the users about investing through our initiative called Varsity. After Investopedia, I think it is the most popular resource online for education on capital markets.'

The education efforts are already showing returns. Zerodha is penetrating deep into the young trader segment. While other brokerage firms have their HNI clients (high net-worth individuals) and low net-worth clients, Zerodha treats all its clients the same and offers one deal to everyone.

'75 per cent of our clients are less than 40 years of age. Almost 50–60 per cent of the new accounts we open are for the first timers. So most people who are trading through us are yet to make large money for themselves. They are trading with less than ₹5 lakh in their accounts.'

Team Building and Hiring

'Most of our team was formed accidentally. Venu and I were living in the same apartment. I had once helped him out of a fight when he was much younger. Don't know why he remembered, but he called me back after a decade and asked if he can work with me—this was during my Reliance days. He now heads our compliance and operations. Hanan was losing money to the markets and joined us to learn how to survive trading; he heads client relations. Karthik went to Europe to do his MBA and joined us back after couple of years. He takes care of all education initiatives. Seema is my wife and we met at a call centre. When things went up for me, I decided to marry her so that she sticks around with me.'

Financial services industry is known for rigid targets, and people are programmed to make money off their clients. Nithin believes that this causes people to miss-sell and even miss targets, which leads to this bad energy.

'We are perhaps the only brokerage firm that does not have brokerage targets. Today we are 700 people and we have multiple offices. What happens is that it gets hard to control what that leader in that office is trying to do. But generally, we are a fun company, and people have the independence to do what they want. We are more like a start-up than a financial services firm. The thing is our entire business is quite simple to manage. There is one rule for all the clients, and operations are straightforward. The only complex component we have is in our technology and risk management layer. We do not necessarily need people from IITs or IIMs. We don't go for experience, we mostly hire 20–22 years old people and groom them. There is churn happening at the lower end, but the first 100–150 people who joined us have not yet quit.'

Out of the 700 employees, 400 are sales managers and handle marketing, 100 are in account opening and quality, 50 are in the tech team and the remaining 200 handle customer support and other issues.

'Our marketing team is the one who calls you back when you visit the website. Because the thing in India is, people are still lazy in signing up. So we need to follow up very actively for each visitor. Second, once the account is opened, our managers will call the client up and ask for referrals, etc. The sales team also helps us with setting franchisee and corporate partnerships.'

Infrastructural Woes and the Painful Nights

When Zerodha moved to its own technology platform and away from NSE Now, the last-mile problems were reintroduced.

'What happens is every broker is connected to the exchanges through a lease line. The order goes to their system and then to the exchange. Now, there is a limit on how many orders this line can support. We have been working on increasing our lease line capacity and adding backups but it takes six months in India. As we have scaled, we became a car that is going at 200 km per hour on a road that can only support 100 km per hour. There are restrictions on bandwidth allocation, how many messages can a lease line handle and more.'

When Brexit happened, Zerodha was in the middle of its infrastructural expansions.

'Exponentially more orders came in. It started at the lease line and moved on to the risk management layer (we use Thomson Reuters execution layer). All of them just could not handle that kind of order volume and we were down for a couple of hours. It was a volatile day and you cannot be down on a volatile day.'

Nithin remained silent for a few seconds.

'We got a lot of fire for that. We had two to three incidences within that two to four months expansion period which cost us hard. Now, we are changing the way our entire back end works. We had sixfold growth in last year and a half, and some of these unimaginable things happened because of the infrastructure issues. It has influenced how we think now. We have redesigned our app Kite so that we make a server request only if something changes at the client side. We are avoiding any unnecessary load.

Other platforms such as ICICI and Sharekhan have been around for much longer period than us and they have seen issues related to load already. So their systems might be more prepared. But they have had their own problems. You saw what happened to NSE earlier in July, right? They had to halt all FNO trades due to a technical glitch. We have the redundancies in place, but many of these issues are unpredictable. With us, it is more crucial because majority of our population consists of active traders rather than investors.'

What Makes Nithin so Successful

As expected from someone who has closely seen the ups and downs, Nithin's answers are well measured, weighed and disciplined. His parting advice to budding entrepreneurs reflects the same sobriety.

'Many people come up with ideas on a coffee table and start a business. But with me, I had done 20,000 hours of work in this industry before even starting something. That had given me an edge over those who just understand it theoretically. There are managers who have degrees from great colleges, but what I have is the hands-on knowledge. Trading was the only thing I had ever done or thought about in my life when I decided to build something around it. The odds of hitting the mark were higher. If you want to improve the odds of success in your business, try working in that industry for a few years. You cannot just pick up an idea in a coffee shop and hope it will become the next big thing.'

Reflecting upon the three key decisions that made Zerodha what it is today, Nithin doesn't have to think too hard.

'First would definitely be getting Kailash on board. Second is launching the Kite platform. It defined the ecosystem that we are trying to build. We also opened up APIs for developers to build over Kite. Today, there are six to seven start-ups who are using that. Third would be when we went for zero brokerage in December of 2015. Those have been the defining moments for us.'

Venu Madhav, Hanan Delvi, Seema Patil, Nikhil Kamath, Dr Kailash Nadh, Nithin Kamath (left to right). Taken at Zerodha Headquarter, Bengaluru in 2015

Key Takeaways

Person

- *Domain expertise:* Nithin has spent years trading and working in capital markets which gave him an edge when he built Zerodha. Experience with call centres came in handy when required to cold call and acquire initial customers.
- *Long-term vision:* Investing in finance tech start-ups personally and through Rainmatter fund, and opening the APIs to developers are ways to grow the finance ecosystem and improve Zerodha's longevity.

Product

- *Building on a clear opportunity:* Spotting an arbitrage opportunity with NSE Now, Zerodha was launched with a good quality platform that came free of cost.
- *Features based on real customer problems:* Nithin focused on the problems that he himself had faced as a trader. Features such as flat transaction fee, no advisory and simpler user interface came from his own experience.
- *Strong technology foundation:* Moving away from white labelled platforms and developing in-house hi-tech systems such as Kite gives more control over user experience.

Marketing

- *Viral word-of-mouth publicity:* Taking a popular yet strategic initiative such as going zero fee for equity investors helped in 6x growth over 1.5 years without much downside.
- *Educating the audience:* Realizing that Indian retail trading market is shallow, Zerodha focused on educating and training initiatives that can grow the size of potential market. Additionally, it helped in search engine optimization (SEO).

Pricing

- *Disruptive pricing:* Keeping a flat initial brokerage fee and zero fee for investors later on was unprecedented in India, and attracted a lot of young traders and investors.

Dripping water hollows out stone, not through force but through persistence.

—Ovid

3 Paras Chopra: Visual Website Optimizer (Wingify)

After four start-up failures, all Paras wanted was to earn ₹50,000 to prove to himself that he's not destined to be a start-up loser. Then VWO happened, and now he's running a US$15 million annual revenue bootstrapped company (and he still thinks he has just begun).

A/B Testing Tool
#pivoting #product #marketing #pricing #bootstrapped #saas

With a background in computational biology, machine learning, online marketing and web technologies, Paras started Wingify in early 2009. Twice featured in the Forbes list, the 2014 Forbes India '30 Under 30' List followed by the 2016 top 'promising young leaders and game changers' under the age of 30 in Asia, Paras does not remember a time when he was not building something.

Wingify's flagship product VWO allows marketing professionals to create different versions of their websites to check out which one produces maximum conversion/sales. What started as a complicated prototype that drew a lot of flak on *Hacker News* was pivoted and sculpted based on feedback to give birth to a free and simpler A/B testing tool called VWO. Paras quit his job without knowing whether he would be able to attract paid users, but his content marketing prowess helped him gather 100–150 paid users quickly in the first two months. The product successfully competed with and exposed the flaws of the Google Website Optimizer and went on to be loved by the marketers across the world.

Figuring out the art of SaaS pricing and sales, Paras helped scale VWO from a simple tool to a marketing solution with a robust subscription model. Today, VWO is used by 4,000 businesses across 80 countries.

The Unconventional Engineer

Paras's love for programming started in eighth standard with Visual Basic 6.0 which created a workable programme from drag-and-drop windows.

'Naram Cheez was my website that I had started when I was 13. It just means "software" in Hindi. Whenever I built something, even tiny, I would put it on there. I was not in favour of spending the two-year time for the preparation of IIT exams. I felt it was unnecessary to spend all your time studying for an exam. I got a decent rank in the Delhi College of Engineering entrance test and chose to study biotechnology. Since I had been programming for a long time, I thought that I should learn something totally new.'

This is not the only unconventional decision he would take in his life. In college as well, he did multiple research internships, convinced his principal to send him to Singapore on a fully sponsored conference, wrote his first paper on a complicated topic on operons and started reading Founders at Work and Paul Graham's essays.

'I thought *ki start-up karni hai*. I created a music listening platform for independent music bands called Kroomsa in the last year of college. I just assembled things together on WordPress, and before every song we inserted one ad. That was the whole business. But very quickly, I realized that there is no money to be made there.'

Very few young entrepreneurs talk about money at such an experimental stage. But Paras has no qualms about it.

'Yes, I wanted to make money. For me that is what a successful start-up is. And I am not mentioning money or wealth because I needed it. What I mean is if someone is giving you money, it is like a big statement that you have created value for that person.'

There were other projects during his college life, but Paras took a regular job at Grail Research upon graduating.

'It was the research arm of a consulting firm, and they assigned me to life sciences division where they had a lot of pharma clients. I told them I don't want to do that because I was done with bio and all that by then. But they told me that I cannot change my area. At that point, I realized what it means to be in a job.

That just ignited a fire in me—I realized that I can never work where other people expect things from me. So I quit that within three months, and luckily I was in correspondence with Varun Aggarwal. He had just finished his master's in machine learning at MIT and had come back to India. He was planning to start Aspiring Minds and offered me a position of R&D engineer. The offer was interesting to me, and I went on to work with him. But I remember that on day one itself, I had told him that I would start my own start-up soon. So I worked on my things only in the nights or weekends. And he was fine with it.'

A Bumpy Start to VWO

Paras registered the domain 'wingify.com' in 2008 right after his graduation. Once he started exploring things, he decided to do something in marketing because that is what he felt he had done well in his previous start-ups. 'I started reading about online marketing. Google Analytics was fairly new back then. There was SEO and all that. So I thought of writing a software for marketing.'

Paras hacked together a PHP (hypertext preprocessor)-based software that combined A/B testing with targeting and analytics. But in his enthusiasm, he overdid it, and the end product was complicated piece of software with a ton of hard-to-understand features.

'For example, I added a thing called context sense which could tell what a page is about from its URL. So it would tell that a page is about computer advertising or about India, or Apple as a fruit and not Apple as a company. Then there was visitor sense. We would install code on your website and it would tell what visitors were doing from an API perspective. I just did what I thought was interesting.'

Since he wanted to get some feedback before making it paid, he put it on *Hacker News* in the first half of 2009 to showcase it to others.

'I was very nervous, and then feedback started coming. People would log in to the website and they would say "What the hell is this!" No one understood it and I got brutal feedback. I felt horrible.

It was a Javascript that people had to embed on their pages, but the interface itself was very complicated. There was no onboarding. When you would log in, there would be 30–40 links. I had written a help page and I assumed that people would read it but people do not read help pages! And then, I was using terms like real-time conversion optimization framework and I thought I was doing a good job. That is when I realized how important onboarding and user experience is. It's funny how one failure can teach you so many different lessons.'

The good thing was that he got 30–50 comments and also a few sign-ups. About 10–15 people tried it out sincerely, and those were the people who became his guiding point for further feedback.

'Patrick McKenzie was one of the people who tried the first version. We talked about user experience and how features are not everything. So I tried to distil some business sense, and that was very valuable early on. I am very thankful to him for that. From all the feedback, I knew that I needed to simplify the product.

Meanwhile, I had tried Google Website Optimizer and I struggled using it myself. That was a mini light-bulb moment there. If I was finding it difficult, other marketers must be finding it even more difficult. I thought I could write something that is simpler. So I made a simple version of this new product in one month. Since it was like Google Website Optimizer, I decided to call my product Visual Website Optimizer (VWO). This time, I did not spend too much time and showed it to a lot of people like Patrick and all and got a lot of positive feedback. That is what told me that it's on the right path this time.

Once I had more confidence, I launched it again on *Hacker News*. I got a lot of sign-ups on day one itself. I think it was around 100–150. Then, Patrick wrote an article called "A/B Testing for Fortune 5M" and did a detailed review of my product. That again got a lot of sign-ups and the ball started rolling from there.'

Besides the Google Website Optimizer, there were a couple of other A/B testing tools that were more focused on enterprise customers. Products like Adobe Testing Target were very expensive. So VWO became a low cost and more usable alternative.

Launching the Paid Version

A lack of formal computer science background was starting to limit Paras.

'I was able to teach myself the concepts on server load, distributed computing etc. But I had also started involving Sparsh Gupta who is now our CTO (chief technology officer). He is from DCE too, and when I was building VWO, he was in London for his MS in artificial intelligence. I started showing him what I was building. I think it was early 2010 and he used to help me part-time. After Patrick's posts, there was a lot of positive momentum in VWO and he understood that. We could feel that it is something real. Deciding to quit your job and coming back to India is a very big deal.'

When the product reached 1,000 active users, it was still free. Paras was finding it increasingly difficult to do support, marketing and coding as a one-man army. 'Around March–April 2010, I had some level of confidence that I will be able to make some money. That is when I decided to quit my job and made the product paid.'

A visitor could do a free trial of the product, and if he liked it, he would sign up using a credit card. 'We had a 30-day free trial limiting to 1,000 visitors. If the test was successful and if they went beyond 1,000 visitors, we would pause their account and ask them to pay. They immediately paid.'

Meanwhile, he received an email from someone at Microsoft that he has gold in his hands. There were many other similar emails commending their approach to A/B testing. What was it that made the product gain such a quick traction?

'There was no difference in the methodology of A/B testing itself. But the way it was applied and the ease with which a user could apply it was different. Usually when you want to run an A/B test, you might want to change few elements here and there but not all of them. Google WO required you to upload two webpages on your server and then it would split the traffic between the two pages. We knew that uploading the page on the server itself required involving an engineer. And marketers are perennially not able to get their hands on the engineering resources. So even a simple change would take weeks or months depending on the availability of engineering team. What we did was that we just asked marketers to embed Javascript code on the website. Then they simply had to use our interface and they could change anything—text, button colour, image—and make it live immediately without involving any engineer. That is the reason it got so much traction.'

Whenever Paras describes his user, he talks about the marketer. 'Yes, I always targeted it for marketing managers or people who were responsible for marketing in the company.'

This clarity of his target user profile helped him add specific features that the marketers ended up loving. The usability of VWO lay in its utter simplicity.

'You needed to touch the code only once. Then, it would load the complete page in our interface and you could change anything. The marketer did not even have to specify what you want to change. It was that generic. You put in the code once, and then you could run any number of tests. They absolutely loved entering the website URL and seeing the editor where they could change anything. See, most of them were marketers and they never had the ability or power to change anything on the website. They had to coax or bribe the developers to get stuff done. So a lot of people actually started using VWO just for changing things on their website and not even do A/B testing. [Paras chuckles]'

Furthermore, his machine-learning background helped him understand the statistical concepts used in A/B testing and added more credibility to the results.

'Like if you did the button colour test, then you would see that the blue button resulted in 500 visitors and 50 clicks and the red button got 550 visitors and resulted in 100 clicks. Then you would see that red button as a percentage click rate was way higher compared to the blue button. And it was not just the click rate but also the statistical significance that said whether the results are fluke or statistically significant.'

Growth Through Content Marketing

Paras has, over time, grown to be a content marketing expert. The journey started organically from the VWO blog. Often, entrepreneurs wonder how to write good content. Paras swears by case studies!

'There was a very neat trick about case studies that I bumped into. If someone got a good increase in conversion or sales through their A/B tests, we showed a pop up asking if they want to be featured as a case study on the Wingify blog. So I got a lot of inbound interest of people who wanted to be featured as a case study. And it was happening even while I was sleeping. These were small businesses and they valued any publicity. That way, I got a good backlog of interesting studies and I didn't have to chase anybody or build relationships. That worked great because if somebody increased their conversions just by 20 per cent with VWO in five minutes, that is a very attention-grabbing headline plus the great thing is that it is based on actual results.'

Paras also started blogging very frequently about A/B testing because many marketers did not understand it fully. He wrote about the best practices, how statistical significance is calculated, etc. 'I also started guest posts, so I was contributing to *Smashing Magazine*, SEO Moz blog, Kissmetrics. A lot of places were writing about A/B testing, and from there I would link back to our case studies. That generated initial traffic to the blog.'

For other lead-generation mechanisms, Paras tried Google AdWords as most entrepreneurs do, but he realized that not a lot of people were searching about A/B testing. Volume was a problem.

'We were always running AdWords, but it never brought us a lot of leads. I think you have to experiment different ways. We tried LinkedIn also but, in the end, content is what worked for us really well. We did try outbound marketing and sales, but for that to work, I think, your brand has to be quite significantly known. Outbound would work only if they know you. For example, you would open an email from Microsoft or IBM, but not from an unknown vendor. I did not see outbound working so well.'

Value-Based Pricing

Patrick McKenzie is an expert on SaaS pricing, and that is where his early days' feedback immensely helped Paras in pricing VWO. Another influence came from 37Signals which was a posterchild in SaaS and was also used to write about pricing, etc. 'Entrepreneurs tend to price on the lower side. I feel it should be either free where you do it as a charitable cause or you should charge a respectable amount. Anything in between is confusing.'

'How do you determine the respectable price for your product' is the question!

Paras recommends going by value instead of cost perspective.

'I remember that I had no idea how to do the pricing. It could be US$9 or US$99. Patrick said that US$9 is too low and the rationale really came out to be this. Let's say that a developer costs around US$100 per hour in USA; so if you are saving even 30 minutes with VWO, then one should gladly pay US$50. Of course, VWO was saving much more. If you can calculate how much revenue you are helping them make or what cost you are helping them save, then it's very easy for you to put a number. For example, if you are making a product for e-commerce and you are increasing their sales by 2–3 per cent on an average and helping them make extra US$10,000, then I think it's okay to take 20 per cent of the value that you are creating.

Plus, I felt that someone who is not willing to pay even US$50 per month will not be a good person to have as a user. You don't want to be perceived as a cheap product because a lot of mid-market and enterprise people know that if the product is priced too low, they are not going to get a good service. The fact is you realistically cannot provide customer service and support at US$9. So we started at US$49 per month. Next plan was US$129 and the highest was US$249.'

Feature-wise, there was not much disparity between the plans in the beginning. He would even put few packages as 'coming soon' just to gauge interest.

'You need to see how a user would benefit from your product, and then chunk the pricing according to that. A lot of products would have standard enterprise plans, and then within that, they would have another axis in terms of number of subscribers or users. I have seen three to four plans working pretty well. The highest plan is for your salespeople to use and it won't usually be the plan that sells the most, but just because it's there, the second most expensive plan becomes very attractive. The lowest plan is simply for you to onboard a customer.'

Team Building

Paras had a simple logic for hiring. Whenever he ended up spending too much time on something, he decided it was time to hire someone for that job.

'A lot of my time was going into customer support. We have been very obsessive about keeping customers happy. I didn't even want to differentiate between free or paid, or whether it's a dumb question or intelligent. I felt it was my responsibility to answer everyone comprehensively. So I didn't want to see anything left unanswered, but then, that was taking too much of my time. The questions could be "how does this work", or a bug, or pricing or anything. So I and Sparsh hired our first employee in March 2011 for customer support.'

Paying competitive salaries was not an issue since the product was making revenues. The next two employees were engineers from DCE, and one of them is still with them. About 1–1.5 years later, he hired his first salesperson. 'It was worlds apart from how an engineer would think. Earlier he focused on the inbound interest. Then, he also ensured that no lead gets dropped.'

Hiring is another area where Paras's online brand and presence has helped immensely.

'Nothing sells like success. Many founders are shy about sharing their success and approach. Whatever talks I was giving, articles I was writing helped a lot in getting people to know about Wingify. So even if your customer base is not in India, the founder should invest in building a brand just for hiring sake. Remember, your company is not only competing for customers but also for talent. I just feel that recruitment should be taken very seriously because a good employee attracts a better employee, and a bad one always pushes and doesn't let good candidates come on board.'

Consultative Sales and Global Success

VWO hit a million dollar in cumulative revenues in 18 months, and reached 1,000 customers in two years. Today, it is one of the poster-children for Indian SaaS companies that have sold extremely well on foreign soils. And that takes more than organic marketing. At some point, Paras realized that targeting enterprises has to be a part of the company's strategy. A salesperson that Paras had hired convinced him that they need to create a tailored plan for enterprises.

'That's the thing you know, if you hire a salesperson, his incentive is to sell more and more. They are the ones who guide you into entering the enterprise sales and suggest pricing plans. And once we started selling it, it actually made a lot of economic sense. Enterprises love to pay for priority support and integrations a lot more than the small businesses. Even if you keep the other features the same, you can increase the pricing to offer better customer support. For each enterprise client, we assigned a customer success manager. Another thing I observed was that the higher a customer is paying, lower is the churn rate. This is very counter intuitive, but I have seen this in so many companies now. The highest paying companies are the most loyal ones, and the people who are paying less probably don't care much about the product and can leave anytime. So the best customers are the ones who pay the most.'

Entrepreneurs start with one or two-member teams. They relate better to SMBs, but they don't understand the enterprise or mid-market customer problems, and that is what restricts their pricing power. Paras suggests anybody who is starting a SaaS should try to understand what an organization of 100 people looks like and how their priorities are different from a 5–10 people company.

VWO can be looked at as a product which is just required once or a couple of times. Someone might test how his landing page is looking, and then buy the plan for three months and do all the testing he needs. Turning such a product into a strong monthly subscription machinery has taken both persistence and creativity. Paras attributes this to his consultative sales strategy.

'If you understand the customer needs and establish a better product fit, they stick with you longer. What that means is to guide the prospect on the value of A/B testing itself, making him understand the commitment required to see the results. So we try to be on the prospect's side instead of blindly selling the product. Unless we have the commitment from them in terms of time, budget and resources, we know that the process will not be successful. So we are now focusing more on advisory role rather than sales role. To clarify, I don't mean we are providing consulting services. What I am saying is that we don't even have sales conversation in first two/three calls, we first understand their business, where they are coming from, etc. before talking about the product.'

Today, Wingify generates 99 per cent of its revenue from overseas sales and serves customers including Microsoft and Rackspace.

'I think being in India is a cost advantage. And since the clients in the USA are buying over phone or emails or online, location does not really matter.

We have one person in the USA but he is not in the sales team. We have been doing the sales part entirely from India and it is working fine.'

Coming to hiring non-technical staff in India, Paras talks about India-specific challenges.

'In Silicon Valley and Europe, you have people coming from Salesforce or other mature organizations. They have seen a start-up going through the growth phase and maturing. In India, that ecosystem is missing. So it is extremely challenging to find a head of sales or marketing. You will find people from FMCG (fast-moving consumer goods), but adapting your knowledge from there to a SaaS B2B company is...I don't know. So when we hire customer success managers, it is a SaaS concept and we don't know where to find this person. So we have to rely a lot on training and coaching.'

Saying NO to External Fundraising

One of the things that anybody notices immediately about VWO is that it has never raised external funding.

'If your goals are to grow very fast, then not taking funding can be a disadvantage, but if your goal is long-term sustenance, then it's an advantage because you are in control. In my case, I simply never understood why I should take venture capital. We were always profitable and growing. So I thought we are doing fine and what is the point of taking someone's money. Also, I am not much into mentors or advice myself. I read a lot of books, so I get that knowledge from reading.'

Venture capital does help in growing fast and VCs have funded competing tools like Optimizely.

'In hindsight, we could have grown way faster by not only fundraising but just realizing that others were growing faster. We were happy with growing 100 per cent YOY. I read that it is a good growth to double in size every year. But our competitors were growing three to four times every year. So that knowledge was not there. I feel we could have brought in more salespeople and hired a bigger marketing team earlier than we did. And it's not even the question of money because we had the money. Instead of hiring one salesperson initially, we should have hired three salespeople. And that is my evolution as an entrepreneur. I just did not know, and I was not ready to have mentors or advisors. I was figuring a lot of things myself.'

Parting Advice

For someone who has not yet touched his thirties, Paras's self-awareness makes him clearly stand apart.

'I should have read more business books than start-up books. People get hooked on to start-up conferences and reading start-up books; it becomes an addiction. But after a certain stage, they should graduate on to reading *Harvard Business Review* (*HBR*). I'm relating to this because the problem set completely changes after sometime. You have to think of strategy, you have to know what a VP of sales really does, so on and so forth. So I should have read more business literature. I would recommend *HBR* and their booklets called Top 10 of Leadership, etc. which give a good foundation for an entrepreneur to transition to CEO. I think that phase is very difficult. You have never managed people and you don't know what the word "strategy" really means.'

Another advice he gives is to hire two people instead of one even if you need one.

'Because if it is only one person, you don't know if the job is being performed at an optimal level or not. What if that person is not good enough? Lastly, I should have hired a senior person and let that senior person build a team rather than hiring very junior people. Because when you scale, finding a manager later on becomes way more difficult. If you start with senior people, they can support you as you grow. I am not saying very senior either, so you have to look at culture fit too. But if you are getting the culture fit, go for a senior person.'

Dark Side of Having No Boss

'The biggest challenge was that there was no one to coach or mentor me and I was the first-time CEO. I never had a board of investors or anyone whom I was answerable to. So the challenge was to not get lulled and fall into chasing a local maxima. How to build a company that endures as opposed to just making profits in the short run? I had to disorient and push myself repeatedly to keep acting like a VC-funded company. To act like a mature CEO when I was not. For example, we could have still been profitable in short run if we did not hire sales or product people. We could have just played it more tactically and not tried to learn more about business building because there was no one to guide us. If you are profitable from the first day, complacency can set in.'

What Gets Paras Going?

Paras is a bookworm and a self-taught manager.

Paras working on VWO in 2012 in Delhi

He diligently reviews the books he reads on his blog and lists his top favourites here:

- *Zero to One* by Peter Thiel
- *The Vital Question* by Nick Lane
- *The Beginning of Infinity* by David Deutsch
- *The Innovator's Dilemma* by Clayton M. Christensen

Additionally, he recommends *HBR* and Stratechery's articles.

Key Takeaways

Person

- Sticking fearlessly to his own gut and priorities.
- Building fast and building many things, and observing what sticks.
- Staying optimistic through negative feedback and turning it into a better product.
- Developing awareness through reading.

Product

- *Get validation early:* By spending too much time building without seeking user feedback, Paras risked creating a product that was not useful.
- *Pivot based on validation: Hacker News* comments and feedback from few users told what features should be kept and what should be eliminated.
- *Know thy audience:* Paras was clear on who he was building for (marketers) and what mattered to them (simplicity). This clear targeting helped him find the product market fit early on.

Pricing

- *Value-based pricing:* Designing the pricing based on the value created for businesses made it easy to convince the customers.

Marketing and Sales

- *Early focus on B2B:* Salespeople driven by right incentives helped expand in enterprise space. Creating features highly valued by the enterprises helped getting bigger companies on board at higher price points.
- *Innovate ways to generate content:* Turning successful user tests into user-written case studies generated more and free content, and better SEO.
- *Branding to attract talent:* By public speaking and blogging, Paras created a brand not only attractive to customers outside India but also to employees within India.

Fundraising

- *Clarity on his priority:* Take external money only if you want to grow superfast in short term and don't mind risking long-term sustenance and free control.

Oil is valuable. Many people would love to own lots of oil. But owning lots of oil won't make you rich. It's understanding how oil can make you rich that brings wealth.

— Robert Kiyosaki

4   Nikhil Rasiwasia: Fashiate

How do you monetize a technology without having to go through the grind and risk of a start-up? It's simple—you create a prototype and get acquired! That is how this scientist did it.

E-salesman for the E-commerce Websites
#ideation #exit #acquired #e-commerce

Fashiate was founded in November 2014 by Yahoo! Labs India employees—Dr Nikhil Rasiwasia, Dr Gaurav Aggarwal and Deepthi Singh. Unlike the start-ups that are kickstarted with a specific problem in mind, the motivation behind Fashiate came from the scientific brains of Nikhil and Gaurav (among other founders) who have earned their PhD from premier schools in the USA in the field of computer vision and imaging.

How can their image expertise be applied to a commercial problem? Chasing this question, they built prototypes around the use of image technologies in the field of fashion. What started off as a coffee-break discussion morphed into an e-salesman for the e-commerce websites that help shoppers in finding items that look 'like that'. In a roller-coaster four-month ride, Yahoo! shut down its India office, the initial founder list changed numerous times and the founders found a way to sell their prototype without ever launching the product live. Fashiate is an outlier in every sense of the word.

Nikhil is not your typical hyper-ambitious and single-minded entrepreneur. He is an academician at heart who had a clear exit strategy from day one and does not pretend to be anything else. He has a good story to tell to those who are more excited by ideas and problems to solve than 'living the start-up'. He exemplifies that fundraising and making it big is not the only way to think about it. *Do what feels right to you.* Every few minutes, he reminds me that 'we got lucky', but I have never seen luck coming to those who did not have the nerve to stay in the game.

The Start-Up Itch

Nikhil got his BTech in electrical engineering from IIT Kanpur. It took a small start-up in college and management stint at ITC to make him realize he does not like to 'manage' people. So he headed to the University of California at San Diego (UCSD) to pursue a PhD focused on vision and graphics.

Never feeling at home in the USA, he accepted an offer from Yahoo! Labs to join a research position back in India in December 2011. He also had an option to join as a faculty at IIT Delhi.

At Yahoo! Labs, he was solving intellectual problems for the corporate side, building upon new ideas and then trying to integrate those into the live products.

'But I felt that there was a disconnect between the research and product teams. So we would build things and solve problems but our solutions never saw daylight. Besides, there was a dissatisfaction in terms of the recognition our work would get due to politics or whatever. So despite liking the kind of work we were doing, we were just dissatisfied because our work was not creating the impact that would drive us. Plus, Yahoo! was especially struggling in India. So after three years, I started yearning for a change in the kind of work I was doing.'

September 2014 is when the coffee-table discussions began with friends where people started floating ideas. All of them were working in machine learning and computer vision. Five of them were serious about starting something.

'Out of five, three of us had PhD in this area. Another was a software engineer who had worked with us and the other was a master's in the same area. So we were all technically inclined, and we had a niche kind of technical expertise. In retrospect, it is not a good idea that everyone has the same niche, but back then we felt comfortable with each other. It was also comforting that we were all taking similar decisions.'

Hailing from a computer vision background, they started exploring areas where images play a central role in businesses. 'Luckily for us, it was also the time when computer vision was going through a changeover. Newer technologies had come into place and these were giving some good results. These technologies came in about 2012. So 2014 was when it became commercial.'

The technologies Nikhil is referring to are image classification, image annotation, image retrieval, etc.

'"Deep learning" was the term that became popular in 2012. It slowly gained momentum as one of the best algorithms out there to understand images. Those algorithms made it easier to build commercial business ideas around this field. Earlier, the performances of image-based systems weren't very high. People used to start companies but they would struggle to reach an accuracy that is commercially viable. Even now it is not 100 per cent there, but it was possible to build a product with current generation of technology that could be commercially successful. That is what we wanted to do—figure out an area where we could do that.'

Reverse Engineering Commercial Viability

The wave of e-commerce was very strong. So the team zeroed in on fashion because images are the most important consideration in the fashion purchase.

'If I am buying a laptop, I don't need to know what the laptop looks like. But if I am buying a shirt, I need to definitely look at the make of the shirt. At that time, a couple of research papers came in the area of fashion imaging. We thought that no other company had such a technology. Then, each of the ideas was evaluated from a market point of view. Is the market big enough? Shaadi.com or Matrimonial or travel business online were not as big as e-commerce, and our contribution would be limited. The second step was to validate. Here, I like the phrase of vitamin and painkiller. Is it a painkiller for you or a vitamin for you?'

He next spoke to his cousin Amit Agarwal who had successfully exited Via.com, an online travel firm. Nikhil remembers talking to a popular VC from Bangalore.

'He was a B2B guy. He said, "If you are going B2C (business-to-consumer), I don't want to be associated with you. B2B is not scalable but it's safer". Another VC from Hyderabad was a B2C believer. We realized that B2C market size is much bigger than B2B companies but it has higher risk potential as well. B2B is more stable. Here is how someone explained B2B to us. If there is a gold rush, people may not find gold but they all want to dig. For that, they need spades and hammers. You should build hammers because those would definitely sell. It boiled down to what we wanted to do because both the directions were possible.'

At the end, they zeroed in on two different problems. The first was the user fashion experience on online portals. The second was a B2B product that helps sellers put their images online more easily and in a way that meets the standards of the e-commerce websites.

To explain it better, Nikhil elaborates,

'The first product was about the online shopping experience. When you go for shopping physically, the salesman listens to the customer's needs. That is the e-salesman we were trying to build based on what users clicked on, what they like or what is the next set of things to show them. See, here was the problem—if a user clicked on a shirt that has checks, the e-commerce companies had no good way of understanding why he clicked on that shirt. Was it because the image looked nice to him or was he interested in checks?

Nobody was analysing images back then. They were only categorising it by brand, price and other tags. The tags may or may not contain checks. Or the kind of checks could be different. I as a user am clicking on it because of the shape, the pattern, the colours of the image, but the system doesn't understand that. It just knows the brand and the price tag, and all. So that was the place where we could make a difference. Especially when making an offline purchase, there is a salesman and you tell him what kind of shirt you like. You ask him to show more of a certain kind. That was the initial thought process back then. This was the first product idea. It could be a B2B or B2C because we could always sell the technology or build our own website.'

The second idea was for the sellers who were selling through Amazon and other e-commerce websites.

'Let's say I have a shirt that I need to sell online. My first problem is that there are three or four websites, I have to talk to them separately. The second problem is all the information about the product that I have to enter in a specific format. A bunch of it is like, what is the colour and size, and after that upload the images. All these websites have a standard for what the image should look like. They should have a white background, it should be on a model, the model should not be ugly, it should be of a particular size, etc. The seller doesn't know how images operate. Good quality images are hard to take, and editing it to a particular standard is a big problem. They usually hire a company to do this. We were happy with our technology part and felt we could solve these problems. This was purely B2B.'

Somehow, the team leaned towards the first idea and proceeded with it. The idea itself was not novel. There was a company, Like.com, which tried doing the same thing in 2006, but the technology was not good enough.

'When we did a pilot, we were happy with our set of research. Technology was taken care of. We knew we can do something with it. I personally divide start-ups in three parts: technology, product and the business. The product around this idea had already been built earlier. We were not the first people to do it. But the business aspect had never been cracked. Nobody made a huge amount of money from this kind of an idea. Our novelty was not in coming up with this idea. But I feel what we got right was the timing and the application of the technology for the right product. The new generation of technology came around when e-commerce in India was growing. We had spent three years working in Yahoo! Labs where images comprised of 50–60 per cent of our work. So things fell into place.'

In parallel, the team kept on building the technology. Since there were five people, they could still keep on improvising on the technology and simultaneously do other things. 'Technology would be the same in all or everything we do. The product could be different; the business could be different.'

And then one fine day, Yahoo! announced that it is shutting down the India centre.

From Idea to Minimal Prototype: Fashiate

Yahoo! gave two options: Go out with a severance package or relocate to the US office.

'This brought a period of turmoil because some people were not sure anymore. Others kept going back and forth, but I and Gaurav had decided that we will not go to the USA. We two were always together. So it was down to two of us now. Gaurav had done his PhD from the University of Maryland. Both of us were researchers who didn't know how to build products. There were days when we thought that we might not be the best team to do a start-up because we needed someone to build the product.'

So they also started considering switching jobs in India. One of the companies they got a call from was Flipkart. By that time, they also had a very minimal prototype of the product. So when they interviewed with Amod Malviya (CTO of Flipkart at that time), they told him that they are starting a company but would be happy to work with Flipkart in any form.

'We could work as a contractor or exclusively for your company while doing the start up. We are even open to the idea of a full-time employment, but you have to respect the fact that we are building a start-up and we have to negotiate on that front. He was positive about it because the kind of problem we wanted to work on was exactly the kind of problem Flipkart needed a solution for. Amod said, "But I still have to take an interview. I would not be able to give you an offer without an interview because you guys don't have much to show". We then started with the interview process of Flipkart.'

However, the process was delayed because Flipkart did not have a PhD in computer vision to interview them.

'Meanwhile, there was another colleague, Deepthi, who earlier wanted to be a part of our team. But we were already five people, so we had said no to her. She had reached out to us again, and since Flipkart was taking some time with the interviews, we also had spare time at Yahoo! That "allowed" us to work on our own idea.'

Nikhil and Gaurav had read 10–15 research papers around the core technology. They spent time figuring out which papers to read, trying to find any open-source code available, experimenting with the code on the dataset they wanted to work with. Deepthi helped in building the back end and front end of the product. In all, it took about two months to get to a workable demo.

The wireframes and PowerPoint demo were ready by November. 'We kept on building the product. In parallel, Flipkart interviews were going on. Around the end of November, we had built a prototype that was good enough to show to the people.'

The working prototype was meant to be shown to investors or companies they were interviewing with.

'So we never had to do the hard work on the product like marketing or getting users. We got lucky in that. Had the acquisition not happened and we had decided to take the venture capital, then we would have built a company. Our USP (unique selling proposition) was in two things.

One was the idea of e-salesman itself. Technology behind that idea was the second USP.'

Preparing to Exit

Nikhil was clear on his priorities. He personally had a backup option if things didn't work out. 'I always had an exit strategy if everything failed. That, in my case, was to do a job or be a professor somewhere.'

An interesting turn of events played out as the team had finished their prototype by now. They started calling their prototype by the name Fashiate.

'We just went to Flipkart again and said, "We are starting a company now and this is what we have built. Can we consider this as an acquisition?" Amod was not very happy with that but what he agreed upon was that Flipkart would keep in mind that we had already built something and account for that in our job offers.'

What gave them confidence was that Amod had looked at the product and said, 'I have never seen something like this.' That made the team very proud that they had pulled off a technology that nobody else was doing. Nikhil elaborates, 'The technology was still a little nascent. We were not really happy with the technology part, but it was a demo which was working fine. Even Amod knew that the technology part is hard.'

The praises for their demo had lifted their hopes. Meanwhile Yahoo! announced that 15 December would be the last day for the Indian office. Finally, the reality crept in—doing a start-up is not only about doing a start-up: it is a lifestyle choice. The team was still battling the dilemma whether to go the start-up route or not when Flipkart made them an offer.

'That offer was better than a standard employment, but it was not as good as an acquisition target we were hoping for. There were two components—one is the monetary value of our product Fashiate which they were likely to pay through a bonus and some stock options. The second component of the deal was regarding our employment that would reflect in the salary and stock options. So stock option is common for the product, and the employment and bonus is effectively for the product. Flipkart came to us with three numbers: our bonus, our stock options and the salary. All three were not up to our expectations.'

The Big Moment: To Sell or Not to Sell

The team had planned to raise US$500,000 in case they did not get acquired. There were three investors who were showing good interest.

'We were open with the VCs. We told them we were talking to Flipkart and they were okay with it. All these VCs wanted us to go the B2C route because they wanted to play a bigger game. We were comfortable with that. We needed funds to go B2C route. It takes a lot of marketing to succeed in B2C. Gaurav had started leaning towards the Flipkart offer but Deepthi was not interested. She wanted to continue building our company. I was in the middle and not able to decide.'

Nikhil was thinking about his family.

'Parents always want their children to be on the safer side. Although they did not say it, but I felt they would get troubled with the idea of me not having a salary for some time. I got married the same year, and my wife supported me and said I should do what I want. But I could see that their comfort level was not as high. Or maybe I was just doubting myself, I don't know!'

They had asked Flipkart for a better offer by 14 December since 16 December was everybody's last day. On 15 December, Nikhil got a message from his friend Anuj who was heading the buyer experience in Snapdeal. He said, 'I know you guys are working on a product. Why don't you talk to people at Snapdeal also?' Seeing no harm in that, Nikhil called him up and next day went to Snapdeal to show the demo to their CTO.

That very day, within a few hours, Snapdeal decided that they had an interest in the product and they also knew that Nikhil had an offer from Flipkart which he was about to take.

'We even discussed the valuation on the same day. This is 17 or 18 December. Since they had started a conversation after we had built a product, it was a pure acquisition for them. Plus, Snapdeal was growing a lot back then, and they wanted to be Flipkart's competition. So I did not have to do much of negotiation there. They came with a number. We offered another number.'

Finally, Rohit Bansal came down to Bangalore and met all three of them and saw the product again. He gave the final nod.

'This was almost the end of December—25th or 26th. So a week went by. Flipkart had come up with another offer which was better than before but again Snapdeal was slightly better than Flipkart. Flipkart was giving independent offers to the three of us because they were hiring us. They were not buying our product. They were just compensating the product by giving us bonuses. Snapdeal's offer was an acquisition offer. This created some disagreements on how to split it amongst ourselves. Since I was negotiating with Snapdeal, I was just thinking how we can do it so that all three of us are happy and the gain is equal for all of us. In retrospect, we should have had an agreement before we went into any negotiation with Snapdeal. In the end, after a couple of discussions, we finally reached an agreement.'

In the end, the team decided to go with Snapdeal and split the acquisition in a way that was beneficial for all of them.

Life after Acquisition

Upon being asked the details of the acquisition, Nikhil hesitates, 'We have signed an NDA (non-disclosure agreement) and my co-founders will probably not be happy if I disclose that kind of information.'

But he is more animated when talking about what unfolded next.

'We joined in February and were made to start a new team called multi-media research lab. We ran it quite like a start-up itself. For three months, we kept on trying to integrate our idea but it did not work. A couple of months after we joined, Chief Product Officer Anand Chandrasekaran had joined Snapdeal and realized the value of our e-salesman idea and noticed how things were getting delayed. He recommended that we launch a new website itself which could be Snapdeal branded until they are ready to integrate it with the rest of the system. So we launched findmystyle.in to showcase our technology. By July, we had grown to seven people.'

However, e-salesman uses machine learning which takes time and needs more data to work well.

'We had built models based on our understanding and latest technology, but the product would be more effective once more people were using it. I believe current websites are doing user matching based on user clicks and textual components of products alone whereas we were trying to also use visual component of the products.'

Findmystyle did grow for a while. They were getting around 100 orders per day without any additional marketing.

'To really make it work, it had to be better integrated with Snapdeal because we faced issues like items being sold out by the time orders were placed, we did not have basic filters, etc. that Snapdeal had. We ran for two years but we just had to shut down in end of May 2017 because Snapdeal was cutting costs at that time.'

With the benefit of hindsight now, Nikhil has a better understanding of how bigger companies work.

'Once a bigger company acquires you, it is hard for them to integrate your technology into their existing systems. There is a lot of politics, and a company always has other things of higher priority. We felt that Snapdeal would want to work on this idea as soon as possible because they have spent money on us but that was not necessarily true. It was not a lack of desire; it was just that there were too many things for the company to focus on. So beware of that.'

Another important advice he gives is to hire a lawyer during the acquisitions, because they suggest a few terms that an entrepreneur may never think of by himself.

Finally, he recommends discussing the roles very clearly and who you are going to work with.

'When we came in, we did not know who to talk to because till then we were talking to mostly co-founders or very senior people. We took some time to understand the landscape. I wish we were introduced to those people earlier so that we could move more quickly.'

Connecting the Dots in Hindsight

The Fashiate story is an outlier, and it shows how one can commercialize niche technology. There are a few professors and academics who have specialized knowledge and they think of how to monetize their research. But they are rarely motivated to go the full start-up route. Nikhil chimes in, 'I believe the motivation is different and they realize that they need more skills than their academic knowhow to make it really big. Also, they already have well-established careers.'

At the time of writing of this book, Gaurav had joined Ola and Nikhil was heading to Amazon. They had to spend at least two years according to their Snapdeal contract for their cash component to fully vest. 'Our stock component was vesting over four years but I am not sure what would be its value now. Deepthi, with her start-up interests, might do another start-up.'

Nikhil finally has found his comfort zone with the idea of start-ups.

'If I am given a chance to go back in time, I would still do Fashiate. I would make the same decisions. We were lucky that we were getting paid while experimenting and making mistakes. Timing was quite perfect for our product which helped us in getting such a quick exit. Could Snapdeal have done better with our technology and us?—Yes, but I understand their constraints. We used to get frustrated initially but now I am more mature to understand why things happened that way. For that matter, even we were not very good at working within corporations. We could have found ways to get things into production earlier, but our mindset was also different. Our idea was eventually executed and we got to work on that which is great. And I don't think I regret not choosing Flipkart either because we probably would not have had that kind of authority, seniority and freedom in Flipkart.'

Nikhil thinks he will try another start-up when he has the right team.

Gaurav Aggarwal, Deepthi Singh and Nikhil Rasiwasia (left to right)

'Start-up teams are like marriages; it takes certain sacrifices to make them work. I now know what growth and sustainability mean. I would do a start-up for a lifestyle choice and not strive for a billion-dollar company. This means I am not necessarily looking for funding potential. I am happy to do a "business" now—something that would give me a better lifestyle. Start-up is just a glamorized word anyway.'

Key Takeaways

Person

- Clear priority and exit strategy.

Product

- *Ideation:* Founders' expertise was considered, and a set of problems was chosen that could be solved by leveraging the current technologies. By talking to other entrepreneurs and investors, the idea and target segment were refined (B2B vs B2C).
- *Validation:* Comments from Flipkart CTO Amod validated the promise and novelty of Fashiate technology. This gave the founders a confidence that they can pursue the idea if acquisition does not work out.

Exit

- *Leverage:* By leveraging the Flipkart offer, the founders managed to get a better deal from Snapdeal.
- *Negotiation:* The founders carefully negotiated until they got the terms they wanted.

NO SHORTCUTS

PART 2

Traction and Virality

I was thinking that if three people can be so effective that we were getting a million views a month, imagine if more learned people start sharing their lessons.
—Gaurav Munjal (Unacademy)

Paul Graham asks, 'What makes you think we would want this?' Evan replies—'Because we have two million users.' They were shocked.
—Prasanna Sankar (LikeALittle)

We realized that the real growth came from long-term page views and therefore we should invest in content which has longer shelf life.
—Ankit Maheshwari (Instablogs)

Traction is basically quantitative evidence of the customer demand. It's the Supreme Court definition of porn. You'll know it when you see it.

—Naval Ravikant

Beyond validation comes traction, and it is easy to see it in action when you are focusing on a small segment. Facebook blew up in Harvard and Twitter blew up at the SXSW (South by Southwest) conference. I notice a similar trend in the interviews where start-ups that grew very fast found their traction in niche user groups. Unacademy, one of the youngest start-ups in this book, has already crossed 20 million in monthly views and built a two-sided market fairly quickly. If you look at it deeply, the major part of its growth came from Roman Saini's video lessons on UPSC preparation—a niche segment that lacked online prep resources until then.

Not too far off is LikeALittle's insane growth acquiring two million users in the first six weeks and alarming Facebook and Google in the process. They gained traction on the Stanford campus before spreading onto others.

In a milder and slower form of traction, the Instablogs story shows the power of community as Ankit and Nandini succeeded in relating to their audience and inducing loyalty. In a pre-smartphone and low-bandwidth era, they created a YouTube channel with two million monthly views and blog content that generated half a million dollars in yearly revenues.

Risk more than others think is safe. Dream more than others think is practical.

—Howard Schultz

5 Gaurav Munjal, Roman Saini and Hemesh Singh: Unacademy

From offering free UPSC lessons to building an app so that anyone can teach anything, the 20-something founders behind the youngest start-ups discussed in this book are working to make self-help books and paid courses obsolete.

YouTube for Learning
#traction #product #edtech

Unacademy started off as a YouTube channel in 2010 when Gaurav Munjal explained a computer science concept to his friends over a video. Enter his close friend and confidante Roman Saini, the young AIIMS doctor, who cleared the prestigious Civil Services Examination in 2014 in his first attempt. With the popularity of Roman's UPSC preparation courses shooting through the roof, the Unacademy channel crossed a million views within a month. This is when the idea struck—how about building a tool that will allow anyone to start teaching? Gaurav quickly convinced Roman, and the product brain behind his previous start-up Flatchat, Hemesh Singh, to join full time. Soon, Sachin Gupta joined as the fourth founder, and Unacademy's new avatar was kicked off in August 2015.

Subsequently, Unacademy created an educator app and a learner app that can run on any cheap smartphone even in places having poor data connectivity. This educator app was launched in May 2017, and several successful candidates all across India—even backward villages—created lessons that would help thousands more. Founders claim that they have slashed the course creation time from five hours to a few minutes. With 40,000 lessons on their platform, 20 million monthly views, more than 1,000 educators as of June 2017 and celebrity educators such as Dr Kiran Bedi and Dr Shashi Tharoor, Unacademy has already attracted nearly US$18 million in funding from Sequoia, Blume, Nexus and other well-known angels.

Gaurav's stint with his previous start-up Flatchat has made him a better CEO, and he knows how to charm his audience. Will he be able to execute this 'YouTube for Learning' vision? Can Roman inspire more people to create more lessons? Can Hemesh and Sachin build a robust app and strong content discovery that will underpin the usability of the Unacademy platform? They have the cash and runway but how well that is spent and how well it translates to business sustainability remains to be seen. It is Unacademy's 25 per cent month-on-month growth that is promising, and it is the founders' young blood and fiery energy that has raised the hopes. Will they be the poster children that Indian edtech needs?

Roman Saini: From AIIMS to IAS to Entrepreneurship

Roman became friends with Gaurav in their Class XII chemistry tuitions. Coming from a family of doctors, he drifted towards medicine. In 2008, he joined AIIMS, but within two to three years, he started preparing for civil services. This was partly motivated by his senior Shena Aggarwal who had secured first rank in IAS. On 31 August 2014, he joined the civil services foundation programme in Mussoorie.

In a small entrepreneurial stint, Roman had started a medical tourism start-up when he was at AIIMS.

'The whole idea was that the medical facilities in India are way cheaper than in the West. For example, a liver transplant that costs US$300,000 in the USA can be done for much cheaper in India, even after including the cost of travel and accommodation. But the concern is, how do you find a good doctor? What if they take out your kidney? So we were connecting patients from the Middle East with IVF (in vitro fertilization) facilities in India. In 2011, there were five to six IVF doctors in Delhi that we talked to. Then, we got someone to create a very basic app which would help connect clients from Iran, Afghanistan and Iraq, etc. to the vetted doctors in Delhi. We helped around 42 patients in two months. After that, I again got busy with college and UPSC preparation. You can say that was my first experience with a start-up.'

In 2010–2011, Gaurav had started Unacademy as a YouTube channel, and later asked Roman to make videos on his channel to help IAS aspirants. Roman had used both coaching and self-preparation for IAS, and noticed that there were not many online resources at that time.

'Starting August 2014, I started actively creating videos for the platform. Meanwhile, I continued to fulfil my duties at the academy, where we learnt district administration, management, relation with army and CRPF, laws, what are our powers, CrPC, etc. Then I was posted as the assistant collector in Jabalpur. In September 2015, I made the decision to resign and join Unacademy full time.'

Gaurav Munjal: Born with an Entrepreneurial DNA

When Gaurav did not get selected for the editorial board of his school's magazine called *X-rays*, he walked up to the principal and convinced him to let him start the online version of the school magazine. He agreed and gave Gaurav a computer, a room and permission to carry a digital camera to the school every day. Gaurav founded his own team and conducted vox pop videos on various topics, such as who are the favourite teachers among students or what they would like to do when they grow up, and uploaded that on school website. 'Eventually, e-X-rays became the official website of our school (Xavier's, Jaipur). It was then that I realized that I love creating stuff from scratch.'

When the time came for engineering examinations, he gave the test to enrol at the coaching institute Resonance. 'To enrol there, you needed to take a test, and I failed that. So forget IIT, I had even failed to clear a test for coaching centre for IITs,' he chuckles. 'My AIEEE rank was 66,000 but I was ecstatic because heck, it wasn't more than 100,000!'

Gaurav ended up going to NMIMS, located in Juhu, Mumbai.

'I always sensed a unique entrepreneurial community developing in Andheri and Juhu. When I was in the third year, entrepreneurs like Kunal Shah would come and judge our college events. I met Ankur Agarwal of PriceBaba and I was writing blog posts for him as an intern. I would study enough to pass the examinations, and spent most of my time in coding and participating in competitive coding websites like TopCoder and CodeChef.'

In his second year, he was organizing an event and wanted to get sponsorship from CodeChef (a business unit of Directi). So he went to the office of Directiplex in Andheri East, and fell in love with the place. 'It was the way start-up offices are now but this was in 2009 when "start-ups" word was not that common.'

In his third year, he built Flat.to in college and launched Unacademy as a YouTube channel. 'My first video for Unacademy was uploaded in December 2010 for my friends who were sitting few kilometres away in Mumbai and wanted me to explain an engineering concept to them. So I said, why not do it over YouTube?'

He had a Dell laptop and a study table. He bought a whiteboard and recorded a simple video on a concept in computer graphics. That video has over 120,000 views by now. These are Indian engineering topics which are not very popular outside India. No one was explaining them online.

'I did not even know what content creation is; I just liked starting new things. I even started a fashion blog called Fashionama, and my friends will vouch for the fact that I do not know the F of Fashion. But the point was that I was earning ₹1 lakh per month from that blog using AdSense. I would pay a stipend to my friends for writing posts for it. All this time, I also kept uploading videos on Unacademy.'

Tasting Success with Flatchat

'When I got selected for an internship at Directi, I met Pratik Tandel, who is one of the India's best coders. He was so good that Facebook had offered him an internship in California. Right now, he is very senior guy at Twitter. During this time, I helped a friend find a flat through a broker. In return, the broker gave me a 10 per cent commission. That led me to the idea behind Flat.to—students need good brokers because *unko ghar dhoondne me* difficulty *hoti hai* and brokers need leads. If I can earn ₹4,000–5,000 by referring one friend, what if all the college students rent their flats via me? That is why I talked to Pratik and we built this Flat.to prototype. It was a map-based website and we had started that one year before Housing.com. But things did not hit off. Both of us were engineers, *kuch samajh nahi aaya*. Again, I called Roman and asked him *ki tu Delhi me sambhal le*. He started trying but *do din baad, he said ki mere bas ki nahi hai*. Flat.to sort of died out after that.'

In December 2013, Aakrit Vaish of Haptik gave a talk at NMIMS and mentioned that he invests in start-ups. 'So *jaise hi wo bahar nikla, maine use pakad liya*. I introduced myself to him, showed him the website and the next day he offered to invest in Flat.to.'

Flat.to had helped with 100–200 flats by that time and it was running smoothly. Gaurav had also received a job offer from Directi. While he was excited about it, he was also considering building up Flat.to.

'Somehow, I ended up joining Directi because it was a good offer and parents were also saying *ki apna kaam 1 saal baad kar lena*. Things are much different now. When my younger brother wants to do something, he is given more freedom now because my family has seen me.'

Gaurav joined as a software developer for the media.net project at Directi that was later sold to a Chinese company for US$900 million. While it was the same stuff that he had worked on and enjoyed as an intern, he had changed as a person by the time he started his full-time job.

'*Ye samajh aa gaya ki* this is not what I wanted to do now. After six months, I read that Housing.com launched and realized that I had made a big mistake. It was also a map-based service and I knew that if we had continued working on Flat.to, we would have only improved at it. I called up Aakrit and I asked him if his offer was still valid. He told me that I should make a product first and he will join me as a co-founder. So I called up Pratik and told him that I am going to work on our idea and if he can transfer the domain names. He was gracious enough to do that without any hassle. Aakrit had told me that he would transfer the money after I quit. So I took a no-objection certificate from Directi and started building the Flat.to product. After one year, I quit and started with Aakrit. We worked on it for around 10 months. Meanwhile Hemesh joined us; he was our first tech hire in Flat.to in June 2013.'

The challenges followed. While they had ₹20 lakh in their account when they started, they did not know how to spend it.

'We hired too many people and burnt too much money but we built a good product. I was the marketer. Hemesh handled the product and design very well. People respected us because it was a good product, but sales, ops were not as good. Housing.com *ki wajah se hamara blood pressure high rehta tha.* Here is a company that was buying a domain for a million dollars and we had a total of ₹20 lakh. Just imagine. We needed to raise more money.'

A few angels were interested but most of them were doing traditional businesses, and Gaurav did not feel excited to work with them. Then, he met Sumit Jain from CommonFloor who said, 'This is a really good product, let me acquire Flat.to. Keep building whatever you are building and give us 80 per cent stake.' They gave a 5X exit to Aakrit and invested more for 80 per cent acquisition.

After selling Flat.to, Gaurav moved to Bangalore where he developed Flatchat, which lets people looking for a place and people looking for flatmates to chat with each other, as part of CommonFloor. An internal round of funding was done, because Flatchat was doing really well. The whole idea was to make it more convenient and quick for the users.

'Just like Tinder, we should have a quicker way to house hunt. I believe that if you don't change with time, you will start hating your product. You need to outgrow yourself. That is what we did with Flatchat. There are businesses that are purely tech, and then there are businesses like Housing.com and Flat.to which are largely determined by the efficiency of your operations. What I realized is that I enjoy the tech part of it which doesn't require operations.'

Refocusing on Unacademy: From Educational Content to Edtech

During this time, Gaurav was also talking a lot with Roman. And then, Roman cracked the IAS!

'That is when I thought that now is the right time for him to start teaching. So he started making videos and Unacademy started growing very fast. Note that programmers have lot of reference material, but IAS aspirants have no resources available online. Growth was good and I really wanted Roman to join, but he was keen on joining the civil services. We were also working on Flatchat at this point. Although Roman had not officially joined or quit civil services, he continued making videos on Unacademy. At some point, I think everything fell into place. I left CommonFloor somewhere around August 2015 because Roman and I decided we would start Unacademy. Afterwards, Quikr acquired CommonFloor, and Flatchat also went to them. When I make enough money, I may buy Flatchat back from Quikr because I believe that it is a really good product. It solved rental problems. I had spent a lot to get that domain Flatchat.com as well. So that was that.'

Unacademy remained a YouTube channel till December 2015. Other than Gaurav and Roman, Ravi Handa was putting up videos on CAT preparation. While it would get decent views (1 million per month by December) and they were monetizing by YouTube ads, the biggest problem was that only three people had made videos.

'We needed more. The best minds in India were not even teaching online. If they started teaching, what a difference it would make! But existing tools make it very difficult for people to make videos. It takes hours to prepare for it. Our whole discussion came down to—can we make it quick and simple for anyone to make videos? Can we bring this onboarding time down to a minute? That is how we came to a solution to use a smartphone. I thought we should build a way where people can make a complete video using a smartphone and nothing else. When I shared that idea with Hemesh and Roman, they were immediately sold on it. This was in August 2015, just when I had informed Flatchat that I would be leaving. Hemesh's college friend Sachin also joined us as the fourth co-founder.'

There are multiple ways one can go about learning and education. Creating content alone did not seem to be a big vision.

'I was thinking that if three people can be so effective that we were getting a million views a month, imagine if more learned people start sharing their lessons. I could open studios like every other education start-up and I could call educators and create videos. Or I can build a tool which I can send to a lakh educators in our country and who can make their own videos. We have 20 million views every month, and we have over 40,000 lessons created by more than 1,000 educators from all over India. This has been possible because of our educator app, created by a team of 50 people.'

Staying away from an Udemy kind of model was a deliberate choice. 'We could think of monetizing in other ways—for example, premium membership for clearing doubts with the educators. Since day one, we wanted to build a learning platform where anyone can join and teach for free.'

Once the team was assembled, the work on the educator app started. Hemesh was looking after the product and design, Sachin was looking after the engineering, Roman was looking after the content and Gaurav took care of everything else—from fundraising to marketing to whatever was needed.

This shift from YouTube to app redefined the value of Unacademy as a product. Today, the founders believe that Unacademy's true value proposition lies in creating this educator app that has enabled educators to create content easily.

Hemesh chimes in on the technology aspect.

'We have an educator app for creating the lesson, and we have a learning app for people who want to consume the content. The educator app had a lot of complexities. We needed to support features like importing the content, images, editing the lessons, etc. Then, we need to ensure that it runs smoothly on all kind of phones. We need to be careful that things upload quickly. Our biggest concern was to stabilize the app to a great degree before even making it public. We were in beta for more than one year. In fact, we launched our app only in May 2017. Before that, we used to invite educators over emails.'

Defining Key Product Features

Many people are recording lessons on a laptop, processing it and selling their courses on MOOC (massive open online course) platforms. Unacademy is hoping to simplify the process as well as the technology knowledge required to do this. The three co-founders add their perspective.

Gaurav adds why they think smartphone is the solution. 'You need three things for a good course—content, your voice and interaction with the content. We realized that it is all possible through a smartphone. I can upload the content, take pictures, can highlight the content using touch and record my voice.'

Being a non-techie, Roman understands the value of simplicity.

'I will tell you that as a non-techie, it used to take me four to five hours to create a video before. And you need to spend money on a microphone, a tablet, a good laptop, good Internet speed to upload GBs of data and so on. *99 per cent log itna effort kyun karenge?* With this app, I can create a course in a minute. You need to just upload your presentation, start recording, and interact or annotate your presentation through touch. We provide interaction tools like highlighter, laser pointer, etc.'

Hemesh shows what is going on behind the scenes.

'One major thing we have done is created our own video player which helps reduce the bandwidth and it buffers much faster too. We have also paid attention on how to make the product more relevant, and one of the things we noticed is that short videos tend to do better. So we encourage educators to create bite-sized videos that a learner is more likely to see because no one wants to see a two-hour long video. So we force a limit of 15 minutes on a lesson. It also helps because once the educator has created and finished one lesson, his enthusiasm level is high, but if he has to create a very long video right away, then people feel discouraged.'

Roman shares an example,

'While we put a limit of 15 minutes on one lesson, a course can have multiple lessons. For example, we have an 11-hour long course on signals which has 60 lessons. The guy got rank 152 in GATE and he created this course that covers practically everything on signals.'

A demo follows. I see the vision in quick swipes, clicks and tools. The founders talk excitedly and share stories.

Gaurav shares the journey from the YouTube channel to Unacademy.in.

'We launched the website Unacademy.in on 10 December 2015. After chasing the owner of the domain for months, we finally bought the .com domain for quite a lot of money. When the educator app started working, those videos that were submitted on our website were played on our learning app. We still have the YouTube channel but we use it as a marketing platform now. Five per cent of the content is still there. We put a few lessons on it and if the user wants to see rest of the lessons, we ask them to come to our website.'

Organic Traction

An Alexa rank of around 500 in India and 500,000 downloads of their Android app without spending anything on marketing, is impressive by any standard. How did they achieve this?

Good quality content is very crucial to the platform's success. Roman understands his target audience very well.

'We had a million monthly views on our YouTube channel before we launched our app and we knew we had a lot of educators right there. We put up a form on our YouTube page and we added a "teach" button where people could volunteer to teach. With the educator app, it is very easy for them to start teaching. *Aap samjho*, there are people who are teaching these concepts to people around them anyway. Now with Hemesh's tool, they can click pictures of their notes, add explanations and quickly share it through the educator app. *Ye wo log hain jo khud bhi padh lete hain aur doosron ko bhi padha dete hain.* They were our initial educators. Many of these people have gathered a million views on their courses on Unacademy. That gives them a whole lot more motivation.'

Talking of motivation, Roman shares the story of Dheeraj Singh Chouhan from Saharanpur, located between Dehradun and Delhi. He ranked 27th in SSC CGL 2015. That exam is a smaller version of the UPSC.

'He does not even get 2G properly and he does not speak English very well. He is teaching on Unacademy using our app. When he was posted in a remote village in Chhattisgarh, on day one, someone approached him with a *mithaai ka dabba.* They told him Sir *aapka course dekh ke hamare bacche ka selection hua hai. Isse zyada aur kya motivation ho sakta hai?*'

It is not a coincidence that they have been able to find people like Dheeraj. Gaurav has learnt from Flatchat that one needs defined processes to run things smoothly. Following this philosophy, Roman heads the content section and has created two teams.

'One that brings in the educators and takes care of them. We call it our "educator care" team. Another is "category leader team" which is responsible for growth and diversity, but things are changing very fast. We try to bring in educators, influencers and celebrities. We have a strong brand recall value, and people want to work with us. We have influencers like Dr Kiran Bedi and Shashi Tharoor.'

Gaurav shares that they have spent no marketing dollars.

'My belief on social media is very different for each medium. YouTube is about sharing education lessons. Social media is about life experiences. Rather than selling on social media, we shared our stories, and that just built a following. Roman and I developed a good following and our answers get many upvotes. The thing is, we have kept hustling and sharing our journeys. Photos were important on Facebook, so when we met Akshay Kumar, for example, we posted that photo. Marketing is not about creating posters anymore. You need to understand what the people really want. If there is an exam and you share what will help people pass that exam, that is what the audience wants now.'

How has Unacademy managed to get to these celebrities and influencers? It boils down to the capacity to hustle. And Gaurav is a natural at that. He says,

'I emailed one of the leading entrepreneurs in Gurgaon (name I cannot disclose) so many times, but he would say *kyun milna hai* and kept delaying. I was at this StartupIndia event in January 2016. Somebody called my name and it was him. *Mai to chalu ho gaya* and pitched him. He said email me again. So when I reached back in Bangalore, I emailed him. He said, "I will meet you for 15 minutes". So I flew all the way to Delhi to just meet him. I valued his time, so I prepared five questions that I was going to ask him. The advice that he gave to me has really stayed with me all this while. He said, traction is as important as the product. 50 per cent of your time should be spent on the product and 50 per cent on traction. Advice number two was to grow one per cent every day. This has translated into a mandate to the content team to grow 25–30 per cent month on month. In last 1.5–2 years, we have had a consistent growth and that is the result of that 15 minutes meeting. I like to make things happen.'

Apart from the government examination preparation and computer programming, English lessons became another big area on Unacademy. In computer programming also, people have started teaching in Hindi too.

'And I don't think anyone is teaching programming in Hindi. In the beginning, category development was happening by chance. Roman created a course on willpower. So one part is the structured approach where we know there is demand for competitive exam preparation. Second part is *ki aap kisi bhi acche bande ko le aao*. There is Vaibhavi Rangarajan who scored 336 out of 340. She created a course where she tells a story in which she has covered 330 English words. So people can learn new English words through that story. One course got one lakh views. It was so innovative.'

Incentivizing Course Creators

It is tough to build a two-sided market. To succeed, Unacademy needed not only learners but educators. But Gaurav had the experience of doing that.

'Even with Flatchat, that is what we were trying to do. I thought that if we market it properly, both sides will come automatically. Renters and tenants will come. In Unacademy, we had built a following already when I and Roman were teaching. We have grown from 100,000 subscribers in September 2015 to 800,000 subscribers in June 2017. It was easy to invite more educators once the channel became popular.'

Once the app went live, people could submit their courses.

'We did pay some money initially but it is not the primary incentive. It is the same reason why people write on social media platforms and blogs.

Many have gamified the process, offering badges of recognition; similarly, we have top educators every month. We give out recognitions if you cross so many views, etc. We are also thinking of regional events for educators, award nights, etc.'

Eventually, Unacademy's vision is to go global, and they have chosen Brazil as the next stop. 'We saw the population and possible market size. We are using YouTube first with Brazil-oriented content to see how it does. We have gathered Brazilian educators who are delivering lessons in Portuguese,' Gaurav confides.

They did pay the initial educators in Brazil to create relevant content. In the long term, however, they think the right educators would be the ones who are motivated by recognition and not money.

'Ultimately, we do want to figure a revenue model where educators are making money using Unacademy. But we want them to be excited by the fact that their videos are being seen in the parts of world that they never imagined. The impact has to exceed the revenue making. That is what Facebook and Twitter are about.'

Monetization and Fundraising

The big elephant in the room is the question on monetization of edtech. How long will Unacademy keep getting/spreading content for free? The founders have been pondering upon it.

Gaurav shares his preliminary thoughts.

'We have some thoughts. Personalization of content, mentorship and features are three things that we will monetize on. For example, we launched a feature where you can save offline lessons for a subscription. We are one of the top-grossing apps on the Playstore in the educational category. We can also charge for real time Q&A sessions with an expert educator and it will have limited seats. So people might want to pay for getting that chance to directly interact with and ask questions to an educator.

We experimented with an event called UTalk where we invited our celebrity educators. It was a paid event and was sold out pretty soon. We can try more events around people who are expert in their areas. For example, if there is a music educator, we can do live concerts with him/her which will be paid.'

In October 2015, Unacademy raised a seed round of US$500,000 from Blume Ventures, Rajan Anandan, Sujeet Kumar, Sumit from CommonFloor, Phanindra Sama and few others. In April 2016, they raised a pre-Series A of US$1 million from Blume, Vijay Shekhar Sharma, Ashish Tulsian and others. January 2017 is when they raised a US$4.5 million Series A round led by Nexus.

'August 2017 is when we did Series B of US$11.5 million. Blume and Nexus have participated again, and our angel investors took a secondary exit. I like investors who are pull rather than push. Push means probing repeatedly whereas pull means they are there if you need help. Another thing I have looked for is—are they truly interested in a global consumer company? We have wanted to focus on global from day one.'

After using some of the funds for office space, hiring and scaling up □heir operations, the company still had a comfortable 30–32 months of runway as of 2017. The growth helps in attracting interesting people, the kind who have made Unacademy popular in the first place. Roman got his senior from AIIMS and a few others to join as full-time employees. One of them was handling growth strategy for Indonesia.

Gaurav doesn't believe in splurging on above-market salaries.

'If someone comes to me saying that he has a ₹17-lakh offer, I offer him ₹16-lakh package. If he joins us at that package, then I know he is joining because he truly believes in us. I also make sure that I push them out of their comfort zones. Richa Mathur is handling our operations. I met her at 5:00 PM in Mumbai and told her that your next interview will be at 10:00 AM tomorrow in our Bangalore office. She was living at Powai and there was only one flight left that night that she could take. I told her that only if you make this next meeting, then I will interview you further. It was an overstatement but it was about seeing how she reacts. She actually made it and started working right after that. I believe that we are here together for next 5–10 years. It is important that they believe in hustling and pushing the way we do.'

Most of the hiring has happened through references only.

'We are hiring interns in different categories. For example, someone who is good with English is told to build a community around English. Scaling content through staff-on-demand interns rather than full-time people is a great hack. It reduces the burn rate and you can grow much more quickly. I can hire 50 interns for two months, and even if half of them work well, it is great.'

The Moment of Truth

The ride has just started. As the number of submissions rise, Unacademy had to step up the moderation process. Roman shares,

'We reject around 80 per cent courses. We do not approve anything that is not 8/10 on quality. Also, pushing harder on someone's first course ensures that they try harder when they resubmit it. We have noticed that when people submit for the second time after getting rejected, that course quality is really good.'

While the team did not share how many courses one educator is creating, they inform that there are around 600 videos/lessons being uploaded daily. To scale the moderation of so many videos, the team has thought of assigning credit scores to the educators. 'Someone with high score can be approved directly. We can catch technical flaws such as bad voice, etc. in our product itself.'

They are aware that the app can solve the creation part, but discovery and distribution are going to matter as much if not more. Gaurav adds his final two cents.

'Let's say you have an affinity for low-pitch voice educators. Can we show courses by those kind of instructors? If you repeatedly heard your astronomy lesson from a science course, we should be recommending you good astronomy lessons. I think a recommendation engine would be crucial because we are already nearing 40,000 lessons. We will soon reach a million. What three lessons do I suggest to a user out of those million? We have started gathering data but we have more things to do than we have people who can do it.

Sachin Gupta, Gaurav Munjal, Hemesh Singh, Roman Saini (founders) (clockwise from top left)

Whatever works for first 10,000 views does not work for first 100,000 and then 500,000 views. It will be interesting to see how much we can keep growing without spending significant marketing dollars. I have the budget, but can we still grow without spending much is the question.'

On the whole, the team is looking ahead at the mountain of challenges with cautious optimism. And if their past drive is anything to go by, this would be a fun ride to watch.

Key Takeaways

Person

- *Gaurav's natural bent for selling and forging connections:* Helped in finding co-founders, mentors and investors.
- *Gaurav's leadership:* Assembling a founding team with diverse core strengths.
- *Roman's expertise and reputation:* Helped building an initial audience and attract other educators.
- *Long-term vision:* Instead of competing with others on content, taking the approach of building a product that content creators can use.

Traction

- *Validating in a niche segment:* By focusing on UPSC for which the preparation material was not readily available online, an initial audience reeled in.
- *Building two-sided community:* Once the founder videos started getting a million views from learners, attracting more educators became possible.
- *Understanding social media:* Intelligently leveraged different social media for different purposes.
- *Hustle and networking:* Being able to persuade celebrity influencers added to the credibility of the platform.

Product

- *Market research and understanding:* Knowing that many quality educators hail from small towns, the team designed product features to penetrate this specific market. Having created YouTube courses themselves, the founders knew the pain points to be solved.
- *Proprietary platform:* Designing the video player and educator apps allowed more control on these features including lower

bandwidth consumption, faster buffering and compatibility on any basic smartphone.

Operations

- *Creating content team:* Actively scouting good educators and popular topics on platforms like Quora replenishes the supply of content creators.
- *Leveraging interns:* Scaling content and learner community around a topic through short-term interns interested in that topic saved time and money.

Challenges That Lie Ahead

1. Figuring the right revenue model.
2. Keeping educators incentivized to add quality lessons.
3. Building an intelligent discovery and recommendation mechanism to help the users find what they want.

The difference between perseverance and obstinacy is that one comes from a strong will, and the other from a strong won't.

—Henry Ward Beecher

6   Prasanna Sankar: LikeALittle

From building an app that attracted two million users in six weeks to calling it quits in three years, Prasanna saw more action in his short-lived start-up than people see in a lifetime. Funded by the who's who of the Silicon Valley and rejecting US$50 million and US$100 million acquisition offers from Facebook and Google, LikeALittle is the most exciting start-up you may never have heard of.

Anonymous Flirting Platform for College Students
#traction #product #social_media #failure

LikeALittle was founded by Prasanna Sankar, Shubham Mittal and Evan Reas in October 2010 after trying out a lot of other failed ideas. Sometimes known as 'a flirting website for college students' for lack of a better description, LikeALittle was a platform for posting anonymous comments about people in your vicinity. Inspired by FitFinder, a similar idea that had become popular in London School of Economics, LikeALittle gained traction from Stanford and quickly replicated to other schools in the USA. As frivolous as it sounds, this is the start-up that was threatening Facebook with its growth at one point. LikeALittle would see a lot of such peaks in a short lifespan.

The viral growth of LikeALittle reflected in the 20 million page views in the first six weeks and attracted funding of

US$7 million from Andreessen Horowitz, Ron Conway, Mark Pincus, Paul Graham and such others. And then it started going down. In a soap opera-ish plot, the music stopped and no one knew how to dance anymore. The founders tried to pivot before shutting it down. Prasanna left it in 2013. What happened and how?

The man behind it all, Prasanna is a TopCoder and Google code-jam programming prodigy who found inspiration in Paul Graham and valley start-ups. In a candid chat, he paints a most realistic picture of founder ambitions, pressures and fears. He takes a dig at the buzzwords such as lean start-ups and growth hacking. In a world that elevates funding and traction stories, he wonderfully reminds us that the norm for start-ups is to fail and perhaps we need a better definition of success.

The Programming Prodigy

When Prasanna fell in love with programming, he started writing viruses.

'I pranked my friends. I would give them a game CD which was infected with the viruses I created. So then their computer would start showing pictures of Rajnikanth. It would countdown to five minutes, and then ask them to email me for getting the antivirus.'

Fast-forward to his days at NIT Trichy. He was ranked number one in India on TopCoder and won the Google Code Jam from India in 2005. This gave him a chance to visit the Google HQ in the USA.

'I was looking at all these volleyball courts and swimming pools. Crowd was super young. I knew I just wanted to work at Google after that.'

He did intern at Google twice and got a full-time offer from Google and Microsoft. Due to issues around H-1B, he could not get the US visa on time. Joining Google meant waiting 18 months.

'Meanwhile, Microsoft came in and matched my salary and offered to post me in Vancouver. My friends used to call me "Google Prasanna" all the time. So it surprised everyone when I ended up joining Microsoft.'

He joined the fledgling team for Bing (the Google search competitor created by Microsoft) when it had only 50 people.

'I saw insane growth there—from 50 people to 3,000 people in 18 months. This was my first experience of a hyper-growth product. It was not really Microsoft as we know. It was a start-up within Microsoft that had taken off at that time unexpectedly. Steve Balmer then started investing in TV ads, etc. The time when they hired me, they were actually breaking many rules such as "Microsoft USA hires from the USA and Microsoft India hires from India". My code was running on 100,000 boxes. A small bug that would be triggered once in a million times could still occur once a day because volume was so high! It was a dream for a computer geek like me.'

His friend Shubham Mittal who had interned with him at Google India had joined Bing as well.

'He is the smartest guy I have met so far. He was JEE ranked 2, IIT Delhi topper, President gold medallist and what not. Later, he would become my co-founder because we really liked each other. We used to discuss that we would go to Bing and then start a company together some day.'

Six months down the line, things were getting comfortable. Just when his manager wanted to promote him, Prasanna started feeling that he was a misfit.

'I didn't want to climb the typical corporate ladder in Microsoft. I thought I was super special. Back in college, I was ranked in the top 50 of the world. I did not want to do what everyone else was doing. I was also making decent money in college days just by winning these coding competitions. So I was working to buy my freedom. I was seduced by this American dream that Paul Graham was writing about and I wanted to give that a shot.'

It took a bit of work convincing Shubham, but Prasanna managed to do it. In September 2009, the duo quit Microsoft and left for a

YC[1] interview in Silicon Valley. They crashed at the Stanford hostel with some friends.

Reality Check with Paul Graham

Prasanna's voice grows more animated as he remembers those days.

'It was stupid looking back. We were living in our own bubble and knew nothing. The idea that we were pitching to YC was for this software that we had worked on for three months while we were in Microsoft. It was an exe file that the user would pay for. It would take a video of your computer screen every 200–250 milliseconds and index it. It made it totally searchable, any text on the screen. Let's say you read an obscure article yesterday and you remember some words from it. You could go back to that article by searching for that word.'

As soon as they said it was an exe file that the users were supposed to pay for, Paul Graham interrupted them and started laughing. He said, 'You guys look smart but this is 21st century and people don't really pay for exe anymore. Do you have any other idea?' And I was like, 'No, no, you are wrong, Paul. Dropbox worked, right?' Prasanna laughs.

Not so surprisingly, Paul Graham was not convinced and they were rejected. YC rejection sent them down the spiral of self-doubt and anxiety.

'We were not sure anymore what we were doing. But at least, we were already in valley and meeting these incredible people like Jawed Karim. He had gone insanely rich after selling YouTube to Google. We met some young billionaires too. Talking to all these people made us realize that we were wasting our time with this product and we lost conviction over time.'

---

[1] YC (Y Combinator) is an American seed accelerator, started by Paul Graham, Jessica Livingston, Trevor Blackwell and Robert Tappan Morris.

The Quintessential Start-Up Ride in the Valley

A common friend connected Prasanna to Evan Reas, a Stanford Business School student, who had raised venture capital for his idea ProFounder, and offered Shubham and him more than 10 per cent equity each. It was a website that helped small businesses raise funding.

'Small businesses are a huge part of the American economy and most of them raise money from their friends and families. But they did not do the paperwork properly and it was time consuming. We knew that our original idea is not going to work out and we need something else. Evan and his team already had a list of customers ready. He had even convinced a well-known person to become the CEO. She was Jessica Jackley and was famous for starting a company called Kiva. The team already had commitments to raise around US$300,000 for a US$3 million valuation in January 2010. We could see that it might become big.'

As it happened, the co-founders had a rift and decided to part ways. When they split, Jessica continued with the original idea and raised money from the same investors but at a lower valuation. Prasanna and Shubham decided to stick with Evan. 'Evan was a smart, convincing and super dedicated person. Now that he had split with his other two co-founders, we all became equal partners and started afresh.'

This is when a phase of aggressive experimentation started.

'That was the time of lean start-ups, we were caught into that. So we were just rapidly experimenting. We would come up with ideas on whiteboard, would try to sell even before we build a product and so on. I and Evan would walk down University Avenue which had a lot of businesses and we were signing them up for this product called discountly.com which was a chain marketing platform for restaurants. If you bring five people to this restaurant, your meal is free. And whenever those people came again, you would still get the reward. We thought the Amway style of marketing works, and so we sold the idea to local shops and signed up a few of them. I don't even remember why we gave up on that right now because we were trying too many things. Then, the iPad came up. We were convinced that this would be the next big thing. Our common friend Ankit Gupta had generated significant revenue from his Pulse app within a few months!'

Living in a hyperactive circle like Stanford has its own pros and cons. Sometimes, there are too many distractions and noise that can influence you. Prasanna wholeheartedly agrees.

'Looking back, five years after, I have learnt a few things. One is, I would never do a lean start-up thing again. I don't think ideas are brainstormed. I don't believe that any outlier success comes from brainstorming of ideas. You need to have deep commitment and domain knowledge to whatever you are doing. It comes when you care for something for long regardless of its commercial benefits. I have met hundreds of founders by now and I see it consistently. The guys who did not switch ideas too frivolously may not be VC-level hit stories, but they are the ones who are doing great for themselves. In fact, my own college roommate started HackerRank. If we ignore outlier outcomes, we have many second-level outcomes like HackerRank and Dr Chrono. They are US$10-million ARR (accounting rate of return) kind of companies. They stuck to their industry and kept working on and on, even when things were not going great. The Internet itself being a growth industry helped them double or triple every year and the growth added up over a long time. If you triple every year, you may not be VC investible, but you are still a successful lifestyle business.'

Prasanna is an avid reader. Having read the books of Peter Thiel, Warren Buffett and Paul Graham, he also had the golden opportunity to closely witness the start-up action in the valley.

'A classic outlier is half insider and half outsider. Insider in the sense that you know enough about the bigger things that are happening in your space. But you are enough of the outsider that the noise is completely ignored. You are just sitting out till you are compelled by the merits of an idea to act. If you take Paul Graham, he was far away from Sand Hill Road (where all VC offices are) and was not trying to start anything. And he was doing everything differently. He would decide to invest within a 10-minute conversation. He was putting in US$10,000 when people were putting in US$10 million. He was looking for students who wanted to try something over the summer, whereas VCs were looking for proven people and seasoned professionals. And he found a winner by doing these things.'

Prasanna rues the fact that he listened to too much noise.

'We were too much of an outsider when we were at Microsoft, but at Stanford, we became too much of an insider. Then, Evan is from business school; he is the epitome of a connected person. He was meeting investors who are talking about next big trends. So he was always chasing that investible idea. And he is doing that even today, which is pretty sad.'

The Light Bulb Moment: The Idea Presents Itself

It was now 1.5 years since they started.

'My girlfriend was studying in Cambridge at that time and taking a class with Professor Doug Richards who was an angel investor on the TV reality show called Dragon's Den (UK's equivalent of *Shark Tank*). He mentioned his most recent investment in a start-up called FitFinder—it was a web app created by a student at University College of London that started as an inside joke. This guy showed it to four/five of his guy friends and whenever they spotted a hot girl, they posted it on this app. But what happened was that this joke spread really fast. So it was a classic case of "they built it for themselves and it turns out that more of the world had a similar taste". They had a million page views in a month and became a rage in all London campuses. Then, the London School Chancellor asked the guys to shut it down because people were complaining that the app is objectifying women. So the FitFinder founder thought that he is graduating within a month and he can always restart the company once he gets his degree. When I heard this, it was clear to me what I needed to do now.'

Prasanna saw a clean product market fit. Market was begging for the product and the product was being taken away. It was the perfect 'hammer finds a nail' moment. 'We had to build it right away because we had to beat the FitFinder guys to market. So we just decided whatever domain name we could get within an hour.'

That is how LikeALittle was born. Evan was not convinced immediately. He thought it was silly and did not want to do an app that was considered to be objectifying women. He did not want to make money that way. 'I told him, let us give it a week. If, within a week, it does not take off, we can switch.'

'I had also started thinking that I cannot do it by myself because I am a weird Indian immigrant dude and the idea was not fitting with my personality. You know when these white people would post, sometimes I would not even understand their slang and why it's funny. So I needed Evan if this was to work.'

Prasanna just built the website overnight, and next day went to Stanford with Evan to try and launch it. The website had a simple text box.

'You choose a location, let's say Stanford Green Library. Then you would type something like—"Hey, girl in blue dress, you look cute". Or you could say something sarcastic about something that you are seeing right now. You hit on post and it would go on the Stanford page. So it's a single page with a text box and whatever you post goes on the page. That is all. Everything is anonymous and public. No registrations.'

LikeALittle Conquers Stanford

They kept going back to Stanford for three to four days, trying different marketing ideas. 'All we knew was that FitFinder worked this way. So we had some sense but we did not fully understand what to do with this product. And it was not taking off easily,' he chuckles.

'We went to the campus and we showed the website to students and they said it's cool but nobody used it. Every day we would try something and every day we would come back and write 10 different ideas that we can try the next day. We talked to people but it turned out that you need certain kind of weird person to start this and we were not finding those people. We would try writing "www.likealittle.com" on a class blackboard before the lecture started hoping that somebody would check it out. But even if some people checked it, they wouldn't understand what to do. Next, we thought we would scrape Stanford directory for student emails and send them emails all at same time so that when they are in class, they could start using it simultaneously. We set up the homepage of all computers in a lab to likealittle.com. So we tried all these ideas but nothing was working. It was almost Day 5 at that time and my one-week deadline to Evan was coming up.'

Day 5 started from Stanford's Green Library.

'We had decided to take all the risk we could, even if it meant getting banned from the library. So Day 5, we went and took a lot of postcards and behind each postcard, I wrote, *Experience high-quality 3D flirting for the next 30 minutes on www.likealittle.com*. We made 50 such postcards and Evan went and sat among other students in the library. He had made a list of 50 comments about the place that he would post pretending to be a regular user. He had this list ready and I went on the door and handed out these postcards to everyone entering the library so that people don't know that Evan was a part of the team.'

Prasanna distributed the postcards and went to a corner and started refreshing the website on his laptop. Evan made five quick comments and Prasanna kept checking the apache logs. Hits were coming. Evan continued to post his stuff and people were refreshing to check what the new post is. After one or two hours, Evan stopped posting. There was just one other meaningful post and two people had liked it by clicking the like button on the top of the website. It appeared to be another failed attempt.

'Before I went to sleep, I went to the site and saw a third like on the page. I would have slept four to five hour, and in the morning I saw seven likes. By the next evening, we had 50 likes. There were three to four new posts but mostly new likes. So we decided to try out the exact same thing the next day. We went to the same library and gave out these cards. Now, it clearly started taking off. New people were starting to come to the library by reading the things on the website. At that point, we knew this was big. End of that day, we had 2,000 likes or so. Within next two days, we had 20 per cent share of the web traffic in Stanford.'

Thank God, they had the like button! Being an anonymous website, most of the posts were created by a guy hitting on a girl or vice versa. 'There were also a few comments like "How LikeALittle sucked" in a demeaning way.' But the team had all the validation they needed.

'You know we had no time to feel or sleep. There was so much to build. We were getting so much traffic, this one server was not enough anymore. From that point to almost next few weeks, we were sleeping only two to three hours every day. We were just hungry and sleep deprived. I was just drowning with work. The site would break; we wanted new features. You have to remember that we were not even sure that we had made it. We did not know whether the users will keep coming back. We were shit scared that they would leave. So I was quickly building features like you could sign up with your Stanford email so that you can get notifications. I built a commenting system so that each time you comment, you get a unique fruit name assigned to you which one could use to have some identity in that conversation alone. We added more locations based on the frequency of what people were posting.'

Evan was doing moderation as well. 'Like if somebody said, "Your ass is big" or something tasteless that could spoil the community, we would delete that. He was doing some level of customer support, getting us food.'

They were scared that the FitFinder thing would come to the USA. 'I was sure they would launch, I didn't know when. We just knew that something has worked and we have to grow fast.'

Scaling to Other Campuses

The biggest problem was that founders did not know if the same approach would work in the other campuses. 'Ideally, we wanted to figure out a formula that we could replicate.' The same library experiment failed to deliver in Berkeley although by the time they reached there, Berkeley students had already heard about them.

'Now, we were wondering how to scale it. I knew that a lot of other campus students were visiting our website. So I put up a button where people could request to open LikeALittle in their campus. We started by focusing on five campuses this way. These people would become campus ambassadors and manage it. Few of them worked well such as University of Wisconsin and University of Michigan. First, we understood what motivated them. The people who submitted these requests liked being called the CEOs of these chapters and wanted to put it on their resume. It would be a matter of pride for them. Also, we started seeing correlations that if a girl is in a super popular fraternity and she becomes the ambassador, it had much better chances of taking off versus a techie guy. Techie guys were the worst case.'

Next, they made a one-page playbook on 'How to make LikeALittle chapter thrive in your campus' and mentioned tips such as putting fake posts, attracting popular friends, etc. That was Week 3 or 4 and then everything broke loose. 'Once we added this button and released this formula sheet, growth was through the roof. Every day, we were doubling.'

In the first six weeks, LikeAlittle had astounding 20 million page views and two million visitors.

Along with the popularity, came in a flurry of harassment posts on the website.

'Because college-going students are like that. They post anything they want. There were suicide threats, there were drugs like Adderall being sold. I didn't understand half of the things that these people were talking. Like I didn't even understand the slang. So anyway, all these things were happening and there was a lot of backlash from the college administration. There was this love–hate relationship with the website. And it bothered Evan a lot. It didn't bother me that much. I really didn't care what people thought about me. But everyday cops would call us and they would ask for people's identity. There would be some college kid threatening suicide. And they would be trying to locate them. So all this was happening and Evan was handling all of these because I was in the tech. And he used to hate it.'

As a result, Evan was always pushing for adding more identity to the website so that people wouldn't do such mean things. And Prasanna was totally against it. 'I thought that anonymity is the fire. That was the biggest reason the website was working.'

Investors Take Notice and Acquisition Offers Pour In

Evan had a mentor-ish relationship with Scott Cook, who started Intuit.

'He knew that LikeALittle was taking off like crazy. He would say things like "This two-people house is actually the centre of the world. The world just doesn't realize it yet". He wrote a cheque for US$100,000. Then, he connected us to Marc Andreessen, Sequoia, etc. and we realized how hot we were. Everybody wanted to invest.'

Just few weeks before this, Prasanna had applied to YC with another idea and received an interview call. By the time they went there, the idea had been completely changed.

'I remember going in there and pitching Paul Graham on this new idea. And Paul Graham says, "What?? You post about this girl?" And they were like come on, it's hopeless. Paul Graham asks, "What makes you think we would want this?" And that is when we turned it around. Evan told him, "Because we have two million users". They were shocked. They said, "You changed the idea from the time we had called you for interview to the time you are meeting us for interview. Less than two months. And you have so many users that soon?" We said, yes. They were like "Oh, My God! Let's see the website. What's going on?" They were totally into it.'

To get a perspective, Facebook hit 100,000 users by its second year. It was rare for a social media to take off the way LikeALittle did. The funding was a matter of formality afterwards.

'We didn't need any pitch line. There would be no conversation. They would ask us, "Tell us what you do". We would open the website analytics and just show them our traffic graph. And there was no more discussion after that. There was no talk about monetization. They didn't care about backlash. What they cared about was how big the founders thought it could be.'

Finally, LikeALittle did join YC for their Winter 2011 batch. The investment terms were standard—US$20,000 for 5 per cent stake. Additionally, they raised around US$1.5 million at US$10-million valuation through Andreessen Horowitz. The other offer was from Sequoia and that was for a million dollars at a US$4-million valuation.

'Unfortunately, we never spent a lot of time in YC because that was the precise time when growth was really insane and the site was going down every day. So we weren't even getting enough sleep. We weren't going to any YC meetings. Once Paul Graham emailed us and said, "I don't know why you guys aren't coming to any of our meetings. You are not doing one-on-one with me as well. It seems, this is not normal. Our successful companies are the ones that took YC seriously and you guys aren't". And then we met him and described our situation. Then he understood. But we never had time to work on the problem. We were constantly afraid of the problem but everyday there used to be bigger problems. Cops would call us, the site would go down.'

Soon thereafter, Facebook CTO Bret Taylor had expressed an interest to work together.

'This was another way of saying that he wanted to buy us. Bret said you know the price could be like US$50 million. Evan said thanks but no thanks! Marc Andreessen once said Mark Zuckerberg was pretty concerned that we were growing really really fast and we were competition to Facebook. And therefore, Marc Andreessen should not be on our board because he was on Facebook's board.'

Investors were not the only people they were attracting. They had hired two engineers and two non-engineering folks by this time. The website was for college students and a lot of people reached out saying that they wanted to work with them. Prasanna and Evan didn't have any time to filter and said no to everyone.

'But there was this one girl, who was probably 16 years old at that time. She was studying in some school. She said, "I am coming over". That was her email. I said, "Sorry, we don't have any opportunities at this time". She said, "No. Coming over". Next thing I know is that she was in front of our house and we were just blown away. She just came and said, "Don't pay me anything. I don't need any money. I will just help you". We were still hesitant and said, "Please don't waste our time, we have lots of things to do". And she just sat with me and Evan for like 10 to 15 minutes and she asked what were the top things that were bothering us on the website. She immediately started adding value and we hired her.'

Hitting the Ceiling

'We were facing a big problem,' Prasanna finally gets to the darker side of the tale.

'We noticed that after two or three days, user activity used to go down a lot. And this was true even within the first month of our launch. In the first two days, we used to completely take over an entire campus. In Stanford, it meant that there was a new post every time we refreshed the page, it was that crazy. Third day onwards, the post frequency would become one in three hours and so on. It gradually worsens and might stabilize around 2 per cent of the users using the site on a monthly basis after five to six months. Now, our choice was to spread quickly to more campuses and kill the path for any other site like FitFinder or keep focusing on retention. We did have ideas on how to address the retention problem such as letting users enter their emails and be notified of new updates, etc. But we could only focus on one strategy at that point.'

They decided to continue expanding and in six to nine months, they had acquired 70 per cent of the US market share.

'We had good share in South Korea, Hong Kong schools. At our peak, we were doing 10 million daily actives or perhaps more. We were a really hot start-up. We had one insane statistic that Facebook was super jealous of—if a user came to our site thrice, there was a 50 per cent chance that he would come back to our site 100 more times. This was like crazy. So in three visits, the user was addicted to us. But it also turned out that the drug fades away with time. Within three months, people were getting cured.'

The founders panicked for the first time when growth actually started slowing down. 'At one point, we also saw a drop in daily active users. The overall number of page views and user registrations started coming down. At that time, it became very clear that this retention problem is serious'.

Three months down the line, they started to add superficial user profiles so that one could put in the email address for subscribing to the daily posts.

'Everything hit us simultaneously. We also had administration and moderation issues. We had to build automated techniques to flag bad posts. We were wondering if those were causing the retention issue, so for a long time, we just paid attention to moderating offensive comments. It was not feasible to keep doing this manually. There was no time to hire or manage people, where would we even start looking for people to hire for moderation? Only option was to delegate the job to campus representatives. We built tools, a list of banned words and advise that worked well enough so that these reps were now able to handle the situation on their own. The problem was that no external person could do it because even Evan was not understanding the slangs that these kids were using. UrbanDictionary did not have those definitions, so we would never have been able to moderate it. Self-governing was the only option. But unfortunately, the retention problem did not seem to be resolved even after moderation success.'

Rift Between the Founders

Plush with cash, investors started recommending ideas to keep growing. Marc Andreessen suggested spending US$10,000–100,000 per campus to ensure LikeALittle completely sticks. With less than 100 elite schools in the USA, they could completely take over by spending less than US$5 million.

'Yishan Wong who had just retired as the director of Facebook was advising us those days. Later on, he went on to become the CEO of Reddit. I remember all discussions were going in the direction of adding more identity on the site. Marc Andreessen thought that we should put in more identity and I told him we are never going to do that because anonymity is what is working for us. Evan agreed with him. Everyone looked up to Marc Andreessen, and Evan is a guy who really cared what other people thought of him and validation from Marc Andreessen was like a powerful drug. This started straining our relationship.'

By early to mid-2012, the traffic was going down and iPhone was dominating.

'Since there was GPS and most people were carrying these iPhones, we had to go mobile. We decided to pivot to an app called Circle which was more about location. And we couldn't completely get the transition right. We just could not move our desktop users to mobile. The traffic on the desktop was also slowly decaying. And there was this constant pressure that Evan would come up with new ideas that he wanted to try and we thought this thing wasn't going anywhere. There was a lot of friction in the team.'

To be fair, the desktop-to-mobile transition was painful for everyone including Facebook.

'It was not clear at that time in 2012–2013, whether the winners in desktop are going to win the mobile game. We had only about 0.5 per cent users on mobile and I could not justify investing all my engineering resources into that. We were adding more and more identity stuff on the mobile, and that was all driven by Evan. But nothing was working. By that time, I didn't have any good ideas left. Anything I said was not working. I knew what ever was working had stopped to work. So I just went along with their ideas. We launched a lot of different apps on the mobile and we just pivoted a hundred times and failed.'

Accepting the Failure

Despite the world's finest investors behind them, the party came crashing down. What do the investors do when something is not working?

'Investors don't really get frustrated. They just stop talking to you. They just stop wasting their time. They write off the investments and move on. This has happened a lot of times to them. It is the first time for us. So they are just trying to focus their time on things that can return their entire billion dollar fund. And they just stopped meeting us.'

In one of the board meetings, Jeff Jordan was representing the Andreessen Horowitz firm.

'At that time Marc had nearly made up his mind to invest another US$10 million in us. So in this meeting, we were showing our mobile app to Jeff and putting up a face that things are going great and the new app will be a great success. I think it was pretty clear to Jeff from the numbers that we are not getting anywhere. He did not say much to us, but he must have told Marc that we have lost our product market fit and we don't deserve any more money. Marc decided to give us US$5 million instead of US$10 million on a US$30 million valuation. I am sure he just wrote it off in his mind. He gave that check just to keep his word.'

It was beginning of 2013. Prasanna was feeling burnt out and didn't believe in the idea anymore. He was sticking around because he had taken an oath with Shubham that they would do this for five years no matter what.

'I wasn't being productive. I was reading a lot of other books. There was a lot of friction between Evan and me. Around mid-2013, we had a confrontation. It was clear to everyone that we had already delayed and I should leave the company, and it was already too late at that point. So I left in August 2013.'

Shubham, Evan, two employees and a designer—everyone else continued. Prasanna was the only one who left.

Lessons Learnt

When you lose, make sure you don't lose the lesson as well. Prasanna, for sure, did not. He believes there are some ideas that have a shelf life and there is nothing much one can do after that.

Looking back, Prasanna feels that they were the kind of entrepreneurs who decide that they would start a company before they decide what they are going to work on.

'Precisely the kind of entrepreneurs who fail. My belief right now is that nobody is a genius when it comes to going against fundamentals. Not Paul Graham, not Marc Andreessen. If a user is coming to a site to do something and that doesn't last, then you can be just happy with the reduced frequency. That's what the fundamentals dictate. Many people that I meet in the start-up world, ask me, "So our site doesn't have engagements. How can I increase engagement?" As if it's a standalone problem! There is this term called *growth hacking* which became famous around the time when Facebook grew. I think that's the biggest thing that I fundamentally disagree with; people have this misinterpretation that you can somehow growth hack your way to success, you can somehow turn knobs and make it successful. But you have to understand that user behaviour has certain patterns and constraints in the way it works. You have to just understand it and come to terms with it. You can't engineer your way out of any of the constraints.'

Could they have done anything differently?

'I wouldn't even try adding a ton of things. We had a lot of money sitting in the bank. We were not running out of money anytime soon. I would have just focused on user behaviour and resigned to the fact that engagement is going to reduce and hit a new low after three months on campus. And may be that means just a million or two million page views from campuses. We needed to think of which other places we could have catered to and tried to serve them rather than trying to institute a different user behaviour. I would just keep it at two million or three million page views, and put ads and make US$10,000 or US$100,000 a month and be happy.'

The journey could have drained anyone. After an acquisition offer from Facebook at US$50 million valuation, there was another by

Marissa Mayer (who was at Google at that time) for US$100 million. And they didn't sell in both cases. At that time, Facebook was valued at US$6–7 billion. They were giving most of it in stocks at US$50 million which would be a billion dollars today.

'We were somewhat blinded in the pressure of proving that we are a big deal which we weren't. The world had changed. We were the top start-up in our YC batch. I think every time I met a founder or YC colleague from my batch, it all started feeling really fake to me. The conversation always started with how is it going? And socially you are expected to give a very rosy picture and at one point I felt like saying, "Dude, cut the bullshit. It's been three years since we left YC. I know you are up to no shit. I am up to no shit". Of course, I can't say that because my employees would quit. I was literally wasting their lives. I was in between a rock and a hard place and it was burning me out.'

After quitting, Prasanna sold a little bit of his LikeALittle stock and did things that he never had time to do before.

'I made around a crore and started travelling around. I came back to India and met my old friends. I was just chilling. I got married around that time. My wife got a job in Netherlands. So I moved to Netherlands. We took a year off. Mostly just investing my money in stocks and that went really well because the Indian markets in August 2013 quite predictable.'

This hiatus from his entrepreneurial explorations is now over, and Prasanna is currently doing a start-up called Rippling with the ex-CEO of Zenefits.

Prasanna Recommends

He thrives on books and shares his top five reads:

- *Zero to One* by Peter Thiel
- *Antifragile* by Nassim Nicholas Taleb
- *The Snowball* by Alice Schroeder
- *You Can Be a Stock Market Genius* by Joel Greenblatt (despite its corny title)

Shubham Mittal, Evan Reas, Prasanna S. and friends (from right to left)

Key Takeaways

Person

- Strong aptitude and talent for computer science and programming.
- High ambitions and very high degree of self-awareness through reading.
- Ability to step away when he lost confidence in the product.

Product

- *Ideation:* Earlier ideas were started with a motivation of making it big rather than a real need. Inspired by FitFinder that had already been a rage on London campuses, LikeALittle was a validated idea that the market was begging for. In hindsight, Prasanna emphasizes that best businesses are built on need, persistence and a rare insight.
- *Understanding the audience:* The decision to keep the website anonymous helped the cause of flirting that the platform was known for and led to rapid early adoption.

Traction

- *Validating in a hyper local zone:* By focusing on Stanford alone, the merits of the idea were proven before expanding elsewhere.
- *Building a community:* By letting students become 'CEO of a campus', the community developed and scaled fast.
- *Reality of user behaviour:* Sometimes, you need to accept the constraints of user behaviour that are inherent to your product and realize that it cannot be mutated.

Challenges That Took the Company Down

1. *Frequently chasing the next big thing:* Pivoting sometime works in a start-up's favour, but excessive pivoting worked against in this case. Prasanna and his team were never able to stick to a vision and got distracted too often.
2. *Conflict in the founding team:* Prasanna and Evan were at loggerheads on the topic of anonymity, and caused a deeper rift in the long run.
3. *Unrealistic expectations:* When insane growth and traffic slowed down, it led to unmanageable pressure on the founders, and eventually the team collapsed.
4. *Lack of patience and focus:* Giving up on the mobile app and the website when new features were not delivering, they misread the market and lost patience.

When you find an idea that you just can't stop thinking about, that's probably a good one to pursue.

—Josh James

7   Nandini and Ankit Maheshwari: Instablogs

The first multiblog network of Asia was the brainchild of a serial entrepreneur couple, Ankit and Nandini. At a time when no one knew what blogs are, how did they manage technology, content and hiring in India to build a global audience?

Multiblog and Citizen Journalism Platform
#traction #product #business_model #acquired #content

Instablogs was founded in October 2005 by Ankit Maheshwari and Nandini Rathi. What started out as a blog network of 50 blogs around niche content, soon added a conversational platform based on news from around the world with a collaborative journalism approach. Breaking even in five months, Instablogs drew two million monthly page views and half a million dollars in yearly revenue by 2008. Nandini's innovative marketing brain and Ankit's technology expertise helped create a content platform that was successfully competing with the high-profiled blogs of USA. Key decisions such as building their own back-end platform and relying heavily on analytics paid dividends in growing the content as well as the community. Instablogs was later renamed as Instamedia, and it raised US$4 million from the Times of India group.

The down-to-earth husband–wife duo overcame a lot of criticism and lack of experience to create data-driven content marketing strategies that are, till date, followed in the blogosphere. Generating more AdSense revenues than bigger media houses and becoming the third largest YouTube channel in India, Instablogs garnered commendable feats to its credit before winding down operations in 2012. Although not the biggest of exits, Instablogs story throws a sparkling spotlight on the endless possibilities of a persistent and resourceful mind.

Nandini was pursuing CA but loved reading blogs, and Ankit was working with small companies, getting a taste of code, design and databases. They married and dreamed of doing a start-up someday. That day arrived soon.

Trailblazers of Blogging

In her college days, Nandini had launched a web directory called Webatlas which made good money for every listing.

'That was my first online start-up. I was charging few dollars for every listing, but then it got banned by Google due to excessive link building. This failure taught me a very important lesson—to never do any business that is totally dependent on Google.

I started following a blog network called Weblogs Inc. which was later acquired by AOL. That was the only blog network on the Internet at that time and it was based in the USA. I was particularly following their luxury blog called Luxist. That is when I decided to start a luxury blog of my own. I discussed it with Ankit and it turned out that he was also interested in content but he had a different idea in mind. He convinced me to launch a blog network instead.'

Ankit and Nandini started participating in digital marketing forums and connected with US entrepreneurs like Aaron Wall who had written the famous SEO book. Ankit admits,

'Nandini would answer questions on marketing and I would answer on technology, servers, databases, etc. We did not have a clear idea, but I ended up resigning from my job. So we started taking on outsourced projects. Our initial projects came from these forums. Someone needed help with ranking higher on Google or revamping their websites. It was those kinds of projects. Nandini got a project from Norway and it was a six to nine months' assignment. And more work started coming our way. Honestly, in those days, I had no idea how different it is to run a product and service start-up, and what venture capital is.'

Ankit found his interest developing in a citizen journalism website.

'One thing that struck me was that every news story has a different impact on people from different parts of the world. So global perception around a news item is different from its local perception. For example, Benazir Bhutto's assassination had a different reaction from people who live in Pakistan than from people who live in India and other countries. So we created a website where every news story had two columns—global impact and local impact. If news is from France, then comments and opinions from French people will be seen in the local column. We observed that the local opinions sometimes were so different from an outsider's viewpoint. The bias is mostly propagated by media and politicians.'

They launched Instablogs in 2005 with two parts: One of the parts, www.instablogs.com, was the citizen journalism platform and the other part comprised of few blogs with their own URLs. Ankit remembers the initial struggle.

'Interestingly, when I first started the citizen journalism project, I did not know how to go about sourcing the opinions. Through various forums, I got in touch with people from the Middle East, Europe, South America, etc. We got our initial audience from there. At the same time, Nandini was building her own team to handle her blogs.'

They took care of the cash by maxing out their credit cards. But hiring remained the biggest challenge because they could not afford to hire journalists, and blogging was an alien concept for Indians. Nandini finally managed to crack the hiring puzzle using her innovative mindset.

'We hired freshers from good colleges and then trained them for blogging. Nobody knew about business-to-business blogging but everyone knew about Amitabh Bachchan's blog because it often came up in the news. I used to ask them [potential employees] if they had read Amitabh Bachchan's blog. If they said yes, I told them that he writes it as a diary but we will do it professionally. Initially we hired 15–20 people. I was writing content on BornRich myself. Apart from content, we needed a few tech people too because Ankit was building our tech platform.'

Ankit's decision to create their own back end instead of using WordPress, etc. was a conscious choice that played to their advantage later on.

'WordPress was not as advanced in those days. It did not have the multisite capabilities as far as I remember. That is why we started building our own platform. Since Nandini wanted a network of blogs with multiple authors anyway, we had to build that. I started the citizen journalism part a bit later using the same technology.'

They launched in 2005 and due to the good PR that Nandini had planned, they got so much traffic that the servers crashed. 'I remember working for 72 hours straight, coding and making sure that everything worked,' Ankit reminisces.

Turning Criticism into PR

Nandini shares more details about her PR planning.

'We didn't have the budget to advertise in order to bring traffic, and social media wasn't like it is today. So we devised a PR strategy to promote our launch. The first strategy was to create content for each site beforehand so that when we do our public launch, our visitors will have interesting content to read. The second strategy was to make an outreach to all the popular bloggers. We created a mailing list and sent out our press release to everyone on the list. The list had bloggers, SEO people, other contacts we made from forums, etc. When we finally launched, reactions started pouring in.

Few people were ignorant, few were very critical. One of the harshest reviews labelled us as cheap Indian writers on steroids for publishing so many blogs on every site. But we didn't lose hope. We gathered all those critical reviews and created an interesting comic strip. The strip showed people gathered around an elephant; someone was pulling the elephant's tail, someone his ears, and saying what they think about that part. The idea was inspired from that joke about blind people feeling an elephant by touching one part and describing what they think an elephant is based on their partial experiences. We wrote the stuff that critics had commented about us in the blurbs and then we personally acknowledged every single critique very politely. We told them that we might not be good but we are going to deliver. The idea was to show that they are missing the bigger picture about us. Interestingly, that worked out great! Our critics ended up feeling bad that they had said all those mean things about us and we ended up building great connections with a lot of people because of that.'

Scaling the Content

Launching 40–50 blogs meant churning out a crazy amount of content. Nandini pivoted to avoid content burnout.

'Creating content every day but having no one to read it is disheartening and demotivating. Organic traffic takes a lot of time to build. So I decided to pivot BornRich away from just a luxury blog like the ones I was following. I was already developing a knack of finding good scoops on the Internet— new product launches, lifestyle news, etc. I was simultaneously building my own RSS (rich site summary) reader and had a good idea of what kind of stories are preferred by the top blogs. As soon as I used to break a new product launch, I started submitting the same to the relevant blogs. This strategy fetched wonderful results. Popular blogs like Gizmodo started linking to us on a daily basis. Soon, we realized that we don't have bandwidth for so many blogs. So we reduced the number of blogs to 15 and then later on to 10.'

Using tools like Statcounter, Nandini noted where the visitors were coming from and started to pitch to other similar websites.

'This helped us immensely to plan a broader outreach. I noticed a lot of interest from gadget blogs, and that's how I expanded our coverage to cover big boy toys. Soon we were on every gadget site's news reader. We started getting a lot of backlinks from almost everywhere. We built a news hunting team to pick up interesting news earlier than the popular blogs in our niche, and we used to tip them and get a link back in return. Our news hunting team would look out for breaking news and stories. I trained them on building a database. There were three to four people in this team, and they would send these news stories to the editor one day in advance so they have stuff to write about first thing in the morning. The respective editors would then approve or disapprove it. This freed a lot of bandwidth for the writers. They were able to create more number of stories that they knew would be well-received. The time zone also worked in our favour. We realized that we could be America's morning news. We streamlined our blogging process a lot. I remember Gizmodo editor Brian Lam once told me that I have an eye for news and it is really impressive.'

Not too long after, BornRich was ranked amongst the top 100 blogs list curated by PCMag. They were also featured on *The Times*, *NY Times*, *The Guardian*, *Business Insider* and almost every big publication.

Innovative Viral Marketing

Getting quality backlinks is not easy. And building a global audience sitting out of a Third World country is another beast. Unknowingly, Nandini was figuring out the viral marketing strategies that are so popular in the blogging space now by trial and error.

'I had built a list of bloggers that I wanted to network with and I used to pitch our stories to them. But we couldn't be begging for links every time. So I decided to interview these bloggers. Instead of interviewing ourselves, we reached out to our blog readers and asked them to send us questions for our celebrity blogger. The crowdsourcing interview concept turned out to be a big hit right from the start. The bloggers we interviewed loved it! They promoted our blog in return. We named the interview series "Cool Geek of the Week". We interviewed the who's who of the whole blogging community. Also, we had multiple blogs—each with its own domain, we could cross-link our popular posts and pass on the link juice to each other.'

That is not all. Similar to Forbes' list of the richest people, Nandini created a list of the rich and the famous who are known for their lavish lifestyles. 'There wasn't a single site that was doing this. So we started collecting interesting personal information on billionaires like Larry Ellison, Russian billionaire Roman Abramovich. For example, the cars they owned, houses, vacation destinations and so on.'

Ankit helped her in building a 'wiki' for BornRich where they listed few celebrities and curated a lot of news about their luxurious lifestyle.

'Opening the wiki to the public allowed our community to add content as well. For example, there was this Russian billionaire who owned the world's most expensive yacht. Anyone who was writing about him used to stumble on our wiki and ended up linking our page. That sent our traffic through the roof.'

Ankit chimes in,

'Talking about traffic, I remember another thing. We were featured as a case study for Google AdSense because we were making more money than some of the mainstream media companies. When Google published that case study on their AdSense blog, we got even more traffic.'

Growth of Citizen Journalism Platform: Tech and the Community

Initially the in-house team posted news on www.instablogs.com. Gradually, Ankit built features to support community journalists.

'One of the biggest challenges we faced was that it was very hard to find English speaking or writing citizen journalists. We started searching for bloggers and bumped into platforms like globalvoices.org which already had a community. What I would do is approach people whose articles I liked, and I would also comment on these websites. These were pro-ams, a term that had become popular around that time. It referred to someone between a professional and an amateur. Slowly, people started joining us, and eventually we even attracted reporters from BBC and *The Economist*. They liked our vision and participated.'

Instablogs started picking momentum around 2007.

'A girl from Pakistan who worked with Geo TV Pakistan joined us and her articles attracted many followers from India also. There was this Buddhist monk who had run away from Myanmar to Sri Lanka, and he shared his own viewpoint when the emergency was imposed on Myanmar. Stories like that struck a chord with people. So I think it was a great experiment because we did succeed in our vision of presenting different viewpoints. In six months, we had more than 4,000 citizen journalists from across the world.'

In 2007–2008, Instablogs launched its YouTube channel where citizen journalists sent their videos from all around the world.

'We had set up a procedure that they had to submit their stories by 12:00 GMT, and our video team worked on it and published a five-minute news bulletin out at 3:00 GMT. We used to do that four to five times a week. So that brought a level of professionalism in the community because the fact was that we could not afford to pay them. But we realized that money was the least motivation, people just wanted to express and contribute to this community. They were passionate about their voice being heard. It was a concept like open source. When we started, we were doing 50–60 articles per day of which 80–90 per cent were being produced by in-house team. When we reached our peak in the end of 2008, we were generating more than 3,000 content pieces per day and almost 100 per cent was coming from the community. All we did was moderation.'

It is hard to run community-led content and keep the community engaged and incentivized to participate.

Ankit attributes it to their technology platform. They built a dashboard where citizen journalists could see the heat map, and analytics on their posts. They also created a tool to show the parts of their content that people are highlighting the most and so on. Adding gamification stuff such as leaderboards and a proper admin panel for the journalists kept things organized. 'Also, we used to hold webinars to teach them how to monetize their content, how to write better. A part of Nandini's job was to empower the community,' Ankit adds. To ensure the content quality, Nandini had built a framework for storyboarding and editorial workflows, and templates to help the writers write good posts.

'Overall, we invested heavily in our tech platform, creating the editorial and content team, and making sure that community grows positively. We had become the third largest video channel in India. We had built a whole studio setup for it. I remember having more than 10 million video views on our channel. We started in 2008 and this was before smartphone era, so that kind of traffic was pretty amazing. The problem was that we could not monetize those views because YouTube had a policy that one could not monetize Indian channels in those days.'

Business Model

Ads were their primary source of revenue even though they occasionally syndicated their content and experimented with sponsored posts. Nandini handled the content advertising and sponsored posts on BornRich. Ankit handled the AdSense part. 'We attracted high-end advertisers such as Mercedes, and all. We were doing well in terms of revenue,' Nandini adds.

Ankit says, 'We stayed away from affiliate because we wanted to stay neutral and wanted to make money irrespective of whether our audience liked a product or not.'

'When we got our first advertiser Shopzilla in 2006 itself, it was a quarterly contract of ₹6–7 lakh. That was the moment we felt that this can grow really big. It helped us break even and we needed that. But to be frank, I think they got a better deal than us,' Ankit smiles.

Within its first four to six months, Instablogs had become profitable. In terms of traffic, BornRich was the biggest blog, followed closely by Instablogs and then the environment or gadgets blog. Revenue was also distributed in the same order, but BornRich revenue was almost twice that of Instablogs. By 2008, they were making around US$400,000 per year mostly through ads.

'We started with using multiple ad networks like Google, and GlamMedia. Even Yahoo! had their ad network that we had partnered with. We had built our internal technology so that we would switch different ad networks based on the visitor IP. Besides the normal features, we also used frequency capping so that the user is not shown the same ad after a certain number of impressions. Initially, we also wanted to show our own ad inventory, and one of our biggest advertisers was Bizrate which was later acquired by Shopzilla.

In those days, online advertising was a more level playing field with multiple players. Few ad networks (other than Google) even gave us a dedicated account manager which helped optimizing our ads. In fact, the revenue from AdSense was probably 30–40 per cent of our total ad revenue. But if you look now, it is almost a Google AdSense monopoly. It took some time to get Google AdSense to work well for us. It used to take time to index the content and show more relevant ads. We also did some optimization around the placement of ads, etc. Once that happened, our revenues escalated.'

In addition, they started promoting content from our other blogs if the user did not click on any ads. Since they had built strong taxonomy, they could figure which content would be relevant to this user. This was their earliest lesson in personalization and user behaviour. 'In fact, that is how we thought of starting our current venture, Betaout,' Ankit reflects.

Fundraising and Exit

Ankit was attending the Proto.in conference in Chennai in 2008. When he told Vijay Anand, who was organizing the conference, that they have two million visitors every month, Vijay didn't believe him. He had to show him their analytics page.

'Once he saw our traffic, he invited us to demo our product at the conference. That is where we met Sameer Guglani who ended up being our advisor. Vishal Gondal liked what we were doing and asked me to meet his partner Sameer Bangara in Gurgaon. I met him, and he helped me understand the business models and how to build financial documents. Till then, the only thing I understood was cash flow statement, but he taught me how to use P&L statements and so on. The reason we were profitable was also because I kept a close eye on our cash flows. Anyway, we immediately hit it off, and raised our first seed round from Sameer Bangara and Vishal Gondal. They had invested US$100,000–120,000.'

Ankit thought that expanding the content team will help grow the traffic and revenues. But the 2008 recession spoiled their plan and their ad revenues dropped despite the growth in the traffic.

'See once you raise money, you either keep raising more money or look for an exit. VCs need higher returns and you need to move extremely fast.' In 2010, they ended up raising Series A round of US$4 million from The Times Group. At that time, everyone was thinking that print media is going to go bust like in the West. People thought that the alternative media is growing, so many media houses were exploring options to get into the digital space. 'In that sense, it probably made sense for Times to invest in a company like us because if the digital space exploded as expected, then they would have cashed in through us.'

But many challenges propped up. They found it hard to scale and keep the content quality high with the freelancers.

'Even big media houses like DemandMedia went down. Google started growing bigger, and its ad network became almost a monopoly. That hurt many SMBs like us. Publishers had little say after that, and our clicks dropped down every month. Our bet was that Microsoft, Yahoo or Facebook would compete with Google AdSense, but they were never able to. In 2012, we also started focusing on Indian content, and we felt that Indian ad revenues will increase because e-commerce was rising. But it did not happen fast enough. With recession hurting our advertisers and Google policies hurting our clicks, our ad revenues came to a point where we knew that it would never make those kind of returns that VCs look for. So we thought we should take an exit and cash out our investors. We were getting few buyout offers. We decided it was time to move on.'

In the end, there were three different entities who acquired parts of Instablogs for an undisclosed amount. One was a Dubai-based media firm and one was from Canada called Valnet. A part of the deal was that Nandini bought back the BornRich property in personal capacity. Overall, the acquisition was tricky because there were different blog properties, and they had a common YouTube channel and proprietary technology. Ankit shares the finer details.

'By the time of exit, we had used less than half of the US$4 million we had raised, so we ended up returning that back to our investors.

We were lucky to find an exit. Not a great deal, but it was decent. I think if we could have stuck to it a bit longer, we might have made some more money because YouTube had become more mainstream and e-commerce eventually rose fast. Smartphones made it easier for people to consume content, and I am sure we would have been more successful but we were just too early in the game.'

Parting Advice

Ankit has a clear thought on how entrepreneurs should decide their priorities.

'I strongly believe that we should be solving the most challenging problems of our company because we are being paid the most. Not in terms of salary, but equity. So we cannot be solving US$12-an-hour worth of problem or even US$100. If we are being paid US$1,000 per hour, then we should be solving that level of problems.'

In hindsight, Ankit attributes a lot of Instablogs success to its technology platform.

'Our decision to focus on analytics, and tracking the user behaviour paid off really well. We invested a lot of time and technology into building that, but I think it was absolutely worth it. For example, it was because of our dashboards that we got a good sense of how our page views were distributed. We realized that the real growth came from long-term page views and, therefore, we should invest in content which has longer shelf life. This is why we invested in the rich-people wiki kind of projects which were more long lasting. I would recommend building an internal dashboard and analytics from day one. It made us very data-driven and that is something which we use heavily in Betaout till date.'

Fond Memories

In 2006, Ankit was visiting Shimla and realized he could get a big office for as cheap as ₹12 per sq. feet. Since Internet and electricity were also available, he decided to move the Instablogs team to Shimla. 'We hired 2–3 guys every year from Shimla engineering college, so even talent was not an issue. Overall, we were able to reduce our costs, run our business without any issues, and keep local people happy!' Although they had to move back to Delhi when they raised the Series A investment, the time spent in Shimla stays close to their hearts. Ankit feels passionately about improving the quality of life and infrastructure in the smaller towns so that the local people are not forced to go to crowded and expensive metros.

Ankit and Nandini are on to their third start-up, Betaout, and they finished Techstars programme in USA in October 2015.

Key Takeaways

Traction

- *Building a community:* Leveraging the forums where Ankit and Nandini were active to announce the launch and invite citizen journalists helped build initial audience for Instablogs. Later on, empowering the community journalists and mentoring them kept the writers incentivized to participate.
- *Innovative PR:* Turning negative feedback into a comic strip won the hearts of the critics. Organic strategies such as interviewing the bloggers and building rich-people wiki drove substantial traffic.
- *Early adoption of YouTube:* As the YouTube platform grew, Instablogs became the third largest Indian video channel. Crowdsourcing videos and adding professional practices around timely publishing helped compete with bigger media houses.

Product

- *Developing proprietary CMS:* Allowed greater control over product features and monetization.
- *Investing in analytics:* Monitoring the traffic patterns helped make smart content decisions such as developing rich-people wiki pages and cross-promoting posts from multiple blogs.
- *Powerful dashboards and moderation:* Ensuring that citizen journalists felt motivated to participate.

Business Model

- *Intelligent ad monetization:* Frequency capping, serving their own ad inventory and cross-promotion of blogs ramped up the initial ad revenues and traffic.
- *Reliance on a single channel:* As Google AdSense monopoly grew, ad revenues went down, adding to the pressure to exit.

PART 3

Business Model and Fundraising

*We thought US$2 million is what we need to start production.
Today, we have raised US$43 million and that is what
it takes OEM to start functioning.*
—Tarun Mehta (Ather Energy)

*One of the mistakes I see Indian companies making is
premature concern about business models.*
—Amit Ranjan (SlideShare)

*When you buy a version 1 iPad which is a US$600 device,
it doesn't do much! If you really want to utilize your iPad or show it
off to people, you wouldn't mind paying US$4 for this app.*
—Ankit Gupta (Pulse)

*The whole idea of raising external money is to accelerate growth.
Otherwise, being profitable itself may not be that difficult.*
—Ankur Singla (Akosha)

Although traction may trump the business model in the beginning, revenue is what matters in the end. You are creating value only if someone is willing to pay for your product/service.

One of the most creative business models is the one that Ankur Singla discusses in Akosha. Very few people know about their B2B business, OneDirect, which generated significantly higher revenue than the B2C consumer complaints side of it. Another interesting read on business models is SlideShare which is by nature a free social sharing product.

That said, sometimes, it is unwise to burden the start-up with a business model until you have built the right user base. Venture capital can help you get there faster. But should you raise money or bootstrap? If you need to do fundraising, what is the right time? Tarun Mehta talks about his fundraising journey in Ather in detail, and shares important advice for hardware entrepreneurs. It is one of the most innovative products featured in this book, and it could have died due to capital starvation.

Another important monetary decision is how to price a product, which can be especially tricky for software products and services. Ankit Gupta's fascinating tale of why/how they priced the Pulse app and what happened afterwards will undoubtedly make you rethink your pricing decisions! You can also refer to Paras Chopra's interview and how he priced Visual Website Optimizer.

To dare is to lose one's footing momentarily. To not dare is to lose oneself.

—Søren Kierkegaard

8   Tarun Mehta: Ather Energy

India has never been known for new product (hardware) development, but that might change with the vision of this IIT Madras duo. Ather is the most serious and promising attempt at creating India's own smart electric scooter and they are here to stay.

Electric Scooter Made in India
#fundraising #product #hardware

Ather Energy is a hardware start-up founded in 2013 by IIT Madras alumni Tarun Mehta and Swapnil Jain. Exploring the existing and dying electric vehicles market convinced Tarun that there is an opportunity to build an electric vehicle that could match petrol scooters on the specs. With a stubborn faith and determination coupled with uncharacteristic patience at their age, the founders left their respective jobs and went back to IIT to start working on the first prototype. A promising start and support from a professor and alumnus helped them to design a new smart electric scooter for the Indian market that bigger brands such as TVS and Hero were not able to. Instead of assembling the vehicle, Ather chose a vertically integrated design approach where every component is designed for the product's need. While this approach slowed their pace of development, it served well in sticking to the original vision and attracting the right investors.

Tarun Mehta is a lethal combination of ambition and patience. The weight of his measured words and lofty vision belies his young age—'*The mission in our case is that all vehicles in the world should be electric in next 20 years and that gives us a different level of motivation.*' Hoping to become the breakout success for India's manufacturing ecosystem, Ather is treading with a cautious optimism. Till July 2017, they have raised US$43 million funding from a formidable line of investors—Flipkart founders Sachin and Binny Bansal, Tiger Global and Hero MotoCorp. This itself speaks of their ability to navigate in a tough segment of hardware start-ups that often die due to capital starvation in India.

However, the road ahead is rife with challenges. Until Ather can ship its first scooter, S340, and deliver on the promises that look so good on the paper, it will be too early to start cheering.

As per Greek mythology, Mt Olympus was the abode of the Greek gods and the site of the throne of Zeus. Air on Mt Olympus is supposedly the purest form of air and is called Ather. 'We fancy ourselves as the purest form of energy,' Tarun shares his vision.

India is not known to be a great place for building innovative hardware products. What made Tarun and Swapnil defy the conventional wisdom?

'The fact that it is hard to build hardware here means it is a great opportunity. If I am sitting in Palo Alto thinking I will build a mobile app, I have got to be worried because every person is in mobile. I would argue that building an e-commerce or an Internet company in India is more worrisome because every guy is doing that. As a culture, we haven't had the opportunity to build strong products because building products takes a long lead time and you need resources for that long when you probably are not even generating any revenue. If you can think like a customer and build it with discipline and vigour, and can deliver consistently—that is much more valuable because it is that much harder for anyone else to do.'

What Tarun is referring to is the fact that if anyone pulls this off, the barriers of entry are insanely high and the reward is significantly greater.

From Ahmedabad to Chennai

Tarun comes from a Marwari family settled in Ahmedabad. His Dad runs a small, one-person company. His inclination towards mechanical and design led him to a new dual-degree engineering design programme at IIT Madras which had courses on mechanical, electronics, management, product design, etc.

'Luckily my rank was exactly right for this. Our department was at a very sweet point and a lot of things fell into the right place. It had not become slow or set like the old departments. We were the third batch and we were just camping in one of the environment labs in the Mechanical department. In our second year, we moved to a new building and were setting things up. Everyone was very attached and felt a higher sense of ownership. Professors also were younger and were finding their way into the systems. The department itself was an experiment. The focus was on product design and engineering. It meant we had to think of a complete product and not just engineering solutions—who would use it and is it affordable. Miraculously, the number of start-ups that have come out of our batch has been huge. Out of 22 people, I believe half of us either started something right away or later on.'

Tarun remained active with a local entrepreneurship club and found them to be 'some of the best mentors that I can think of and people who were truly entrepreneurs at heart'. Swapnil had started working with the Center for Innovation where he started a group that built race cars.

Tarun and Swapnil's first pet project came to be a clean tech project using Stirling engines for one of the courses. They worked on it for three years.

'That did not go anywhere because it was too hard and expensive for undergrad students to build a complete engine. We got to a point where we had trouble hitting the right price point. Hence, we graduated out and took different jobs. I went to Ashok Leyland and Swapnil went to General Motors. But even then, we knew that we might have to wait 18–24 months but we will start something. We were clear that whatever we build, we want it to be a large-impact company; it has to be a tangible product that we can design and shape. Something that we can spend our next 30 years on.'

The Smokeless Ride: Finding Love in the Electric Vehicles

Previously, Tarun had also interned at NID and Mercedes.

'I didn't learn much when I was in NID frankly. I spent lot of time reading on intellectual property. At Mercedes, I realized that they were not doing that much innovation or new product development in India, but it exposed me to their processes and systems. If I had not worked with a brand like Mercedes, I might have kept thinking that maybe Indian manufacturers are not innovating enough but these established global players like Honda would be more innovative. Now I know that is not the case.'

Tarun had an idea of a battery pack design and had filed a patent on it before joining Ashok Leyland. While filing that patent, he explored and got excited about electric vehicles in general.

'There existed a scooter which had top speed of 25 km/hr and 0.3 HP (most scooters have 7–9 HP), and very poor acceleration. Batteries took eight hours of charging time and would run for eight months. So they were underpowered, low-quality and low-performance vehicles. I saw it as a product challenge. You need an electric vehicle which is at par in performance with petrol vehicles. That is the only way people are going to use it. I was also talking to Swapnil that we should start an electric vehicle company and work on the battery. We had quickly realized that a battery alone is not good enough for a business. You have got to build a strong overall product.'

Euphoria around electric vehicles in the Indian market had started in 2009–2010. Tarun found a research that counted around 50 brands at one point because people were buying cheap vehicles from China and selling them in India.

'I believe around 100,000 electric scooters were sold at that time. But reselling is not good enough to become an OEM. What we were looking at was development capability, manufacturing capacity, after sales, brand and everything. It was doubly complicated because most of the products themselves were poor quality. So what was happening is that many electrical vehicles were coming into the market but no one was buying. By 2012, the number of electrical vehicles sold came down to 30,000. The government had also killed a subsidy regime, and many people think that is what caused the decline but that is hard to believe for me. The entire market was dying because the vehicles were shitty.'

Competing Against Themselves

One assumes that existing automobile leaders can enter the market any time and run with it. Tarun theorizes why the real competition is not likely to come from the biggies.

'See, if Tarun Mehta wants to start an electrical vehicle company, he can get a container of 100 scooters from China for ₹50 lakh and sell them in India under any name—Mehta Trading Company (MTC) selling electric scooter named Vaayu (for example). Tarun has nothing to lose. The worst case is he loses ₹50 lakh. People will think MTC scooters are shitty but who cares. No one knows MTC anyway. But TVS has a bigger reputation. They are doing ₹10,000 crore in revenues every year, and if they brought a shitty scooter, their parent brand suffers. They cannot take that risk. So larger OEMs like TVS realized that electrical vehicles are not as simple as they thought. Building it from scratch was not an option for them because they did not have the internal competence in that space. BSA and TVS gave it a shot but quickly pulled out for that reason. Hero Electric is a different company and they continued trying it out because they were run by different folks than Hero Motors. Bajaj and Honda, I think, never tried. Anyway, this is my reading.

What we are very good at is building a company around testing, value engineering, bringing cost down, branding, distribution, servicing and all that. After that, few companies have been able to sustain the efforts from previous generation. They cannot become a Tesla all of a sudden. It is not in the owner's DNA because they are fundamentally not product people. If you are going to quote me, quote me on this also—I am not saying that product people are at a higher pedestal than regular businessmen. I am just saying it is a different DNA. Just like Apple cannot produce a billion phones—they need Foxconn for that. By the way, they don't even have a good ERP (enterprise resource planning) system. The world's largest company doesn't have a good ERP, they run on Excel and they don't care. That is the good thing that they don't care because they focus on what they are good at. So whenever we talk of DNA change, it requires extreme time and dedication.'

This is what Ather is betting on. They knew that most of the people in India are not going to try and build what they are building. Tarun confides,

'We are building a strong technology company which will own all its engineering and can build products from scratch. Can somebody else build the new products like the way we do—perhaps they can copy our first product, but we will launch a new one in two years and this company will always be catching up. What someone cannot copy is the business process itself. How do you get 15 different teams working together—android development to power electronics to vehicle design to plastic to sheet metal to dashboard? What we were betting on is our ability for new product development.'

Bootstrapping and Validating the Product

Ather got its earliest support from Professor R. Krishnakumar at IIT Madras. 'He told us that if you want to build something, just leave your jobs and come back. We will give you whatever support we can.'

So Tarun and Swapnil left their jobs in February 2013 and came back to IIT Madras. IIT gave them project associateship work for a monthly stipend of ₹15,000 that covered their expenses. They also got access to all the labs and could bootstrap. Being incubated inside IIT Madras created a cocoon and shielded them from the noise in the start-up ecosystem.

'The bad thing is that you are disconnected from reality. The good thing is you are disconnected from reality,' Tarun emphasizes.

'If you are in Bangalore, you are going to meet-ups, talking to VCs and other entrepreneurs all the time. You are hearing how advertising is the next big thing or how blah blah is the next big thing. You get influenced a lot by all that. In such an environment, you never get a chance to develop your own philosophy. When your ecosystem keeps telling you that you should spend so much to acquire a customer, you start believing in that. How will you have the opportunity to develop your own school of thought? You will be a product of what surrounds you. Our six months in that IIT Park allowed us to be isolated and develop our own value system.

We took six months to build the very first battery pack prototype and it was a simple version of a scooter with almost no money or external help. We built the lithium ion battery pack and the frame of the scooter. At that point, we were probably one of the very few in India who did that. It was pretty crappy but it helped you get over that mental barrier. If we can build this, then we can probably build a much better version of this too. In September, we registered the company. We got a ₹5 lakh grant from IIT Madras which is given to people who want to start something up. Additionally, we had raised a ₹15-lakh loan.'

Then they started pitching to potential investors, and one of the alumni, Dr V Srinivasan, agreed to give them ₹25 lakh in October 2013.

'He lived in California and has his own start-up there. He had come to IIT Madras to give a lecture and kept half an hour aside to talk to budding entrepreneurs. I told him what we were working on. Within 15 minutes, he got pretty excited. He said that he very much believed in electric as he had just bought a Tesla. He asked me what we needed. He went on and talked to the professor who was supporting us and saw our prototype in the next hour itself. He went back to the USA, and within few weeks, we had agreed on the terms and he invested ₹25 lakh. The only thing we were discussing at that point was to do some sort of basic validation of the market.'

Tarun started pitching a certain spec of the vehicle to others as well. The idea was to see if anyone is willing to put actual money into it.

'I reached out to another professor at IIT Madras who we had been talking to. I said, "Sir, I have discussed the specs of this vehicles—3x top speed, 20x more powerful, 10x longer battery, 8x faster charging, etc. I had already got the design made by a designer, so we know what the scooter would look like. For all of this (which was quite close to the performance of petrol scooter), would you be interested in buying it?" And he replied, "Oh! Absolutely. I would buy it". I asked, "We think we can price it just under a lakh, does that make sense? Activa is around ₹55,000 you know just to compare". And he said, "Yes, I would absolutely pay that much for it". I requested him to put that money out and be our first customer so that we can get there more quickly. He immediately cut a check for ₹85,000. This was around November 2013. It was quite unbelievable. Next four people also gave us ₹85,000 each and after that some people gave us ₹20,000 and so on. So we raised ₹4–5 lakh this way. For a budding start-up, it was a big validation.'

In total, they had arranged roughly ₹40–45 lakh by this time. By June 2014, Ather had first legit prototype with self-built lithium ion battery pack. The product had a top speed of 72 km/hr, and a dashboard to see the navigation and speed. It had belt drive and good accelerator.

'If you ask about first fully functional vehicle, then that we were able to bring it only in 2016. And we have completely changed from that prototype in 2014. The battery position is completely different; it has moved from seat to the floorboard. The first time we built this platform that we are currently using was in March 2015. So that was 18 months from the day we started. Now, we could actually start a proper product design and architect a complete solution.'

Money Management

Hardware start-ups leech money. 'We thought we will be able to start delivering with little money. That was wrong assumption. We thought US$2 million is what we need to start production. Today, we have raised US$43 million and know that is what it takes OEM to start functioning,' Tarun chuckles.

One of the things that stand out about Ather is its savvy money management. The founders had been cash efficient from day one.

'We knew our way around with prototyping. During our five years in college, we had built a lot of things—four engines, construction equipment. The internship at BHEL saw us building another equipment. Swapnil was part of a team that had built a race car. Between us, we had so much prototyping experience that we could build a complete scooter in ₹1 lakh. I mean just a proof of concept. We knew exactly which vendor in which lane to go to. How to negotiate with guys speaking in Tamil—we had done all that in the college. We knew our way around the components and machine shops. And see, it was our ability to build these prototypes and show improvement with each one that helped us raise money too. That was the only way to get funding because we were showing results.'

Another thing that helped them burn less money was just hiring interns for ₹5,000–7,000 per month. Those first interns came from HelloIntern or similar job portals. 'We hired them for six months, then extended another six months and then converted them to full-time employees as and when they finished their colleges. They were super valuable.'

The founders hardly had any money when they started and used the meagre savings they had. But Tarun doesn't think it was a sacrifice.

'I strongly believe that if you feel that you are giving up a lot for your start-up, your chances of success dramatically come down because now you are faced with a massive mental block. You will start resenting that money and pinching pennies for wrong reasons. Even if we were spending pennies, that was all we had, but it never felt like we are pinching pennies. I have seen too many people frustrated or struggling and thinking that they could have been in a nice job instead—that is not a good place to be in.'

Fundraising

'To be honest, fundraising does not take a lot of your time but it takes a hell lot of mental bandwidth. As a first-time entrepreneur, every single round is special and different. They hear your idea, throw you out and you are super discouraged. You again go back. You start understanding who is genuinely interested or not. Over time, you become battle hardened. Finally, you find the serious guy and negotiate and close the round. It takes time and it blocks you out because you have no time to think of other things.'

Initially, they were just looking for ₹2 crore and it made sense to seek angel investors.

'We took introductions and meetings from anybody who was ready to listen. What we realized is that investing takes a certain mindset and risk appetite. Even if people have money, they may not have that mindset and it takes years to get that. For example, we met somebody from a family worth hundreds of crores, if not thousands. For them, investing ₹4–5 crore is not a big deal but it took us two months and four to five meetings to realize that they would never invest. Then there were people who had appetite but had their own idea of how we should do things. And it is tempting to say that yeah if you are investing, we can change the plan a bit. It took fair amount of resilience to say no to them. I can think of at least a couple where we declined the offer.'

Despite sensible finance handling, there were multiple panic moments when they came close to running out of the money. 'One point we actually ran out of money and were surviving on loans. In a month, even the loan would have been exhausted. That is when Sachin and Binny invested a million dollars.'

It all started with a cold email. Tarun sent an email to Sachin Bansal with a pitch deck and telling him that they were having hard time finding investors. 'I think I emailed him on Saturday night and on Sunday morning, I had a reply. He said that it is looking pretty awesome, feel free to drop by when you are in Bangalore.'

Tarun did not know what to expect in their first meeting. Ather was looking at raising ₹5 crore.

'Sachin asked questions about their vision and plan of execution. Luckily, that is something we were very clear on. We were going to reach our vision of all electric vehicles in India by delivering high-end product and great customer experience. So it was always a multi-year, decade kind of a plan. We were not looking to change anything, and I think it worked to our advantage. Sachin got excited with our plan. Also, our understanding of technology is pretty good. So we hit it off and he was very supportive of our "don't change your plan for any investor" outlook also. He connected us to some folks and we followed up with them, but nothing worked out. So after three months, we went back to him. We told that we are still struggling with raising funds and we now need US$1 million. We asked him if he would consider investing ₹30–40 lakh of his own because that would give a lot of confidence to other potential investors. Sachin said, "I would love to invest". So we said, "Great, can you invest half a million?" Sachin smiled and said, "Why don't you let us do the full round? We want to put in US$1 million".'

Sachin was on board now and had advised them to actively raise more money if they have less than 18 months in the bank. Although it meant that they had to be constantly raising funds, Tarun started appreciating the discipline.

'In any other space like e-commerce or software, you can do something even with low cash. You can improve your customer onboarding or something and go back to market. But in hardware, there is nothing you can do just with the prototype. You need money to produce. Hence, if you cut it too close, it is the biggest risk for any hardware company. Once you are into the market, yes you can play with other strategies, but before that, you need to keep raising the money. If you don't have the cash leverage, you will be on the mercy of the investor. If you have 24–30 months of cash, you can wait it out for a better investor. So we raised our next round with Tiger with enough money sitting with us.'

Now, they could actually hire people with good salaries. They made real plans, moved to Bangalore and started feeling like a real company for the first time.

In 2016, Hero MotoCorp invested ₹200 crores for a 30 per cent stake. Tarun is not wary of too much dilution.

'Steve Jobs had 1–2 per cent of Apple? When he came back, Apple was much smaller than unicorns today are and he had lesser stake than many of the founders of today. I don't believe percentage holding is the biggest motivation. I think it is important that entrepreneurs understand that money does not come for free. If your business needs capital, someone needs to make money out of it. You cannot become all rich on your own.

If Ather becomes a billion-dollar company someday, even if I have 5 per cent, that is still US$50 million, which is ₹350 crore. I don't think I will look at that and say, hey, I would have been motivated only if I had more. And I would not reach there because of my sheer willpower or commitment. We got here because there are 100 employees working even harder than us. They also need to make money. There were investors who bet tens or hundreds of millions of dollars on you.'

Decisions That Mattered

Tarun is brutally honest.

'I don't think we were very smart in seven to eight months. Most of the decisions we took did not allow us to get anywhere quickly. But those decisions have helped us stick to our vision even today. They might have slowed us down actually, but they were important for long-term sustenance. For example, had we decided not do practically everything in-house, we could have used an Activa frame and bought a motor and battery pack from China. We could have hit the market in 2015 itself. But we decided that if we put up a product like that, anybody could copy that and we would not be left with any product advantage. Product experience would also be sub-par. So our call was to focus on vertically integrated approach for the next five years, if not longer, and build very strong engineering products in-house. Another important thing is that we stuck with those calls consistently and did not shift our focus.'

Deviating from the conventional wisdom, Tarun is someone who doesn't like the word 'pivot'. 'It should be your last resort. There is no pride in pivoting every six months. A pivot means that there was lot of learning from the mistakes you made. We have had minor pivots but it has been thoughtful.'

Everything comes back to their vision.

'We have never been after money and have always felt driven by a larger mission. The mission in our case is that all vehicles in the world should be electric in next 20 years and that gives us a different level of motivation. You look at problems in a different way then. We don't get stuck and feel that we should change the product itself. If we are stumbling somewhere, we would see that we cannot do this thing at *this* scale, so what else can we do or how can we scale this? Our motivation is that long-term and short-term challenges do not stop us. Let us say, a challenge towards our vision is that no vendor is giving us the batteries we need. Now, do we use lead acid batteries? We cannot because then there won't be enough people buying, and the market will become limited which is against our vision. Simple. Chuck it, build your own battery pack. It takes time, so what? So that is our vision.'

Hardware Challenges in India

Tarun feels it is a mindset and a hiring challenge. New product development is a 'zero to one' journey instead of '1 to n', in the words of Peter Thiel. India has not seen its share of product development yet.

Ather is vertically integrated in design. While they source most of the components from India itself, there are few items that they need from outside because India does not produce certain items like lithium ion cells. Tarun is, however, optimistic that India will start producing them in the next five years.

'China has a massive control over the supply chain. They have most of the raw materials and have massive manufacturing. India has been pretty poor in all of those. That reflects in the cost. It makes it way harder to make a product cheaper in India than it is in China. So if your strategy is to be a low-cost manufacturer, China is a better place.

The work that Indian companies have been doing so far is the value engineering. We are good at figuring out how to reduce the cost of a GM car from ₹12 to ₹6 lakh when they sell it in India. You can change the slider, remove extra air bags, can work with plastic instead of metal or replace heavier metal with lighter metal, etc. We don't need this coating because we don't reach those temperatures in India. Protection from snow is a pretty stupid thing to have in India. So it is not just throwing a feature out, but it is re-engineering and re-conditioning to Indian reality. Our engineers have had a lot of opportunity to do all that. The ecosystem is pretty evolved when it comes to hiring in those areas. Except for Pulsar or Nano or Tata Indigo, new product development has not happened much. That was the case with China too until the right time came and they created Xiaomi and OnePlus. Building a new product is very very different from building something on an existing platform. Every vehicle manufacturer in India started with a technology partnership with a global brand. TVS Suzuki, Hero Honda, Maruti Suzuki. We needed external support to get things started.

For a new product, your pricing is going to look different and evolve over time. The work you have to put with vendors, opposition you will see on the process itself and coaxing them to give you what you need is a different game. Every decision of yours will have a huge cascading effect. That can push you over the edge because the things are always in chaos. Every two months, you might be back to square one. You need mindset, you need patience and you need tenacity to stick. It is a problem to find the people who can do that. I really look for someone who is wise and has patience because whatever we are doing is going to take time.'

Team Building

Swapnil takes care of the technology and Tarun deals with the business aspects of Ather.

Today, Ather has 200 people, but such people are hard to find. Surprisingly, less than 30 per cent are from IITs.

'First 60–70 people were applicants who had reached out to us or came through friends and other employees. Internal referrals worked great because that helped in weeding out the bad people. Apart from the initial interns, everyone else came through a referral. For example, the current head of product was a good friend of Swapnil and they had known each other for a long time. More than a friend, they had worked together in the past, and he knew what we value and how we work. So we convinced him to leave his job at ITC and forego the ISB MBA programme to join us for almost no salary. Our first designer was introduced to us through a friend. We interacted for few months and it was clear that we all shared a chemistry which led us to get him to jump ship and join Ather. And there are times when we sell ourselves too. For example, this intern was about to leave after finishing his six months because he was joining a MS programme in Germany. We convinced him that Ather will be far more exciting for him and he stayed back. So we pitch to retain talent.'

Ather actively gives ESOPs based on the role. Their philosophy has been that everybody without exception, who is staying with them in longer run should have stock options. Tarun says,

'When employees see their holdings multiple by 30–40x in a short time frame, they start valuing the options. This has worked as a retention strategy as well.

The day your company becomes a breakout success, everybody will become wealthy. And if you manage to do that, you will do something incredibly positive to the Indian start-up ecosystem. These people will then go and convince 500 other people that they should work at start-ups; that is the way to get the right experience and get rich. They will invest in other companies and that will be the positive loop. We firmly believe in it. Stock options when rolled out may seem small—like it might be only ₹5 lakh—but when the company becomes 30x more valuable, that becomes more than a crore. That is good enough to make you comfortable.'

Road to the Future

As of January 2018, Ather Energy has raised US\$43 million and is looking at launching their vehicle by the end of 2018.

'I don't want to take my eyes off the fact that a product is yet to come out in the market. It needs to come out, needs to scale and stand in the market, and not fail,' Tarun says. A pause follows. 'We are still focusing on development and testing. We have to finish all that and make the product work. There is no point in having any targets beyond that. We will start a pre-order campaign just a few months before the launch.'

Parting Advice

'Everything was a surprise, not by 20–30 per cent but 10–20 times! How much time it would take, how much money it would take, efforts it would take, everything. Build more prototypes, build them more frequently. Investors can fund you only on the back of those prototypes. You need fundraising and building good prototypes is the only way to get that. Second, find patience. Find patience in people and find patience in capital. It's a long journey.'

What Gets Tarun Going?

Tarun looks up to Sachin Bansal and his IIT Madras senior Achal Kothari for advice.

The recommendations from his bookshelf are:

- *The Silmarillion* by J. R. R. Tolkien

Tarun Mehta and Swapnil Jain with a Very Early Stage Prototype in Chennai, IITM Campus

- *The Hard Thing About Hard Things* by Ben Horowitz
- *The Alchemist* by Paulo Coelho
- *The Innovator's Dilemma* by Clayton Christensen

Key Takeaways

Person

- *Seeing opportunities instead of challenges:* Going after the harder-to-crack segment of hardware start-ups, which offers an opportunity to make a larger impact and higher barriers to entry if successful.
- *Determined and patient:* Sticking to vision instead of short-term compromises.

Product

- *Market research and understanding:* It was Tarun's and Swapnil's experience with vendors and in-depth understanding of electric vehicles segment that led to the design of a product that people are getting excited about.

- *Early validation:* Getting interested users to pre-order the bikes not only helped raise initial funding but validated the price and demand.
- *Extensive and rapid protyping:* Helped in gaining investors' trust and realizing the execution challenges.

Fundraising

- *Fundraising when 18 months of cash left:* Hardware start-ups need a lot of cash and should be constantly fundraising.

I knew that if I failed I wouldn't regret that, but I knew the one thing I might regret is not trying.

—Jeff Bezos

9　Amit Ranjan: SlideShare

Very few people know that the 'YouTube for Presentations', SlideShare, was built by Indians distributed between Delhi and Silicon Valley. Its co-founder and COO, Amit Ranjan, shares all the action that took place inside one of the first social web start-ups from its birth in a BarCamp to its acquisition by LinkedIn.

YouTube for Presentations
#business_model #hiring #marketing #acquired

Amit Ranjan, a mechanical engineer and an MBA, was getting restless in the typical MBA job. Joining hands with his Silicon Valley-based sister Rashmi Sinha and brother-in-law Jonathan Boutelle, Amit left the cushy job to lead a team of software engineers to support the products that they would build.

SlideShare was founded in 2006 by the three of them. When audience and presenters struggled to share their PowerPoint slides in a BarCamp at Delhi, the trio set upon to build a YouTube-esque platform for the slides. But can slides excite people as much as videos? And if not, how do you build traction? While the company successfully figured that piece of the puzzle and attracted 20 million users, the puzzle to monetize the medium was not easy to solve.

Amidst finding viable business model and convincing investors that family-run start-ups can indeed work, SlideShare started to break even in 2011 when it generated US$5 million in revenues.

It was just gaining momentum as the leading professional community in content marketing when the LinkedIn acquisition for US$118 million hit the news. One would always wonder how much SlideShare could have been worth just a year later. What Amit (in hindsight) rues is that they had just figured the right business model and may have sold too soon.

The Accidental Entrepreneur

Amit graduated with a mechanical engineering degree from NIT Jaipur and MBA from FMS Delhi in 1999. Working for leading brands such as Godrej and Asian Paints in sales and management roles, Amit headed to Pepsi in 2003. He had ample operational experience by now but a nagging feeling that he was more of an engineer than a manager at heart kept bothering him.

Meanwhile, his sister Rashmi had joined the University of California, Berkeley, as a researcher and had married Jonathan Boutelle who was working in Silicon Valley as a software engineer.

'Rashmi used to make fun of me. She said why are you working at Pepsi selling coloured water? Incidentally, she was also in a phase where she realized that academia is great but it moves very slowly. She was married to a software engineer in the Bay Area, having seen the dot-com boom closely. They had the access to a very exciting, dynamic ecosystem and they were deep into technology. She had decided to move out of academia, and that's when we talked. It was a little casual talk on a weekend among the three of us when they were visiting in 2004. We all got together and said, "Okay, let's do a start-up". That was the first time I consciously used the word "start-up".'

They finally decided to go ahead with it in 2004 and quit their respective jobs.

'In 2004, Indian families understood the word "business", but business was meant for a completely different class of people. The whole notion of professionals starting a business was not heard of. I had a little bit of savings from my previous jobs. My wife was working full time. I don't think I was thinking too much about money at that point of time. In terms of social networking, the biggest application at that time was FriendSter, and MySpace was just starting.

Rashmi used to write a very popular blog around design.[1] As a part of her design research, she had started organizing a lot of the design-oriented events and conferences in the Bay Area. She was a specialist in human–computer interaction (HCI) and had started doing user experience consulting. Our earliest idea was to build a product for user experience testing and validation based on Rashmi's research. This product came to be known as MindCanvas. It would help in doing customer research, wire frames to show to people and to collect feedback.

We didn't have a lot of money. So the plan was that we would start a company here in Delhi, and we will hire a team of four or five engineers and the product would be built here. And I would need to learn how to manage a team and the product. So that's what we started doing. We rented a very very small office of 250 sq. ft close to IIT Delhi. The rent was I think ₹8,000.'

Initial Hiring

Amit needed to hire engineers fast. But how do you convince other people to work for you when no one has heard of you?

'The thing is, you cannot get the people to work for your company because there is no company per se. So the only reason good people would work for you is if they actually like you and trust you. One of the things that helped was that all three of us were blogging about our respective areas. I had started a blog about how do you start a company. Rashmi had a blog on design, user experience and HCI. Her blog had the most traction. Jonathan used to write a blog on technology. Almost all the initial engineers who we hired were people who used to read our blogs. In fact, the first guy who joined us stayed until 2014. One day, Rashmi posted on her blog that we are starting

---

[1] See http://rashmisinha.com/

a company in Delhi and looking for engineers. This guy came from reading that blog. He was our first engineer and he had a huge part to play in the success of SlideShare.'

Later on, with SlideShare, they started doing a lot of meet-ups such as Ruby and Javascript meet-ups. 'I think that showcased what kind of people we were and made engineers think that we have a good culture. That also helped in attracting talent.'

Amit took an interesting approach in deciding the salaries. The first few hires were freshers because they didn't have a lot of money.

'Our approach was not to sign the cheapest people, but whatever we could afford, we wanted to get the best in that. What I thought was that someone who might have worked for Infosys or Wipro is good enough for us. So I used that as a benchmark. Then we looked at what these companies were paying these engineers. I remember that Infosys was paying around ₹2.1 lakh back in 2004. So what I thought was that we will pay 30 per cent more than what these guys are paying. That became our thumb rule. It worked out pretty well in hindsight.'

The founders were not taking any salary in the first year and started with minimal salary in the second year. There was no notion of MVP (minimal viable product), lean methodology or agile in those days. They closed the room and kept building and building. MindCanvas was launched at the end of 18 months, and some of the team assumptions were proved wrong. With few iterations, they got initial customers including Microsoft and Yahoo! They were making money now. But the founders still felt unfulfilled.

'MindCanvas was B2B and we started questioning that even if this start-up was to become really really successful, how many people are we going to impact with this product? So although the product and the company started doing well and generating revenue, the feeling was that "Yeah, this is okay but this doesn't excite us".'

Managing the engineering team became a personal challenge for Amit but he persisted.

'I was never a software coder. I was the only one from the founding team who was physically present in the Delhi office. Rashmi and Jonathan came down twice a year, and my challenge was to gain the respect of these smart engineers. It is a fact that engineers don't like sales/marketing people much, especially Linux hackers.

The good thing was that I completely understood and accepted the challenge. I knew that respect needs to be earned, and secondly, I need to be authentic and not put up an act. I showed people that I am learning as much as they are. I really worked very hard to pick up technical skills and learnt by observing them. I anyway wanted to get out of this MBA thing. So it started working out gradually.'

Birth of SlideShare

The MindCanvas team kept blogging and arranging meet-ups. They were also getting involved in open-source activities since they were using many open-source technologies in their products. Rashmi and Jonathan had attended a BarCamp in Silicon Valley and decided to do something similar in Delhi. BarCamp is free, open and inviting, unlike the conferences which are structured and expensive, involving high-profile speakers in a restricted setting.

'I remember talking to Adobe who agreed to give us a space for this event. In 2006, we organized that BarCamp and it attracted techies from all over India. At the end of the day, many of the speakers approached us to share their PowerPoint presentations with the audience. Some people started handing their presentations in a flash drive, some in CDs and some said they will email it to us. We did what we could to help share these presentations. But one thing we noticed was that people were using Flickr and YouTube which worked well for sharing videos and photographs. So there was no problem with sharing of photos and videos, but we found that there was no easy way of sharing the presentations.'

AMIT RANJAN: SLIDESHARE

151

The inevitable question was—'Is there a way to share the presentation files with others on the Internet?'

'We decided to build a prototype for this problem using a couple of engineers from our MindCanvas team. We spent about four or five months on it. After building for four or five months, we started showing it to some people. People said it looks good, and we took a decision to launch this product. It took about six months of effort in total, using two engineers. So we launched in October 2006. At that time, *TechCrunch* was the most read blog, and to be on *TechCrunch* was a very big thing. Our product was featured there (thanks to Rashmi's connection with Michael Arrington) and it immediately took off like a rocket. Within three or four days, we knew we had hit upon something big. We got thousands of people starting to use our platform to upload presentations, and many congratulated us.'

They had hit the product market fit. Being a social web application, it offered a chance to make a bigger impact that the founders had always wanted to do. So the team decided not to continue MindCanvas anymore, and focus completely on SlideShare.

Product Evolution

The team soon realized that the reason why something like SlideShare did not exist was that it was technically not easy to convert PowerPoint, keynote files, etc. and make it work seamlessly on all the browsers.

'We took nine months to roll it out, and almost six to seven months were spent in just building that core engine. The social wrapper was built after that. So people would have to create an account and then they could upload the presentation. We asked for some meta information and then converted that file into a player. I remember we took some good technical decisions around the player itself. For example, we had built the ability to get fast playbacks. We were inspired by what Google had told the world about speed—they said that unless you have fast user experience, don't bother with your product. So our player would start playing the slideshow right from the moment the second slide is downloaded and converted instead of waiting for all the slides to convert. That gave the users a fast playback experience.'

The team also explored why YouTube got so popular. Being active bloggers themselves, the founders could see the correlation of blogging and emergence of social platforms.

'Bloggers wanted to showcase their skills and display their personality on their blogs. People wanted to share their videos, photos and presentations. So they used YouTube to upload their videos, and as soon as the video converted, they grabbed the embed code and put it on their blogs. In a way, these platforms were feeding their blogs. The same was true for their photos on Flickr and, later, their presentations on the SlideShare. After six months of uploading your content, you might visit YouTube/SlideShare one day and notice that it has 50,000 views. And you say, "Really? I didn't even know this. I just needed a way to put it on my blog. But this thing also gets you views!" We recognized that the real virality of these platforms paralleled the growth of the blogging. So we made it possible for our users to embed their SlideShare presentations on their blogs.'

Becoming the Product Manager

The team had a sense of urgency since they were the first movers and wanted to make the most of it.

Given Rashmi's background in design, it was decided to make her the CEO and Jonathan the CTO. Amit decided to take on the COO role. In terms of the equity distribution, the founders divided it based on their investments. 'My sister and Jonathan had put in more, so that reflected in the equity distribution as well. We all had an understanding, and we did not see any awkwardness.'

In addition to his operational and recruitment responsibilities, Amit took on the product management role and actively ran the whole product. 'To build a platform from scratch, you need to be open and experimental, and that's how we started growing big.'

He shares few of the most important decisions that helped SlideShare grow bigger and find traction.

'Few months into SlideShare, we realized that PowerPoint was not a medium that excites people as much as a video or a photo. In 2008, videos were exploding all around on YouTube and video start-ups were being funded. PowerPoints are mostly about the professional context or educational context, and they are used in meetings and people hate meetings. So we started wondering how to build a loved community around presentations. We eventually found the answer to that question.'

Amit kept a close tab on what kind of presentations were doing very well and going viral on SlideShare. That is where he found his answer.

'These were visually strong presentations. Most of them came from designers, agencies and web developers who were proud of their sense of design and storytelling. Once we started promoting these on our homepage, it started creating viral loops. Because we sent an email to the uploader that your presentation has been selected from the global uploads, you will be featured for next 24 hours and you can tell your friends about it. What happened was that people really took those as their moments of glory and started blogging about it. They promoted it on Twitter and Facebook, and we were able to create a mass circulation. It started contributing to SlideShare's popularity. Over a couple of years, we built a real momentum to the whole thing. That is one thing we really got right.'

Another thing that helped was that there were a lot of influential people in the Bay Area who started using SlideShare.

'Mark Cuban started posting about us and became an angel investor. Guy Kawasaki is a technologist and marketer, who hailed from Apple. He was well-known in the field of communications. He said, "I have been doing this for 10 years and I always longed for a medium like SlideShare". He suggested organizing a contest for the best presentation (something like the Oscars) and we really liked that idea. So in 2007, for the first time, we organized what we called the "World's Best Presentation Contest". People could upload presentations, and there was voting element to it and we had a bunch of celebrity judges. Kawasaki was also one of the five judges. Finally, we came out with the top 3 from the top 10 presentations. We repeated the contest every year—2007, 2008, 2009 and so on.'

Amit looks at a product manager as someone who owns the entire responsibility around the product. 'He is the CEO of the product. The person who conceptualizes the product, plans on how to build that, how to distribute, how to make money, and then makes all these things happen. That's the way I used to inspire the product managers at SlideShare.'

VC Bias Against Family-Run Start-Ups

There is a taboo against start-ups started by family members among the investors.

Given the traction that SlideShare had, and the kind of advisors or angel investors, it was surprising that the founders had such a tough time trying to raise funds. Amit mentions how frustrating it was that no one talked about it openly.

'A lot of VCs would not even look at us because (a) we were a family (b) we had a woman CEO. The firms just said no or wouldn't give us clear answers. It was only later that we realized what the real reason was. Sequoia and Lightspeed were few VCs that didn't invest. I remember Sequoia was professional and said that they don't believe in some of the use cases, and they don't see the market for that. I don't think their decision was biased.'

In 2008, SlideShare had at least 20 million users. Even the VCs were all using SlideShare.

'In a way, that was always the conversation starter. But anyway, one of the feedbacks we got from few investors was that "you will have to focus on firms which are open to funding women-led start-ups" and that is how we got funded by Venrock. But it took us seven to eight months to get that. Although they have no Indian presence, they have the long history of funding women-led start-ups.'

Amit already knew Dev Khare (who is now with Lightspeed in India but was earlier working with Venrock in the Bay Area) from his MindCanvas days. After launching SlideShare, Amit wrote to him. This eventually led him to David Siminoff who was the partner at Venrock, and his wife had been the Number 2 or Number 3 employee in Yahoo!

'She came from a very strong tech background and was very well-known, and that's what I meant by saying that there are firms that had supported woman-led companies. He really impressed us. Even till now, whenever I or my co-founders are stuck, we reach out to him.'

SlideShare raised US$3 million from Venrock in the end. 'But we were always clear that you cannot let funding be the end goal and you have to focus on what you are building. If you do the right thing, then there would not be any dearth of funding.'

Scaling the Team

The engineering team continued in Delhi until 2008 and then they hired few people in the USA. At the time of acquisition, SlideShare team consisted of 75–80 people out of which 50 were in Delhi. 75 per cent of the employees were in technology. Growing the technology team in India came with its own set of challenges.

SlideShare was built using Ruby on Rails which was just getting popular in 2005.

'It was so new that there were zero people working on it in India. So we decided that we will hire only freshers; they have an open mind and we can mould them the way we want. Another thing is that start-ups have a lot of ambiguity and rework. You do something, then realize that you need something else. Because of all that, it is hard to have very sound coding practices. Since our team was fully made of freshers, we started seeing a problem known as "technology debt". What happened was people started leaving and we were very puzzled. We were doing very well, but many people were leaving. We hired a rockstar engineer from Singapore—one of the best I have ever seen. He left saying that I cannot work in such a shabby company. His departure shook us up and opened our eyes to this problem. It took us that long to even figure out that our codebase had become so bad.'

In 2008–2009, they diligently worked on a phase of technology consolidation. Amit attributes the problem to the relative inexperience of their engineers.

'Only Jonathan was a senior person; rest everyone had joined as a fresher. I think that was a mistake; we should have hired some experienced engineers. Although there are both sides to the argument, experienced people are sometimes not a great fit when you are trying to create a product based on a new concept. Still I think that was a tactical hiring mistake, and we should have seen it coming.'

Amit repeats that they were careful that the team should not feel like an outsourced team. The founders were conscious of keeping a healthy culture.

'Culture does not come from your vision statement; it comes from the way you actually run the company. We gave everyone an equal footing. Second, we used to send people to the USA even when it was difficult to afford it. Third, we gave good facilities such as free ISD calling, broadband connections at home, taxi service, etc. We showed that we cared. Last, the Indian team did not have to take any extra permission or approvals—they were equal owners and it showed in the way they worked. We worked with a philosophy —in Indian time, Indian team rules, and in US time, US team rules.'

When it comes to hiring, Amit differs with most of the other start-ups. He strongly believes in hiring people from different channels—be it job sites, referrals, social media, etc.

'I know many start-ups advocate hiring just via referral but I learnt some tough lessons from that. The problem with hiring just through referrals is that you perpetuate your own type of people. Your guys will get their friends and it ends up being one type of people in the team. I believe in what Darwin said. One of his postulates is that inbreeding weakens your bloodline. The more you mix up people from different races and allow external bloodline, the stronger your bloodline would be. I see that clearly in SlideShare. Initially, it seems good to get all these people together from references, but what happens is when one person leaves, then many others do. If one guy has a problem with the HR practices, others also do.'

Amit makes another interesting remark.

'Steve Jobs in his autobiography says that innovation thrives at the intersection of disciplines. I see that kind of dynamics between myself, Rashmi and Jonathan. We all came from different backgrounds. You should have this reflected at the employee level also. You should have a mix of engineers, designers and product people. You should even mix it up in terms of gender. What that helps with is that every idea is filtered through people with different kind of brains and thinking. You end up making much better decisions that way. So my key learning was that you should not hire from just one channel but mix it up.'

Business Model and Monetization

'There were two ways of building things on the social Internet/web. One was to first have a critical threshold in terms of users and then think about the business model later. The other way would be to think about the business model right from day one. We chose the former. For the kind of thing we were building, you need to get this time to quickly gather that critical mass. You can only think about the business model once you reach a certain stage. When we went to raise funding, we made sure that we were talking to investors who understood and believed in that model.'

Initially, in 2009, SlideShare tried an advertising-led model.

'After two years of trying advertising, we had seen that ads need page views, and SlideShare is a site with limited page views because the page does not refresh even when you are watching a 20-minute presentation. And this is the time when pre-roll and post-roll ads (that YouTube does now) were not introduced. So our experiments with ads did not look too promising. We were doing ads on the sidebar kind of thing and making some money off it.'

SlideShare had its sales team in the USA where they were doing direct advertising. In the rest of the world, they just used Google's ad network. 'The reason is that the price differential is pretty high. If Google's ad network is giving you US$2, then if you sell your own ads, you can make anything between US$8—10 in the USA.'

It was tempting to think of selling their content. But Rashmi felt that it is antithetical to what they have built.

'I mean our name itself had "sharing" in it; all our virality was based on allowing free access to our content, so how could we have a business model that is based on restricting (gating) access to that content? Our VCs felt that we were being academic about it, but in hindsight, I think it was the right decision to not go after making our content paid.'

Around 2010 or 2011, the founders started receiving feedback from the users that they wanted their professional videos to be hosted alongside their PDFs and presentations. This got them thinking that it was better to frame themselves as a platform that caters to professionals, businesses and educators instead of restricting them to slides.

'That expands the market size for us. So another thing we had done was to create a mashup between slides and audio files (MP3 files) called slide casting. Product-wise, we had started slowly allowing people to upload other kinds of formats as well. You could upload pdfs, word document, professional videos for business users, and a mashup between audio and slides for broadcasting.'

They started with a monthly SaaS kind of subscription model with a three-tiered plan—US$19, US$49 and US$249. They offered content marketing features such as adding your branding, banners, etc. They started educating on how people can upload various kinds of formats and use it to market their products.

'Slowly, the business use-case for SlideShare started evolving around content marketing. Companies and a lot of people started using it for content marketing. It was in 2011, and we had tons and tons of write-ups and media coverage about how SlideShare is the big surprise or the hidden gem of content marketing. By 2011, we were making US$5 million. Advertising was contributing 60–70 per cent of that, but it was something we had been running for two years. On the other hand, we had started subscriptions only few months back and it was already contributing 30–40 per cent of our revenues. I think we had started to break even in 2011. And the subscription part was rising quickly. We figured out the real monetization opportunity around SlideShare lies in the content. It was good for us and a little bit of relief, because from 2006, we had kept on building and telling ourselves that we have to first grow our user base and then monetize. At the end of 2010 or 2011, we had some answers to a viable business model.'

SlideShare took a creative approach to encourage companies to use this content marketing feature.

'I remember we took out a list of top 20 content creators based on views. As we looked deeper, there were three people from IBM, two people from Google and so on. We knew from the email they had used to sign in what companies they were coming from. We went to IBM and showed them that data, and asked if they even know about it. They didn't and they were excited. These people were posting some professional and technical content. So we extended to top 1,000 and top 10,000 accounts this way and saw a clear pattern. The insight was that all these big companies with big marketing budgets had an army of content creators already in house.'

So they proposed to IBM that they will create a parent IBM account, where they can link all these top IBM creators and have their content on the IBM page. This would give recognition to these people and IBM will get ready made content. 'We charged a much higher price point for this kind of integration. So we started doing things like this and providing more analytics, etc. that typical SAAS products do nowadays.'

One can say that SlideShare had organically figured out the potential of enterprise SaaS.

LinkedIn Acquisition

In 2008, LinkedIn had created an application platform similar to the Facebook platform where they invited developers to build applications on Facebook. 'However, the LinkedIn platform was by invitation only and they had invited WordPress, Google and us. So we built an application, and it was a mini SlideShare.'

This started a partnership between LinkedIn and SlideShare in 2009.

'For us, the advantage was that there were many LinkedIn users who hadn't heard of SlideShare. So people were discovering SlideShare through LinkedIn. The advantage for LinkedIn was that now there was the professional content from SlideShare flowing in their network. So it was a mutual give and take. By 2012, LinkedIn had realized that out of their 10 or 12 apps, the only app that people were using was SlideShare. Because we had a partnership with them, we used to meet the product team every three months, and were constantly in touch with their engineers and product managers. They already knew about us.'

In 2011, the founders were thinking of raising another US$8–10 million. That is when they were approached by LinkedIn.

'LinkedIn said that they wanted to meet the CEO. First, we thought it is one of the product meetings that we used to have every quarter. But when we went there, they asked if we want to be a part of LinkedIn. We realized that there was a lot of synergy between SlideShare and LinkedIn. LinkedIn was much bigger than us and they had 300 million members at that time. SlideShare had about 45 or 50 million members. So they were five to six times bigger than us. You can argue that everyone who used SlideShare had a LinkedIn account. To us, at a product level, the idea of getting acquired by LinkedIn made a lot of sense.

Another thing worth mentioning is that while we had a big distribution, many of our users were anonymous. We didn't know a lot about our users. A lot of the users who visit SlideShare never log into the platform. We realized that once we got to the business model, we have to quantify the user base. We can monetize well only if we define the user base. When you talk to marketers, you should be able to clearly articulate that this is our user base and their demographic profile. We were weak in that. LinkedIn actually helped answer that part of the riddle as LinkedIn had detailed user profiles. I always say that LinkedIn is the only company on the Internet which has figured out how to get people to fill out their profiles.'

Call it start-up fatigue or strategy, the team was also finding it hard operating half-and-half from the Delhi and San Francisco offices. LinkedIn gave them an out from that.

'We also felt that the employees would benefit financially. So we decided to get acquired. The valuation was about US$120 million. I, at that time, felt that it was probably a low valuation because in 2011 it was just the beginning of our product monetization cycle. I feel that if we had stuck around for two more years, it would have been a different number altogether assuming other things went on well. Unfortunately or fortunately, you become part of a bigger company and your plans just become a subset of theirs.'

Jonathan, Rashmi and Amit (left to right)

The slight tinge of regret trails in Amit's voice.

'I am sure the VCs made good money out of it (I think it was 15 times),' he adds with a chuckle.

Key Takeaways

Person

- *Self-awareness:* Amit accepted what he didn't know and learnt new things with an open mind.
- *Confidence:* Although not a risk taker, Amit had enough confidence to try a start-up in 2004.

Product

- *Start with a familiar territory but shift gears when opportunity knocks:* MindCanvas was born from the team's expertise, but when the BarCamp demonstrated a need, the team was resilient to switch focus to SlideShare.
- *Strong technology underpinning:* SlideShare worked well with any presentation format and the interface was fast.
- *Understanding customer behaviour:* Noticing that users wanted to embed the slideshows on their blogs or that users liked visual presentations helped create product features that lent well to the social nature of the web.

Business Model

- *Monetization for social websites is tricky:* Focusing on traction first proved necessary in the social space. The time it takes to figure out the business model without losing the traction can make or break any social start-up.
- *Experimentation with different models:* Experimenting with ads and realizing that the subscription model can work by positioning the product beyond slides. Eventually content marketing model looked like a perfect fit.
- *Pricing inspired by user behaviour:* Convincing big enterprises like IBM to become a customer by showing the content shared by their employees on SlideShare.

Hiring

- *Attracting talent:* Early employees came because of the blogs of the founders more than the idea. Blogs helped people in knowing the team and building trust.
- *Right salaries:* By benchmarking other companies (like Infosys) where their employees are likely to go, SlideShare offered a 30 per cent hike which worked well.
- *Maintain diversity:* Amit found that relying on referrals alone perpetuated a certain type of people in the company. It worked better to hire a diverse mix of people from a diverse mix of channels. It also proved costly to not have hired any senior engineers when SlideShare faced a problem known as 'technical debt'.

10   Ankit Gupta: Pulse

Influenced by the Silicon Valley culture at Stanford, Ankit created an iPad app for a design class project. The app was picked up by Steve Jobs for a demo and grew into a popular news reading app that was later acquired by LinkedIn for US$90 million. The success came from bold tactical decisions and making the most of a first mover advantage.

Mobile App for News Reading
#pricing #product #traction #acquired #app

All Ankit Gupta wanted after IIT was to land at McKinsey. When that did not happen and he won a Google product competition, he headed to Stanford instead. Pulse was an iPad app that he built with his classmate Akshay Kothari for a class called Launchpad in April 2010. When his professor insisted that the app should be paid and launched soon, the founders were apprehensive. That one decision helped build a loyal community of users and profitability from day one. Laser focus on visual aspects, and leveraging the Stanford ecosystem helped in early traction. It became a viral app when Steve Jobs used it as an example app in a Worldwide Developers Conference (WWDC) demo followed by a controversial episode with *NY Times*.

The strength of its product engineering, interface design and cross-platform availability lent to a robust growth attracting massive interest from top Silicon Valley investors. Key growth came from partnerships with Amazon Kindle Fire and making the app free after raising venture capital. As the company experimented to find the right monetization model, LinkedIn made an offer that the founders could not turn down. The acquisition for US$90 million was announced in April 2013 when Pulse had 30 million users and more than 750 publishers.

It takes more than luck to grow an app from a class project to a scalable business. The young team of Ankit and Akshay represents the quintessential new age entrepreneurs who can leverage the latest technologies and platforms into hyper growth businesses.

Ankit was born in Ajmer but grew up in Mumbai in a small colony. His father ran a computer language training class, and in his sixth grade, he and his parents studied Java together! So computer science became a natural choice when he joined IIT Bombay.

'It is funny but we did not value how much we were learning there. For example, I really did not understand why we are learning operating systems (OS)—going to really low level, designing file system and reading about multithreading! Fast forward, when we were at Pulse, I was the technical co-founder. You know that Pulse is a very visual app. There would be a grid of images. At that time, iPhones were of old generation. It was like iPhone 3G. And when I was writing the app, suddenly the OS fundamentals popped up when I had to move 12 images and download different image sizes in a multithreaded way, using the memory efficiently. So I ended up using a lot of concepts from those courses that I never really thought I would be using.'

One would imagine IIT being the hotbed of start-up in those days, but Ankit denies feeling any desire to start something up.

'There was hardly anybody who thought of starting something. People were excited to get into investment banking and management consulting. There was always an entrepreneurship cell, and the funny thing was that it did not have a great reputation. I think all our seniors, the ones that we respected the most, were going to banks or consulting. We had barely heard of IITians starting companies. The quintessential companies were like Infosys started by Nandan Nilekani, and one of the things he said (I don't know if he actually did but this is what we heard) was that he learnt a lot more from running the cultural festival at IIT than from the coursework at IIT. It is very sad.'

Tasting the Tech

When it came to the final year recruitment, Ankit wanted to get into McKinsey.

However, Google came to the campus for a programme called Google Product Prodigy which was a product development competition. There were many milestones and, in the end, one got a chance to go to Google Bangalore for a Demo Day. 'The prizes were pretty amazing. The first prize was ₹5 lakh. So that was a good platform that I latched on to.'

Ankit built together a team for creating an app similar to Survey Monkey. He called it Polls. The idea was that anyone could create a poll and then embed it on their website and share.

'On the back end, we would have analytics capability, storage of data, focus on using the right data structures, etc. There were three of us and we were very good friends even before IIT. Almost all of our last year was spent on either preparing for our placements or working on this product. I am surprised that we stuck at it so long because everyone around us was having fun and partying. They had gotten a job and there was no reason to study.'

This is also where Ankit paints a contrasting picture between the environment at IIT and Stanford.

'CS at IIT is very theoretical. Teachers take pride that they are teaching the fundamentals and who cares whether you know Javascript or Java! All of these real-world skills were secondary. One should know the underlying theory of algorithms or operating systems and programming languages—that is what professors cared about. Even our own batch mates would make fun of us.

They would laugh that you guys are the top IIT CS graduates and you are writing CSS and Javascript. We didn't mind, but I am just pointing out how different it was from Stanford.'

The competition started at the beginning of the final year and the team kept clearing milestones. Sometime in March, Google flew them to Bangalore for the Demo Day. At the end of the day, the results were declared. Ankit's team had stood second and won a good prize.

'By this time, I had received a consulting job offer, but not from McKinsey. And I had also applied to few graduate schools. We had dinner with top Google Asia-Pacific executives. It is a huge coincidence that I received my acceptance from Stanford the same day. I got rejected from every school except Stanford. At the dinner, a Google executive asked what were we doing after graduation, and most of us said we are going to banking and consulting. These Google executives were surprised that we are the best people in the country and we are not continuing in technology. I wasn't really thinking of my job decision until after this dinner. But I remember, one of the executives (his name is Deep Nishar) said that "Larry Page hired me despite the fact that I come from Harvard Business School". It was 2008, and he said that this year, bankers have lost three trillion dollars.'

That made Ankit rethink.

'I'll be frank that if I had gotten into McKinsey, I probably would have gone ahead with that. And I was very naive. I asked one of my seniors who was at Stanford—"Hey, would I still be able to get into a management consulting firm after Stanford?"' Ankit laughs. '*Wo bhi hansne lag gaya*. And that made my decision easier. That door would still be open, and I like messing around with technology and code. So I thought I will try Stanford.'

Exposure at Stanford

'I thought Stanford would be two more years of IIT but when I got there, I realized how different it was. In my first week, I went to a seminar where the CEO of Microsoft was talking. It was Steve Balmer, but still, you know, the CEO of Microsoft! I had attended a talk by Vinod Khosla that completely blew me away. In the first quarter, I took the hallmark machine learning course by Andrew Ng. I had checked its curriculum before enrolling and felt that I have studied all these things already at IIT, but when I started taking this course, it was almost like I was learning it for the first time. Its problem sets were so challenging that it would take us an entire week to solve them. Overall, we could take courses from design school and biology, and they were all real-world product based courses. I think the social connect network is not the right word—the kind of people you meet is just at a different level. They are so sharp, visionary and risk taking. You just feel that entrepreneurship is in the air. You know the difference between a billionaire and a student at Stanford was just a few years maybe.'

As he got deeper into his classes, Ankit's management consulting dream got sidelined. He adds that the biggest investment that he and his parents made was getting an iPhone and a MacBook. 'It was very expensive. And I got an Apple developer account. I started writing apps right away, just by myself.' Destiny had intervened.

Kickstarting Pulse as a Class Project

Ankit met his co-founder, Akshay Kothari, in their first quarter when both were taking a machine learning class. Akshay recommended him to take a class in the Design School that he had loved. It taught the concept of design thinking and made a great impact on Ankit. 'After that, I took a design class almost every quarter. Pulse started in the last design class that I and Akshay took together. It was called Launchpad.'

It was a unique 10-week course.

'Before you start the class, you come in with a team, and an idea and plan to execute. And you have to sign a contract that you will launch a start-up by the end. Within the first week, you have to create a prototype. Within five weeks, you have to launch your business and in last five weeks, it has to be profitable. Demo day is after five weeks. Roughly 10 companies were there—created by 20–25 students.'

They considered multiple ideas including a group travel booking app but finally decided upon Pulse. The idea was simple—everyone was using mobile devices and reading a lot of news on it. But Ankit believed that the news reading experience sucked. They wanted to create a better and visual user experience around news reading.

'The day the class started was the day iPad launched. We went in the line to buy the iPad and got our first iPad. And it was clear that it can have an amazing news reading experience. Also, iPad app store had very few items. Competition was much lower. So we decided to build our app for iPads. We started coding right away and coded through the weekend. iPad launched on Friday and by Monday, we had a prototype. On Tuesday, we showed it to the class. Even outside the classroom, we showed it to many people.'

Many students try to build apps but not everyone succeeds. And that goes back to some creative validation approaches by the founders. They made full use of the Stanford ecosystem.

'In terms of design, the prototype was actually very similar to what the app became later on. But it wasn't great. People liked playing with the iPad in those days. What we did is this—we didn't really have any office. So we would go to this coffee shop with our iPad. It was a huge device in Silicon Valley at that time. So people would ask us, "hey, how do you like the iPad?" and we would offer it to them to try it out. But we would also open Pulse on it before giving it to them. So they would just look at it and try to use the app. We would look over their shoulders and ask them for their feedback. We could see all the issues they were running into, things that they were not finding intuitive.

We would go there in the morning, change the code in the afternoon and we would have another app by the evening based on user feedback. Very quickly, we got to an app that we launched on the app store. We were proud of our app. I feel it was very usable and intuitive, but at the same time, it had a lot of issues. For example, in the first version, you could only read four publications. Also, if you read for more than three to four minutes, the app would crash. It was definitely a version one. There were memory issues, leaks and, mainly, it was a bunch of stuff hacked together because I had never built an iPad app before!'

Their prototype was working and things were looking up. It was now time to go live—this is when they made one of their biggest decisions.

Unconventional Pricing Call

One of the milestones that the team needed to clear in the class was to launch the app. Should they launch a half-baked app?—that was the dilemma with which they approached their professors. After all, first impression matters!

To their astonishment, their advisors not only pushed them to launch it but also pushed to charge for it. Ankit chuckles. 'It was unthinkable for us. Why would anyone pay for it, right? But they pushed us because that's how we would understand the value of it. You can always bring the price down.'

Team went for a soft launch and released the app on the app store for US$4. 'We create a video and sent to few blogs and iPhone forums.'

The decision became a game changer. Customers became more invested into it. They would wait for improvement. It was a great way to get a group of beta testers. It also pushed the founders to release an update every week. They could have sent an update every day but it took Apple one week to approve the app.

'We were constantly improving the app based on user feedback. Some of the users wanted a more RSS functionality and some wanted more visual aspects. Some people wanted the functionality to mark things read or unread. They wanted the ability to subscribe to few updates. There was feedback to get more publications, more stories and more languages. At one point, we got this feedback from a psychologist who was a huge fan of our app. He wrote us a four-to-five-paragraph email describing the logic of why Pulse's design was helpful. He described how each story being in one square makes our eyes focused on these nuggets of stories much better. How the grid interface enables you to browse faster. And he had these research references. It was like an academic validation of why our interface was so efficient.'

In 10 weeks of the course, Pulse got a few tens of thousands downloads. Ankit attributes that to the user experience as well as novelty of the iPad.

'It was a good news reading app. I am not saying it just because it was my product but iPad was quite new. And a lot of news publications weren't well equipped to write good apps. News apps were typically developed by hobbyist developers. And we kept doing our best. Also, think of this—when you buy a version 1 iPad which is a US$600 device, it doesn't really do much! Pulse was one of the better apps. If you really want to utilize your iPad or show it off to people, you wouldn't mind paying US$4 for this app.

Once we started making some money, we realized that apart from the speed and efficiency of the app, the design needs to be improved. In the beginning, it really looked like a class project. You could see that an engineer had designed it. A friend of ours had gone to the product design programme at Stanford. We hired him for few hours to improve the design of the app. Our first Android engineer, Albert, also was from Stanford. The three of us had done another project together. Quite early we found talented resources at Stanford itself. They had all graduated by then and we paid pretty competitive salaries.'

The Steve Jobs Moment

Right after their class ended in June 2010, Apple was holding a WWDC for iPhone 4 launch. Before launching the phone, Steve Jobs went through the iPad updates and was showing some of the apps. And Pulse was the first app he showed.

'We had no clue that he was going to do that. I wasn't even in San Francisco, I was in New York. I heard about it from people who were at WWDC and they were congratulating us. So I took the first flight back to San Francisco. After I landed, we tried to get into WWDC but we didn't have any tickets and they didn't let us in. That was the first time I felt like the app is something real. Steve Jobs was one of my idols.'

Before they could wallow in the glory of the moment, they were sued by the *NY Times*.

'They sent a letter directly to Apple and from what I understand, their complaint was against us using their RSS feed when the app loaded. They were also unhappy that we were using *NY Times* in our marketing screen. Our app was a paid one and we were not sharing our revenues with the publishers. So they were pissed off. When Steve Jobs announced the app, the app was not available on the app store…[Ankit chuckles] because Apple had taken it down due to this complaint by *NY Times*. That shows the highs and lows of a start-up. We practically went out of business. I was thinking how will we ever fight *NY Times*! We told Professor Dearing that it's over.

And what he replied was, "Guys, this is the best thing that can happen to you! Think who hates *NY Times* the most. The answer is *Wall Street Journal* (WSJ)". So he contacted a friend of his, Kara Swisher, who was a reporter at the WSJ. So the same night when Steve Jobs showed off our app, we gave an interview to Kara. She posted this beautiful factual piece which covered what we did, how *NY Times* took us out and how we were not doing anything illegal the next morning. And this was the day when iPhone 4 was launched. And on Techmeme, iPhone launch story was the second story and our interview was the first. It really blew up and Apple, thankfully, put us back on the app store that very day. We had 30,000 downloads that day. Eventually we also settled things with the *NY Times* lawyers.'

It could have been the end of the road for someone who did not have access to such an advisor or the Valley's influence. This kind of press coverage also triggered new competitors. Ankit recalls their biggest competitor Flipboard announcing its app.

'They were an all-star team, repeat founders who had made US$100 million+ exits. They had acquired a company whose CTO was the founder of Java. One of the co-founders was teaching iOS class at Stanford,' Ankit laughs.

'And they had been working on this idea for many months. They had a bigger head start and the design was amazing. It got a lot of traction very quickly. They had raised US$10 million already. They were a very formidable competitor. As these new players were entering, we had no choice but to focus and listen to our customers, what they wanted and what they cared for. We just kept improving on and on. We were literally updating the app every day.'

Meanwhile Akshay had landed a job offer from Microsoft and Ankit from Facebook. The app was doing well and they kept delaying the start dates. 'I made many excuses, one of which was that I have to go to India for my own wedding,' Ankit laughs.

'I pushed the offer for three to four months and one day, Albert came in. He told us that he has declined his Qualcomm job offer and he is all in. I think that was the point when we realized, "Oh, Albert is all in. We need to go all in too". We used Pulse to file for our H-1B on which we could work full time. Eventually, we got our green cards a few years later.'

From App to a Business

After graduating, they moved into an incubation space run by Professor Michael Dearing in Palo Alto. He also became their advisor and a personal mentor. Within six months, they also released an iPhone app and gathered good reviews. The next step was to scale and they decided to raise venture capital for it and run it like an actual business.

Given the app's traction, there was already a lot of inbound interest.

'It was a fantastic place to be because we did not have to chase anybody. That is why I advise start-ups—try to be profitable. We were getting meeting requests from Silicon Valley investors. In the end, we went with five to six of them in the first round. Mayfield, Lightspeed and few more were there. And we got very good terms. Typically these funds don't invest very little amount but in those early days, VCs were looking to attract good companies. So we had a unique situation where all these top VCs were willing to put in US$200,000 each at really good terms. Also, we closed it very fast and it was a very painless process. Venture capital was like adding fuel to the fire for us. And I am glad we did not raise money too early because may be our app was not ready for that. We raised when we had more confidence in the product.'

The next step was to make the app free.

'Our biggest fear was not whether we will be able to monetize the app now, our biggest fear was the backlash from our paid users. But surprisingly, only a few people complained. Going free helped a lot in user growth for sure. We had a quarter of a million users when we were paid. The day we made the app free, we had a *NY Times* story on that and we did whatever publicity we could. But at the end, we had another quarter of a million downloads that day when we went free. We kept growing from there.'

Different investors helped with different things.

'Greycroft helped with Media, another helped in thinking about the product and many helped with the hiring. Founder of Greycroft, Alan Patricof, is known as the father of venture capital. This fund is very connected with the media entities. And that is why we wanted them to participate when we raised our next round as well. So although NEA led that Series A round of US$9 million, Greycroft participated with a big investment as well. They helped us a lot in getting meetings with the right publishers.'

Getting publishers on board helped in getting customized feeds that were optimized for Pulse experience.

'Clean layout, good visuals, etc. That time, publishers didn't have their websites optimized for mobile and all. So most of the modern publishers actually wanted to work with us. Since publishers were the key players for our ecosystem, we wanted to create a synergy and help them grow their business. Initially, we would help them with getting more eyeballs for their content. Over time, we moved to also helping them with monetizing their content through ads.'

Monetization

After making the app free, the burn rate shot up as well. And competition was rising. Flipboard was aggregating news from a user's social media channels. Publishers also were coming up with their own apps. TechCrunch had released its app. Shortly after their Series A in June 2011, founders became more serious about monetization.

'We tried many models. One was a freemium model where you get most of it free but have to pay for premium content like *WSJ*. So we had partnered with *WSJ* to have an in-app subscription. That experiment did not go too well though. Then, we had bunch of experiments around advertisements. We tried brand ads, sponsored content, etc. Eventually the monetization strategy that we landed on was the sponsored items. So Pulse was a grid-based app; what we did was we made one of the grid reserved for the sponsored content. Brands paid for per impression as far as I remember. That showed some positive signs.'

The team kept experimenting aggressively. They had actually built an experimenting framework within the app where they could A/B test different features or ideas. They were doing social experiments and hardware experiments. One successful experiment was when an intern tried an email newsletter with news stories personalized by user interests. There were many failed experiments as well, such as letting users follow each other.

Hardware experiments turned out more interesting.

'We were experimenting with hardware manufacturers such as Samsung and HTC. They wanted to improve their Android OS experience. In fact, when Amazon Kindle Fire tablet was launching, news reading was obviously an important thing for Kindle because it is a reading device. Pulse was only one of the four apps that were preloaded right on its homepage. So we got almost a million users around Christmas of 2011 through that alone. It was a very interesting time, and we were experimenting with different news reading models, news aggregation models and distribution models. OS kept updating; Android was improving. So the way you built apps was also evolving. Everything was in flux. One thing we stuck to and took very seriously was the end-user experience, and we worked really hard to ensure that user experience kept improving regardless of anything else.'

To maintain an impeccable user experience, the team got real users to come in try using the app in front of them so that they can learn from users' behaviour.

Hardware partnerships started with an inbound interest, but given their success, the team decided to double down on them.

'This is one of the things that Akshay used to handle. Later on, we expanded and built a business development team. It needed lot of meetings with the manufacturer to understand the right product and the right model. I'll tell you about this one partnership that was interesting. So a big hardware manufacturer was launching a brand new device and they wanted Pulse to come on it preloaded. Although their operating system was an Android fork and Pulse worked on most Android devices, Pulse didn't work on theirs due to customizations they had made. It was mostly a HTML5 wrapper around the OS. The device was supposed to launch in a few months and we needed to build a HTML5 app. They wanted us so much that they were willing to give us help to develop it. We saw that as an opportunity to get funded to develop an HTML5 app.'

One of the competitive advantages became that Pulse was available very early on different platforms. They were one of the first apps on Android.

'Every big app was going for iOS first. We felt that we need to be cross-platform from the beginning. It was very tough to get high-quality Android app to perform as well as on iOS app in those days. High-performance visual apps were very tough to build on Android. A lot of people did not even try, and if they did, it was bad user experience mostly.'

Ankit explains how Android OS was developed to work on a variety of phones.

'When you have to account for that range of devices, it is just hard to consistently offer good experience. With iPhones, you can assume to have good graphics card, display and standardization of screen sizes, but you cannot on Android. You have to optimize your app for so many different configurations, even for a very lesser used device. Sometimes you do not even have all the devices to test with and it becomes a theoretical exercise. Today, you can submit your mobile app to a testing company and they will test it on all platforms for you. But that didn't exist back then. Albert did a great job on getting an Android app that worked on this diverse set of devices.'

The result of all that was that Pulse just became the best news reading experience on any mobile. Period. All their competitors were available only on iOS for a long time. And whenever a manufacturer came on Android, Pulse became their natural choice.

LinkedIn Acquisition

In May 2013, they were in the market to raise Series B. The app was growing strong with 30 million downloads at this point.

'We had 300 million stories being read every month. The goal was to raise a large Series B, and try to build out monetization model, sales team, ad business and become profitable. Both of us were excited about it, but at the core, we were product people. We always enjoyed working on the product more than doing all these other things. One of our mentors is Deep Nishar who was head of product at LinkedIn at that time. I had met Deep when I was at IIT. Akshay had just emailed him asking for some advice. We met him on an afternoon and he asked us that "why don't you guys talk to LinkedIn?" It was a new idea to us and we decided to try it out.'

They took a meeting next day with the global head of product, Ryan Roslansky. Eventually, Ryan and LinkedIn's corporate development team came to the Pulse office and checked their status.

'Our culture and vision seemed to align very well. LinkedIn was not as popular and not something that you visit every day. They did not have much of a mobile presence. So from a talent, and product perspective, it made a lot of sense for LinkedIn to acquire us. News is very important for professionals. Plus, we drove daily activity and they agreed to keep the brand name Pulse alive.'

Once the LinkedIn team felt convinced about the synergy, they moved pretty fast.

'We had this meeting on Friday. On Saturday, the head of engineering for news met us. Akshay and I had gone to Big Sur for camping in the weekend. Big Sur is in middle of wilderness. On Saturday night we were told that the CEO of LinkedIn, Jeff Weiner, wanted to meet us next day. And when CEO of LinkedIn wants to meet you, you go meet the CEO of LinkedIn. On top of that, he wanted to meet us at 6:30 AM. So we woke up at 3:00 AM and drove back three hours to meet with Jeff. It was supposed to be a 30-minute meeting but it lasted more than two hours. Next day at 8:00 AM, LinkedIn had an actual offer for us.'

The acquisition happened in a few stages. The first step was an 'intent to acquire', which is an exclusive agreement. Pulse had to open their data so that LinkedIn could do the due diligence on revenues, growth and legal matters.

'Once you sign that exclusivity, they can ask you whatever they want but you cannot approach anyone else. And we couldn't tell our employees that we are in talks with LinkedIn. But of course, they could see that something is up. We were asking for all this data and all, so they wondered. It was a tricky period because the deal can fall through and your valuation might fall down, and it will be harder to get another acquirer as well.'

In between all this, the news got leaked to the press that LinkedIn is buying Pulse. Luckily for Pulse, the press saw it as a positive outcome. In the last phase, the companies discussed how the team would be absorbed.

'At this point, we told our employees because LinkedIn interviewed everyone and then rolled out the offers. We made sure that the employees get a fair deal and helped people get the right role and helped them negotiate their offers. Overall, I would say LinkedIn was a very good acquirer; they were fair and prompt. Everyone was happy in the end. You can see that most of our developers are still at LinkedIn.'

It was a US$ 90 million deal.

Ankit Gupta

In hindsight, Ankit feels that LinkedIn was much better at integrating talent than the product. Pulse had many processes that LinkedIn was not ready to integrate or able to integrate. Pulse is essentially powering what we see as the current LinkedIn feed.

Parting Thoughts

Ankit shares his favourite books:

1. *The Little Prince* by Antoine de Saint-Exupéry
2. *The Unbearable Lightness of Being* by Milan Kundera
3. The Harry Potter series by J. K. Rowling
4. *The Crossroads of Should and Must* by Elle Luna (A friend of mine introduced it to me when I was going through a soul-searching phase. If all of us lived as we must, the world shall be a much better place.)

'When I was little, I remember expressing this desire to be Shah Rukh Khan one day. And someone quite wise gave me an advice. He told me how I will actually become Ankit Gupta, and only become Ankit Gupta. I'm not sure who it was that gave me this advice, but it has stuck with me throughout.'

Key Takeaways

Product

- *Starting early on a new platform:* Since iPad had very few apps and people liked showing off their new gadget, Pulse saw rapid early adoption by launching on iPad first. Same for Android and HTML5.

- *Focus on usability and user feedback:* Preloading the app on iPad before showing it to strangers in coffee shops in the early days or inviting users to the office helped in getting meaningful feedback and improving the user experience.

- *Weekly update cycles:* Releasing new updates almost weekly meant quick big fixes and frequent new features. It helped keep user ratings very high.

- *Design and interface:* Focusing on the visual aspects (aided by bringing in a designer for a clean professional look) had always been the selling point for the app (including attracting the attention of Steve Jobs).

- *Testing features before launching:* Using the experimenting framework to A/B test new ideas enabled a culture of innovation and made sure that only proven features are released.

Business Model

- *Pricing:* Starting as a paid app made the users more invested, the founders more accountable and, of course, the app profitable! Later on, making the app free when venture capital came in increased the number of downloads. Both pricing decisions proved pivotal in the growth of the app.

- *Forging key hardware partnerships:* Partnering with different device manufacturers added new revenue streams.
- *Understanding the needs of key players:* Aligning their interests with the publishers meant friendly synergy and better user experience through customized feeds.

Traction

- *Steve Jobs factor:* Before launching the iPhone 4, Steve Jobs went through the iPad updates and was showing some of the apps. Pulse was the first app he showed. Best endorsement ever!
- *Turning negative news into PR:* Using the *NY Times* attack for coverage on *WSJ* made the Pulse story viral.
- *Attracting users across platforms and devices:* Maintaining cross-platform expertise and getting partnerships with giants such as Amazon Fire attracted wider distribution and faster user growth.

There is no perfect fit when you're looking for the next big thing to do. You have to take opportunities and make an opportunity fit for you, rather than the other way around. The ability to learn is the most important quality a leader can have.

—Sheryl Sandberg

11 Ankur Singla: Akosha

How did a lawyer leave his prestigious job in London to create a legal-tech start-up in India that served three million consumer complaints and worked with 200+ brands? His farsightedness and persistence stands out as he overhauled the way customer woes could be resolved.

Consumer Complaints Redressal Service
#business_model #sales #pivoting #fundraising

Akosha was founded in 2009 by a lawyer, Ankur Singla. After saving ₹14 lakh, Ankur left his job at a law firm in London with a fuzzy idea to start a company by going back to India. The idea went through several iterations, including creating legal documents online, before finding its niche as a consumer complaints redressal platform. That service eventually picked up, and the company processed three million complaints in a span of four years.

With a key decision that the company took about keeping the complaints private, Akosha was able to position itself as a neutral third party that managed to win the trust of consumers and brands alike. While Akosha is usually known for its B2C business where it solved user's grievances against brands, much of its growth also came from its SaaS software called OneDirect, which is its B2B product designed to serve brands. It was never talked about much, but that is the part which was retained after Akosha was pivoted to Helpchat in 2015. As a business, Helpchat floundered from the beginning, with chat functionality not solving the problems as anticipated. The product was quickly pivoted to Tapzo in 2016—an all-in-one app for consumer needs.

Misfit Lawyer in London

Ankur grew up in Chandigarh, reading a lot of business books. A desire to be around smart people in a metro city took him to NLS Bangalore.

'I met a lot of very smart and articulate and intelligent people but I never developed an interest in law. I passed out with very very low grades but I really enjoyed my time outside the classroom. I started a film club. I was also the conveyor of the Law and Technology Committee.'

By the time he graduated, a lot of law firms from London were recruiting on campus. One of them made him an offer he couldn't refuse.

'Within the first 5–10 days of the job, whatever I had already felt before was reinforced—I don't think I'm cut out to be a corporate lawyer. I remember in the first six months, I was made to proofread an insane number of documents which really builds a character in some way. You hate it when you do it, but it really builds a level of attention to detail. Once we had a client who was selling some mines to a Russian oligarch. We went to his house. When I saw this house, it was those palatial houses in central London where you walk in, and there is this huge staircase and big conference room in the house itself. We are sitting there and working on negotiating some deal for some African mine, and what I realized (again) is that in law, the other side is always going to be the one which is really taking the risk and has the life. As a lawyer, I would always be an advisor and consultant. I will never be in the thick of the things.'

In 2008, Ankur read *Stay Hungry Stay Foolish*. It was also in 2008 that he came across Sameer Guglani's blog post on pluggd.in.

'Sameer had guest-posted something about the love of start-up pain and it really resonated with me. It made me ponder that *"ye mai kya apni zindagi kharaab kar raha hun? Kya mai London me baith ke paise kama raha hun?"'*

Next, Ankur somehow calculated that ₹14 Lakh will give him the runway for two years of survival, and he should quit his job in London the day he has saved ₹14 Lakh.

After two years of working in London, he would have qualified as a solicitor (allowing him to practise in the UK). The twist in the tale was when his ₹14 Lakh target was hit in one year and nine months.

'All of my friends were like, three months *baad* quit *kar lena*! But I was like *ki bhai, mujhe to ye karna hi nahi hai*. If anything, *wo karunga to kya pata aur laalach aaye. To maine kaha ki mujhe nahi chahiye* and *mai ja raha hun*.'

Back in Chandigarh, Ankur took a room behind his dad's office.

'I landed in India on 30 May 2009 around 2:30 PM, and I immediately came home and started working. I was thinking of legal ideas. I had thought of starting something like Legalzoom (a US company which allowed users to make legal documents online). I decided to start an online portal where you can make your will.'

The Search for a Tech Partner

Ankur found a DU MCA grad through a job portal and hired him at a monthly salary of ₹25,000. It was decided that the equity part will be discussed later.

'I was myself working very very hard. Those days, I had kept my mattress in the office only. I used to ask this guy a lot of questions about LAMP stack, and front end and back end, and how you build a basic client server application.'

They called their app wasiyat.com and launched it in February 2010. On that website, one could simply click and make wills for ₹1,999 (for comparison, a lawyer might charge ₹10,000 for it).

'What happened was that the idea completely bombed. I sent an email to 35 people saying hey, there is a link and you can make you will. Then people told me that it looked shit and why would anyone make a will. It was pretty brutal but I kept telling *ki nahi, ye ho sakta hai*. I had already calculated that if so many people did so many orders, then it would already be so big.'

Meanwhile, he was struggling after outsourcing tech to a firm in Bangalore. And his MCA hire ended up leaving for another job that paid ₹800,000 in annual salary. Nothing worked for the next seven to eight months. Ankur had even renamed the firm from wasiyat to Akosha so that he could do a lot of other legal documents as well.

Moving to the Metro

Ankur was getting frustrated with Chandigarh. The tipping point came when he made job offers to two people from Punjab University.

'The day they were supposed to join, neither turned up. I called the first guy and he said, "Sir, Mummy *nahi maan rahe, mai nahi aa sakta*". When I phoned the other guy, he also said, "Sorry, *dost nahi aa raha to maine socha mai bhi kya karunga aa kar*". I had studied in Bangalore and worked in London, and learnt this professionalism and *gyaan vyaan*. And hearing this kind of shit made me feel that *is sheher ka kuch nahi ho sakta*. Very soon I left for Delhi and took up a 2-BHK house in Kalkaji. *Delhi me pehle to rent pe jagah hi nahi milti* and then I was single, had no job and, on top of all that, I was a lawyer. This is the worst combination you can have [he chuckles]. *10–15 din to doston ke yahan reh ke roz ghar dekhe. Dhakke khaye ja rahe hain and koi ghar nahi de raha.* I used to call property agent and he would say, "*Accha aap wo black suit wale ho, nahi aapko koi ghar nahi dega*".'

Finally, he found a house in Kalkaji for ₹17,000 monthly rent and lived on as little expenses as he could.

'Initially I used to spend like as I was in London but after four to five months, you get a bit scared that you are not making anything and your money is running out. So then I also started doing some legal consulting for start-ups. I was pretty clear that I just wanted to survive and did not want to go back. I did freelance consulting on legal agreements and all. Simultaneously, trying to build my own start-up. I was very good at legal consulting and a lot of clients used to say that *ye aap kya start-up-vartup kar rahe ho, aap to itne ache lawyer ho. Aap law me kuch aur karo.* Then I used to be like, if you can do a business then why can't I do a business?'

Spotting the Opportunity and Pivoting

'When I had come to Delhi, *us time Airtel ka ₹198 ka 3G pack aata tha.* And you get 1 GB data. So I had called them and activated it, but *unhone activate nahi kiya and mera Internet bill ₹3,000–4,000 ka aa gaya tha.* When you are really tight with money, you get scared and angry when you get such a bill. So I called them and shouted. That time I thought that a lot of other people must also be having similar complaints. Then, there was this other guy in Delhi who came to me saying that *meri sister ka ye coaching institute ke saath case chal raha hai* and they are not refunding her fee. He was asking for help. So I did some research online and there were few small websites who claimed that they can help you with customer complaints. I thought let's try this out. Then I put a fourth button on my website. Earlier we had will, rent agreement and power of attorney. I added a button called consumer complaints.'

The *aha* moment arrived in September 2010, when rediff.com covered Akosha since there were only a few legal start-ups in those days.

'*Usse humein ek din me bada saara traffic aa gaya.* We got 350–400 clicks in one day. Earlier it was two clicks. So out of all the clicks, we got 65 leads on consumer complaints, one on rent and nothing on other two. And it was like one of those lucky moments of finding product market fit. We redid the website, removed everything and made it about consumer complaints.'

Ankur had already met Sameer Guglani (Morpheus Startup Accelerator) by this time and they were keeping in touch. He formally joined Morpheus accelerator in November 2010.

'The good thing was in those days, they use to give ₹5 lakh. By taking ₹5 lakh, I could stop doing consulting. During my first 1.5–2 years, tech was where I struggled the most. After the first guy left, I went through seven to eight different people; they all came and left. Morpheus helped me in tech also. Akosha was the company where they felt *ki founder theek hai but tech ki support nahi milti and isliye kaafi dikkat aati hai*. So we found and negotiated a tech contract with Sarvjeet.'

Sarvjeet ran an outsourcing company that provided technical services for start-ups. He used to manage the tech resources on behalf of a start-up. In return, the start-up had to pay the salaries of these people and give some equity to Sarvjeet.

'Basically, when you are running a small start-up, you cannot attract a guy like Sarvjeet because he is very smart and experienced. So Sarvjeet created this model where he takes the equity, but it will be much smaller than what he would get full time. But by working with multiple start-ups, his risk is also covered. That worked out pretty well for us also.'

Product Evolution

Akosha offered one ₹499 plan and one ₹999 plan in the beginning. Ankur explains some interesting use cases.

'Chances of someone paying would be much higher in a banking or insurance complaint. I will tell you the first complaint we solved. A lady had enrolled her daughter in a IIT coaching centre and they had taken ₹1.5 lakh in fee, but within two days of the classes, the daughter said she didn't want to attend it. When the parents tried to get a refund, they were not giving a refund. So we said that you take our *₹999 wala package*, we will write them a letter that you have to resolve this else we will be forced to take a legal action. The second thing used to be to file a complaint to the consumer court. What happened usually was that the moment we sent the first letter itself, they agreed to refund. So it was a little bit like that.

Another example would be somebody's Nokia phone has been lying with the service centre and it hasn't come back. Those days, Nokia still used to be pretty big. And they didn't know what is happening. Somebody would pay the ₹499 package to request *ki ye theek kara do*. Then what we would be doing is we added a few people on LinkedIn from Nokia in customer support or even from senior management and emailed them saying that we have received a complaint. We have many more complaints. We want to help you win your customer trust back. People who had bad experience with customer support, we would bring them back to you and help retain them. As a CEO, he would always be concerned about his customer service.'

Akosha offered a great solution for customer retention and used to share benchmarking data with the brands—for example, complaints per 1,000 customers for the brand versus its competitors. 'To the customer, we would say, that *ye aap hum pe chhod do*. You are busy, *aap apne kaam karo, ye humein sort karne do*. That was the proposition to the customer.'

After the rediff coverage, traffic again started to wane. This is when Ankur attended a talk by Hitesh Oberoi from www.naukri.com.

'He is Sanjeev Bikhchandani's right hand man. He is himself a great guy and was talking about early days of Naukri. He told that *humein kuch nahi pata tha and humnein ek salary survey kiya tha but humein nahi pata tha ki kaise bechna hai. Humnein 800 chitthiyan bhej di HR heads ko India me and usme se itne logon ka order aa gaya,* and suddenly we got ₹88,000 in revenue when our cost of creating the survey and printing the books was only ₹27,000. We said *ki yaar ye business model to accha hai.* He was talking about the year 1996 and 1997. So that kind of revenue is not bad.'

The thing that stayed with Ankur was that one should find the shortest path from A to B. Applying that to Akosha, Ankur felt that the problem was not that people were not coming to their website but that Ankur was thinking of the shortest way of getting more customers and leads.

'In February, I had some interns coming from NLS, and I sat with them and we brainstormed how to solve this problem. Instead of waiting for the customer to come and file the complaint on our website, we simply started going to other websites where they were posting their complaints and call them. So in those days, *hum mouthshut pe ya consumercomplaints.in pe jaate the,* and we used to see who has posted a complaint with a phone number. We would pick the phone and call them. We had a script—Sir, *hum Akosha naam ki sanstha se bol rahe hain and humnein aapki complaint padhi hai Nokia ke baare me. To log ekdum gusse me [start saying] ki aap Nokia wale sunte nahi ho.* So we used to say *ki Sir hum Nokia se nahi bol rahe hain, ye ek nayi sanstha hai jo logon ki madad karti hai.* Then they would ask *ki* how do you help and we would explain. Then we would say that it would cost ₹499, and then we would get some conversions. I remember we made some 738 calls and got 29–30 conversions.'

One cannot help notice how quick Ankur is with all the numbers. He laughs when explaining why he remembers all that.

'The reason I remember is that even though that was a bad conversion, it was first time we sold something. We could live with that. Slowly our revenue rose up to ₹15,000 per month. Slowly slowly slowly it moved. We used to focus a lot on user testimonials, and then sharing it on social media and websites. *Testimonial se fir trust banta tha kyunki* people thought *ki pehle hi kisi company ne mera kaata hai and ab mai kisi random company ko ₹500 kyun dun?'*

The tech team was still outsourced, and they hired a lot of interns (₹1,000–2,000 monthly salary) who would handle everything from contacting brands on LinkedIn to tracking complaints on Twitter, etc. Additionally, they used Google Adwords to build traction. Google gave them the highest intent customers when they bid for 'Airtel complaint' or 'Airtel customer care' keywords.

'Our ad there would take you to fill out a lead form and that helped us to scale. The good thing was it was a very non-competitive space, so cost of bidding was very low. We would get a complaint for ₹15–18 and that person would take our ₹499 and ₹999 plan, etc. It was a fairly obvious channel but we had to do a lot of hit and trial to optimize it properly.'

Fundraising and Creative Business Model

It took roughly ₹16 lakh to bootstrap Akosha. Ankur believes that one doesn't have product market fit unless someone is willing to pay for it. 'We started experimenting on our website that *chalo 50 per cent logon ko ₹499 ka price dikhaao, telecom complaints ko ₹299 dikhaao, real estate ko ₹999 dikhaao* and so on. Then it gets logical from there.'

Things were falling in place, but there was a nagging feeling that he needed more mentorship. Everyone around him was raising an insane amount of money.

'In 2011–2012, Snapdeal and Flipkart raising so much money made us curious. There were a lot of Morpheus meet-ups during those days—usually at my office in Kalkaji. *Cigarette, daru shaaru hota tha.* We were all early stage entrepreneurs and we wanted to raise money. So a group of 5–10 of us would go to Accel or Kalaari office and keep pitching.'

Akosha was now doing a net monthly revenue of ₹25,000–30,000. Ankur felt he was solving a real Indian customer pain point and they could disrupt the customer care industry. Their burn rate was very low. 'We had 4–5 months of cash flow left when we raised this money.'
Sameer had connected him with Shailendra at Sequoia capital.

'I went and met him in Grand Hotel in Vasant Kunj in Delhi. He is the kind of guy who bets on people. We talked not just about the company but more about my story—why I left London, why am I doing this, etc. He left the meeting saying that we will do something together. One week later, he invited me to present to the committee. I went there and they decided to invest. So they put in US$200,000 and the money came in September 2011.'

Ankur emphasizes on the value of a physical meeting.

'In my experience, whenever I have pitched over phone, it has not worked out. There are times when you meet for the first time and they say that we would love to work with you. Usually it is either on or off. *Aap hamesha milo.* Even if they don't ask you to meet, I say, hey I am in Mumbai tomorrow, why don't we meet physically? If they give me time, then I book my ticket. The second thing is—you should just be yourself. I think VCs have met enough entrepreneurs to know who is genuine. See VC is a market of one. It means that even if 20 VCs say no, and one says yes, that is good enough. Everyone doesn't have to like you; somebody will like you for who you are and that's the right partner.'

As a lawyer, Ankur understands termsheets much better than an average entrepreneur.

'*Hamari jo pehli term sheet thi Sameer ke saath*, that was so liberal and founder friendly. *Khair uski philosophy bhi sahi thi. He thought ki ya to aap kaam kar paaoge—to is sab se much fark nahi padta. Aur agar kaam nahi kar pa rahe ho, to bhi fark nahi padta.* When Sequoia came in, I felt they were also very friendly. It was a straightforward, clean term sheet; there were no liquidation prefs. Whatever back and forth happened was because I was paranoid. I had heard that whatever you negotiate in the first round becomes a template for subsequent rounds. So I was being cautious. But then Shailendra called me and said ki Ankur, *kyun tension le raha hai?* Then I let it go. Also, the thing is back in 2009–2010, VCs used to give bad term sheets. Compared to that, this term sheet was super clean. No tranching, which is the biggest condition VCs usually put.'

Ankur used the Sequoia funds to scale to handle more complaints, figure out B2B monetization model, building in-house tech, etc. 'We worked with Sarvjeet from April 2011 till August 2012. Our CTO, Vishal, joined in June 2012.'

B2B monetization was the real masterstroke.

'We had a beautiful equation going. Customer complaints were two kinds—the first where the volume was high but payment capacity low, like telecom complaints. The second was insurance and real estate where volume was low but propensity to pay much higher. What we did was that we used to monetize from the customer in the second case and from the brands in the first case.'

They created a dashboard called OneDirect where the brands could see user complaints from Akosha.

'And for the paid model of this dashboard, we also showed them complaints made over other social media channels, etc. Brands really lapped it up because this made their life so easy. We just kept quiet and it is working well, so there was no need to talk too much about it. We had big clients like HDFC, Dabur, Ola, Domino's and others.'

A Note on Market Positioning

Ankur, very early on, understood that complaints are tricky things to solve. It was akin to antagonizing the brands. It was the reason that competitors like Mouthshut could not grow.

'People only write when they are angry. If you are a public forum posting these complaints, brands don't like that. It's a tough business.

So we had to do a lot of things to prove to the brands that we have pure intent. We took some strategic calls which were very difficult to follow through, but we did. One was that every complaint filed on our website would be private. *Un dino saara game SEO ka hota tha.* We still decided not to make the complaints public because we felt that the moment we did that, brands would start hating us. Then you just become a forum of negativity, although it can help you in SEO.'

When they took this route, the attitude of the brands shifted.

'They could see that we are not blaming them but building a channel for brands to (a) increase customer retention and (b) get competitive data. For example, I can tell the brands how many issues do they get per 1,000 transactions. *Humne ek bada interesting graph banaya tha* where we would look at the subscriber base of Vodafone, Airtel, Aircel and other players, and benchmark the complaints to subscriber count. If the complaint per subscriber was way higher for one brand, then it was an important insight for them. Within that, we would give them a breakup of how many are 2G, how many are 3G and so on. So it was very important that when we are meeting brands, they should see that we are very different kind of company.'

Of course, it did not always work.

'My learning is that in corporate, "no" does not mean "no". It means "not now". A big company has 20 people you can talk to. If customer care people are not responding, which is obvious because no matter what we do, we are making them look bad. So we shifted our pitch to marketing people and talked about brand equity and sales. We said, *aap gaadi ya AC khareedte ho, to aap doston se poochte ho*. If they say that *iski service acchi nahi hai*, customer doesn't buy but you don't get to know that. To prove that they are losing sales, we built a complicated formula of loss over return of marketing investment or something like that. We showed the search results for "Voltas AC reviews" and how it will impact so many potential customers, which in turn means so many crores of lost sale. When that also did not work, we knew that CEO would still care. We created a mailer that went directly to the CEOs. It would say something like you have 800 complaints pending and here is the benchmarking data. We think that you can improve it. In most cases, that mail would get forwarded to someone and we would get a meeting. So the nutshell is we kept finding a way—*ye nahi to ye, ye nahi to wo* and so on. And we did solve it to a large degree, and that is the reason why we have sold OneDirect to so many brands.'

The Final Pivot

Even after doing 7,000 complaints a day, Akosha was making ₹12–13 lakh on the B2C side and ₹20 lakh on the B2B side. 'Our revenue was ₹30–35 lakh at that time. But however you play it, we didn't think the number would rise exponentially.'

Ankur's vision was clear: if he is building a VC funded business, there is no point in breaking even at ₹35 lakh.

'We could have gone cash positive by firing half the engineering team but the reason you have all those people is that you are building a product for the future. Why are you spending on marketing?—for future growth. So the whole idea of raising external money is to accelerate growth.'

Another complication was that by 2014, mobile had grown bigger.

'Most companies now have more transactions on mobile. And every time I thought of mobile, I felt that there is no way Akosha is going to be relevant on mobile. For the customer, we needed something happening frequently—not complaints which happen once or twice a year. We wanted to be more regular part of consumer life. So we thought, let's launch an app. Now think of this—Airtel gets two crore calls a month and only three to four lakh are proper complaints. The rest are queries like how can we change our plan, etc. or service requests. We said let's start moving up this funnel because that is the only way someone who has downloaded Akosha app will interact again and again with the app. Instead of connecting consumer only for complaints, we thought let's connect for everything. That is how we moved to Helpchat.'

When they pivoted away, they decided to still stick with OneDirect (B2B part) which was generating ₹80–82 lakh per month of SaaS revenue (as of 2017). B2C part became Helpchat in May 2015.

'The reason for renaming was that Akosha was a generic name, people used to mispronounce it as Ashoka, and so on. This time, we wanted a specific name. But the problem happened when our chat part did not really work out. Then we had to move to Tapzo which is a whole another story.'

Start-Up Hurdles

Motivation was never a problem for Ankur. Where he struggled was to rewire his mental model as a lawyer. 'It is so screwed up that your ability to think about the business or world is itself impaired. You don't have any sense of tech. The second challenge is that a lawyer is trained to think of what can go wrong.'

But Ankur persisted and learnt actively. For example, Ankur met Ankur Warikoo in a Startup Saturday and built a connection.

'He kind of took me under his wings. He taught me how to look at Google Analytics and the numbers. How do you actually derive an insight and so on. He also taught me how to use AdWords, how to scale, etc. Key was essentially that I knew what I didn't know and I was very open to asking other people for help. So Ankur, Sameer and Nandini, and Ajay Agarwal (who was also an investor in our company) were the people I used to go for advice on running a company, raising money, how to handle organizational development aspects.'

Be it Ankur's creative monetization approach or doggedness, one can see he has given it all. The Helpchat failure took its toll.

'The most stressful period was when Helpchat wasn't working. For three to four months, I could not even sleep properly and would wake up shaking in my sleep at three o'clock in the morning. It was just a terrible time because there were no easy answers. In retrospect also, I don't know.... It was like my understanding was so poor. Like a sixth-grade student trying to solve calculus. The good thing is once you come out of a bad period, your confidence level grows and your bullshit meter also becomes a lot better. While I don't wish it on anybody, every successful entrepreneur I have talked to has gone through something similar.

In 2015, we got carried away with the hype and ended up raising a lot of money. Right from the Dutch Tulip Mania of the 16th century to the latest real estate crisis in the USA, human beings have been like that. How much money you think you can use wisely is a function of which state of things you are in. I do think creativity needs constraint. Businesses are a lot about creativity, especially like ours. And we used to be more creative when we did not have more money. *Kya kar loge aap paise ka*, you cannot force Airtel *na* (to work with you). So we were forced to be creative.'

What Gets Ankur Going?

Ankur blogs regularly on his start-up journey and thoughts. 'I am a nerd. I don't chill too much. I just love to read and work. There is definitely a book inside me I think. But *shayad* 10–15 *saal baad*!'

Ankur (left) working out of his dad's office in Chandigarh in 2009

From his bookshelf, he recommends:

- *Hackers and Painters* by Paul Graham
- *Poor Charlie's Almanack* by Charles T. Munger
- *The Goal* by Eliyahu M. Goldratt
- *Against the Gods* by Peter Bernstein
- *Zero to One* by Peter Thiel

Key Takeaways

Person

- *Minimizing analysis paralysis:* Quickly chose to move back to India once ₹14 lakh was saved; moved to Delhi when hiring troubles grew.
- *Cultivating mentors:* Good at learning from someone else's experiences.

Product

- *Start with what you know:* By focusing on his legal understanding, Ankur picked up pain points that he could solve with his legal expertise.
- *Pivot based on validation:* By putting all the energy into consumer complaints when validated by Rediff traffic, Ankur could find the product market fit.
- *Understand your potential customers and design the product to serve their needs:* By keeping the complaints private, Akosha avoided alienating the brands and created a robust product in form of OneDirect.

Business Model

- *Clear monetization:* Monetized high-volume/low-margin complaints from brands and low-volume/high-margin complaints from consumers.
- *Pricing:* Figured out the right pricing for consumer complaints by trial and error.

Sales

- *Speaking customer's language:* Sending clear complaints reports and benchmarking data directly to CEOs broke the ice and compelled the brands to come on board when other efforts failed.

PART 4

Sales and Marketing

We explained to all companies that if one GRE test can work for millions of students, one test can work for all the companies.
—Varun Aggarwal (Aspiring Minds)

Business does not happen between companies, it happens between real people.
—Chakshu Kalra (GreyB)

I believe bad product and good marketing can work but good product and bad marketing will never work.
—Deepak Syal (GreyB)

Sales can make or break a business.
Sales can make or break a business.

No, it is not a misprint. I did write that twice because it can never be emphasized enough. If you do not find a way to sell, your start-up will die.

If you do not know how to sell, you must either learn it, just like Chakshu Kalra did at GreyB, or partner with/hire someone who knows it, just like Varun Aggarwal did by co-founding Aspiring Minds with his more business savvy brother Himanshu Aggarwal. Varun has cracked one of the toughest segments known for notoriously long sales cycles—education institutes.

Great sales and marketing lessons are hidden in the story of GreyB. Deepak Syal shows that to win the hearts of your customers, you first need to define the target audience and reach it. Chakshu has designed a whole new framework called friendship sales process that helped win clients such as Apple and Samsung. Together, they prove that you can learn even if you do not have a relevant background.

One common theme that emerges while discussing sales across founders in different sectors is that start-up sales process and the skill set required for it are very different from that in big companies. This brings up a major caveat: hiring a sales manager who sells well in a MNC might not work for you. Then what will work? Read ahead to find out.

If you want to build a ship
don't herd people together to collect wood
and don't assign them tasks and work,
but rather teach them to long for the
endless immensity of the sea.

—Antoine-Marie-Roger de Saint-Exupery

12   Varun Aggarwal: Aspiring Minds

A researcher from MIT takes up the challenge to solve the talent
and recruitment problem of India with a sophisticated adaptive
test. His gumption, originality and humility stand out in a market
where most of the start-ups are copy–pasted from the West.

Hi-tech Adaptive Test for Recruitment
#sales #hiring #product #analytics

Aspiring Minds was founded in 2008 by brothers Varun Aggarwal
and Himanshu Aggarwal with their savings of ₹20–30 lakh. Its
hallmark test known as AMCAT is a GRE/GMAT-ish assessment
test that job seekers can take to benchmark their employability
aptitude. The test being adaptive and computer-based in nature
(level of next question is determined by the correctness of test
taker's response to previous question) was difficult to administer in
the Indian colleges for the lack of proper infrastructure. Improving
its product to work under such conditions, the company created
higher barriers to entry with its execution agility and sophistication
of assessments and machine learning algorithms.

Their emphasis on sales from day one helped them validate the
product with 800 paid test takers within six months. Successfully
battling the 2008 recession with innovative thinking, Aspiring Minds

today claims to be helping over two million candidates find the 'right' jobs every year and is associated with 3,500+ corporations.

The MIT brain behind Aspiring Minds is Varun Aggarwal who wrote the first algorithm for the AMCAT test. A socially driven engineer, Varun admits that technology alone cannot solve the problem; one has to figure out the business and sales model as well. With the product doing well in China, Philippines and other territories now, it seems that the brothers have a shot at creating a solution for one of the nastiest problems for any developing economy—education and employment.

A Socially Driven Scientist

Varun thinks not getting into IIT turned out to be a blessing in disguise because he became more committed to prove himself through his technical work. At NSIT, he worked on everything from genetic algorithms to creating his own *pedometer*.

Apart from academics, he found himself devoted to fighting the rampant practice of ragging.

'Even though I didn't face it, I would admit I was scared of it—by *what if*. What if they take me to hostel and do this and that. I generally have a social bent of mind and I believe that there should be perfect justice. So I founded CURE (Coalition to Uproot Ragging in Education) to help students report ragging incidents.

The biggest achievement was we created a narrative around ragging. In 2007–2008, we published pamphlets about number of sexual ragging cases and number of ragging cases where someone was beaten up. We logged the number of deaths and created the narrative that these are not some fun activities that you see on the campuses; these are way more serious. For the next 5–10 years, the statistics continuously got published in different newspapers. It was brought up in the Parliament in the question hour on ragging statistics. It kind of changed the whole view on how people looked at it.'

A year of working full time at ST Microelectronics made him realize that there is limited learning on the job. He applied to the top four graduate schools and was accepted by MIT. 'I thought it was a statistical error by MIT,' he chuckles.

The MIT Edge

At MIT, Varun found himself enjoying the company of nerds discussing not only science and technology but social issues. He founded the MIT-India reading group where he 'methodically studied socio-economic situations in India and read *a research* by McKinsey that only 25 per cent engineers are employable in India'. This would form the basis for his interest in Aspiring Minds later on.

'What MIT really teaches you is learning how to learn. At the same time, there is a lot of humility in the institution. There are so many achievers that you cannot *not* be humbled. The person in front of you may have a Nobel Prize! The way I took courses at MIT was very funny. In the first semester I took one course in machine learning and one in analog design. In the next semester I took a course in bioinformatics. The next semester I went to my academic advisor and I said I am doing linear optimization. He said, "You are crazy. These don't fit together. The good thing is you are getting all A's that means you can learn it and that's a good skill to have". The next semester I took a course on history and politics in South Asia [he laughs]. What it did was expand my horizon. I got to understand how people think in so many different fields.'

MIT was bustling with entrepreneurs—there were clubs, venture mentoring system, ideas competitions, 100K competition and so on. Soon, Varun had an offer from an analog design start-up which was using algorithms to do analog circuit design but he felt that it's not going to become very big because the technology was not really aligned to what the market was looking for. Instead, he decided to pursue his idea of Aspiring Minds.

Bootstrapping Aspiring Minds

'At a conference, I met Professor Tarun Khanna from Harvard Business School. He was one of the first people with whom I discussed my idea. He became a mentor and encouraged me to do a pilot. So I came back from the USA with a return ticket. There was mutual understanding between me and my MIT advisor that I would be trying my idea in India, and then I would go back for a semester to finish my thesis. But the way things turned out, I couldn't go back at all.'

Meanwhile, Varun's brother Himanshu (a computer engineer from IIT Delhi) had returned from the USA and was also looking for something entrepreneurial. 'I am a more technical/research-oriented person and Himanshu is a more business kind of person with a great software and product understanding too. We were a good combination.'

Varun looked deeper into the employability issues he had studied about India.

'One problem was that the companies struggle to find quality candidates, and the students don't know which skills are needed in the industry. For example, you might be sitting in a small college in Allahabad and you have no idea what is needed to be a sales guy or a software developer or an analyst. This was the first problem. Problem number two was that if you have those skills, how do you tell it to the recruiter that you have these skills. There are 50 lakh people who are graduating from India every year and industries have to filter from these. An easy way for industries is to just focus on the top 200 colleges. But what about the students beyond those 200 colleges? How do they showcase their skills?'

At MIT, Varun had already looked into the science of adaptive testing. He had read how tests like GRE and GMAT are designed. This made it easier for him to decide what tool to build.

'It was machine learning, which was something I knew. It is a statistical model building. So I thought that we would build a GRE or a SAT for jobs—a common standardized test which is technology driven, which can adapt to people and then highlight them to the companies per se. I can't think of a time when I was not thinking of a test. The irony is that I never do well in tests myself especially if it is a timed test.'

Next step was to decide which tests to administer. They chose to focus on English, logical ability and quantitative ability that are important in a wide variety of jobs. 'In addition, there would be specialized computer programming tests for programmers, sales test for sales jobs etc.'

They decided to charge (a) the test takers for joining their job portal and finding jobs, and (b) the employers who want to recruit using their tests. 'All these questions around figuring the right model or pricing was a mix of trial and error and intuition.'

The brothers put in their savings of ₹20–30 lakh at the onset to bootstrap. It helped in building the first version, taking it to the market and reaching the first 800 students. They worked for the first six months from their home. 'In fact, some of the people who took AMCAT later on came to my house. We had made it a testing centre as well. It was just a room and a veranda.'

Varun spent the next few weeks writing the algorithm for the first adaptive test. He hired one person in software from NSIT and one in content who also handled sales.

'The NSIT guy was a capable guy who had missed the campus season and he was looking for a development job. One was my cousin who also needed a job. Himanshu was handling the web product side because he had worked at Sapient and in the Network Appliances.'

Laser Focus on Sales

Many start-ups die waiting for the clients. That was not the case with Aspiring Minds.

While Varun was building the back-end algorithm, Himanshu and the other software engineer was finishing the front-end part.

'Then, we spent a lot of time in the sales because we had to get the pilot out and we needed at least 1,000 people to take the test. I was, at least for two to three days every week, visiting colleges and giving presentations to the students. We needed the pilot to prove the demand so that we can use the data for companies. From day one almost, we started visiting campuses in Ghaziabad, Greater Noida, Faridabad and all. We were meeting the people in placement cells and career offices. First we used to call them and take an appointment, but then I realized that it's better to just walk in. They met only if they were there already and appointments did not really help.

So we slowly started just showing up with a brochure and talked to these guys. We told them, first, we will give feedbacks to students on what they are lacking in. Second, there are seven to eight companies who are working with us and they might hire your students if they score well. These were family and friends companies who had given a letter in writing that said that they will look at the students who take AMCAT tests. Our point was to just get a meeting slot with the students. We used to give a 30-minute presentation on the product, what problem are we trying to solve and which companies are working with us, etc. At the end, we told them that they can take our tests by paying ₹200. So we were collecting leads and conducting the tests in the college.'

These were primarily for IT jobs. For such a small price point, the students did not expect much. So they were pleasantly surprised when Aspiring Minds gave them written reports within a week. The reports were not just scores but also feedback on what areas a student needs to improve upon. 'For the first batch of students, I remember handwriting the reports because our tool was not ready. After the first 100, we developed the capability to print the reports automatically.'

Product Iteration and Market Fit

The first time Varun went to an institute and plugged his laptop, his laptop died due to the viruses. 'It just refused to reboot!' Varun laughs.

'So we added features like if a computer shuts down in middle of the test due to a power cut or whatever, it can be resumed from the same point when power comes back. We had features to deal with virus issues. We made our application so that it can run on very basic configurations. We had to work on our design to handle the poor infrastructural facilities of these colleges. And all these became our value proposition. Corporations who had tried to do this before us were never able to manage it.'

These key features also became huge barriers to entry for any competition. The biggest one was the adaptive nature of the tests.

'In 10 years of our business, there has been no other vendor who does what we do in India. The reason is that it is not simple to design these. You need experience both on machine learning and understanding of education psychology plus a statistics background. There are probably not more than five companies in the world who can do this.'

Varun talks about another product aspect that he thinks was ahead of its time.

'In 2008, there was this company who hired people through us, and after six months, they told us which candidates were successful in their training and which were not based on their internal training results. What we did was that we built a predictive model based on our scores to predict what scores on our tests determine the success ability of the candidates for this company. So we gave them a better criteria and cut-off for next time which will ensure a higher training success. This was the whole feedback loop saying that can you predict the success of a person on the job based on their performance in our tests. This can help make their recruitment criteria more and more sharp. Now we do 30–40 such studies every year and these are called criterion validation studies. These show that our scores can be a predictor of the job performance.'

Varun had returned to India in June. They conducted their first test in August. By December, they had tested the first 800 people. They started speaking to companies and getting them to look at resumes and make some offers. By January, they started working on version

2.0 of the product which was the real adaptive version. Things were looking up, and the founders thought it would be easy to convince more companies to use their platform. But it was 2008 now. Recession had hit the market. No one was hiring!

'Till the end of 2009, whenever we used to go to TCS, Infosys, Wipro, HCL, we were not getting any business. If you go to students, they said, "No one is hiring. Even if we take your test, we are not going to get a job". We were stuck.'

Turning the Tide

In the wake of slow hiring, they started giving away the test for free to the students. This way, they gathered data for 20,000–30,000 candidates.

Additionally, the founders started looking for product diversification. They found an opportunity to work with microfinance companies which were still hiring and not caught up in the recession. They went beyond programming tests and built a personality test that more companies could use.

The efforts paid off, and by the end of 2009, suddenly they received so much business that they had to double their team in two months. 'Thirty people went to 60 people in two months and it was crazy. But before that, it was very challenging time when we were getting no business and thinking how will I ever pay my employees and so on.'

When asked about what kind of companies turned them down during recession, Varun refrains from quoting the names but mentions that they tried the top 10 IT services companies.

'The one company that gave us business was Mphasis. We also did a test validation exercise with them. We were very clear that we will offer free trials if someone wants to try it seriously. But the IT industry was completely in a slump. There were no budget approvals that time, so they did not even want to bother signing up anything.'

Here, Varun points out another problem with the employer mindset.

'Once you start using computer tests which are objective and transparent, the power of recruiters goes away. You need to give the candidate an interview if he crosses the cut-off. There were companies who did not want this because they could not manipulate the process any longer.'

Zooming into the B2B sales process, one wonders what it finally took to get the bigger Indian employers on board. Particularly, do the cold emails work?

Varun nods in understanding.

'That's a very good question. We saw that MIT and IIT names used to sell. So we would say that hey, we are alum from MIT and IIT. We have built this cutting edge product and would like to show it to you. It is fascinating how well emails work. People don't realize it. In our experience, if you send an email to a top level person and if you have a credible story, you will get a response. The rate was one in three or one in four usually. Remember to send a reminder. More responses come on the reminder. You will not get business on the emails, but they help get your foot in. Of course, if you prove yourself to be an idiot in the meeting, you will be thrown out! [he chuckles]. Frankly, I got a meeting with the Gates Foundation just through a cold email. Any of my initial meetings came from cold emails. You just need to be persistent.'

He adds a caution though,

'Corporate cycles are very long. A large company might take three to six months to sign up. Small companies typically converted within a month. We did not know it would take so long and it would be so hard. I often tell people that it was my naivety that I got into this business. As tough as it is, it is also a blessing.'

Aspiring Minds has retained more than 95 per cent of their customers.

Fundraising

Starting around March–April 2008, the founders felt the pressure of raising money soon. They were spending on salaries and rent because they had shifted to an office in Gurgaon. But fundraising at the time of recession was a nightmare. Varun recalls the hustle.

'We were trying to raise ₹2 crore and angel funding used to be ₹70–80 lakh in those days. Only a few angel networks were there, and models involving multiple angels in a round were not figured out. We eventually found one investor after negotiating for three months, but he developed cold feet in the last moment. One of our advisors then made an introduction to a PE (private equity) fund. But he said that their ticket size is probably different and we did not have much hopes on the fund. They wanted us to come to Mumbai but we said that let's first do a call. On the call he said, "We don't give money while talking on phone". So I clarified that we are not expecting that but just need some more information. So my co-founder then went and that deal actually happened. So the funny thing is sometimes least expected things work out well.'

Aspiring Minds ended up raising US$500,000 at that time from the Ajit Khimji group. How does one come up with a right number to raise?

'We built a business model and came up with metrics that are typically needed for a Series A investor. We figured a number that would help us stay afloat for two years. There is no right number but I think you should raise as little as you need, but you should always put in efforts to raise enough. Whatever you expect to take two years will probably take three years in business, and actual cost would be 1.2–1.5 times of whatever you estimate. So do account for all these possibilities in your model. Also, raising a lot at higher valuation may give you trouble in raising the next round.'

Varun gathered some high-profile advisors early on. Arrangement with advisors can be a tricky topic for entrepreneurs since there are no standard guidelines. Varun shares his experience and wisdom.

'See, we had Professor Tarun Khanna who was a mentor and became quite involved; he even became an investor. Other one is my advisor at MIT. She is an expert on machine learning. I cannot disclose the exact arrangement. Our initial arrangement with advisors was that these were the people who were genuinely interested in what we were building and a financial arrangement only evolved later on. That is not the primary motivation for them I am sure. I think it can be a good strategy to have some minimal financial arrangement, but sometimes people get hoodwinked by some unreasonable advisors especially where there is no clear value that they are bringing to the table. Entrepreneurs should not get advisors for their contacts or market reputation but for the value of their advice. Also, I may be wary of any advisor who asks for financial incentives in the first conversation itself. Generally, the rates for an early stage company would be less than 1 per cent. Something like 0.1–0.5 per cent is good. I know people who have given 2–5 per cent to advisors and it makes no sense. A lot of our advisors had no financial incentive for a long time.'

Varun recommends raising money after creating a proof of concept. He advocates the benefits that can come with the funding.

'If you have a good investor, there is governance and business advice. More avenues open up with the connections of the investor. Even hiring opens up because it gives more credibility to the company. So I wouldn't look at funding just for the money. I am not a great fan of bootstrapping and remaining small. I just feel that signals a lack of ambition. I feel better about raising the bar, competing with the best in the world. Funding is a good route if you wish to do this. Yes, as much as you can delay the funding, you can get a better valuation.'

Hiring Advice

'For a start-up, hiring the wrong people can be fatal. You are hiring very few people, so you need to make fewer errors. Type 1 error is when you hire a bad person. Type 2 is when you lose a good person. You can live with Type 2 errors but Type 1 is serious. You have to spend time on hiring, find good people and be objective. I see that the people who have succeeded in Aspiring Minds are the ones who were really motivated by our vision.'

He shares a nugget of hiring advice that has stayed with him.

'Someone told me to hire for the slope and not the constant. He was referring to the equation of the line $y = mx + c$. m is the slope and c is the constant. What he means is that m is the ability and c is the experience. Don't hire for experience. You might hire a sales guy with five years of experience, but if he doesn't understand the product or you well, then it won't matter. For a big company, sales might be commoditized, but it works very differently for a start-up.'

Varun has made his own mistakes and learnt from those.

'Our first sales guy could sell the product where the market was already formed, but he did not get new markets where you have to intelligently answer the questions of the customer. See, many a times, you are selling the product by virtue of selling yourself. The product is anyway invisible and the customer will buy it if he thinks he can trust you. So when you are selling a new concept, you need a different breed of people.'

Varun built a mechanism to figure what kind of people will tick. He stopped looking for education sector people.

'We defined our own competencies, and if someone passes that, we believe that people can learn new domains very quickly. Another thing I did was when hiring mid- to senior-level folks, I give them a chance to ask me questions about the business in the end. And you can get a lot of insights from what they ask. If you know how to sell, you will ask very pertinent questions about that product—what kind of revenues are there, what are the challenges in pricing, etc. If a person has no questions to ask, then he is a clear reject for me. Frankly, a lot of sales guys don't get it. They are just overtly confident and they think that *kuch bhi bech denge*, and I think that does not work. They need to think analytically about the product and they need to understand the commercial challenges.'

Scaling Globally

The next markets they entered into were China and Philippines.

While many start-ups ramp up investments very quickly and put three to four sales guys in new territories, Varun admonishes that may cause the sales teams to bleed very fast in developed economies.

'You realize it only when you have spent a fortune and got zero results. So you should do trials and adapt the product for the market before scaling the sales too much. That is what we did. The China market is obviously tough because of the language issues. We had to do our products in Mandarin there. Our country head there is a native Chinese because business happens there in Mandarin. You need a local Chinese team and you need proper coordination between the Chinese and Indian teams. Other than that, the underlying product is the same. We just translated the tests to Mandarin. Microsoft is using some of our tests in there.'

They are also looking to partner with job portals.

'For example, we are working with biggest job portal in Bangladesh. We have also realized that both our enterprise partners and students want us to provide additional resources for them to use AMCAT in a better way. So we are looking to create those additional ancillary products and services in the whole career/recruitment space.'

A Note on Academicians

At his heart, Varun is an academic, but one cannot help notice how far he has come as a businessman. The journey has not been easy.

'It started as a nightmare,' he chuckles.

'Academics are very different; they call a spade a spade. They have no clue about scaling the sales! They would talk about all the philosophy but the thing is you need to go and sell. Sales training and acumen is so needed and

215214

 so underrated. I learnt all that on the job and it was painful. Sales is very different than presenting an academic paper. You need to handle the objections raised by the customer; you need to be able to talk to different people in their language. There is a different language when you are talking to HR, different when you talk to CEO, different when you are hiring and so on. At the same time, you need to meet the expectations when you deliver the product. You need to handle multiple stakeholders, etc. The good news is now I can do both.'

Another problem he points out is that people coming from academic backgrounds think that they understand business when they don't. 'And this makes them closed to advice. You are in a good position if you know that you don't understand the business and are open to learning it. The problem is, when you think you don't need to learn anything, you will never grow.'

As a parting advice to Indian entrepreneurs, Varun recommends looking at the overseas market rather than India.

'There are many companies set up in India who are selling successfully abroad. The market in India is constrained for technology-intensive products and there are not enough buyers. It is good to expand overseas earlier than later because sales team has to adapt for those markets and you want to build the structure accordingly.'

The Social Cause and Impact

What ultimately is driving Varun to overcome all the hurdles is his social bent of mind. He explains in-depth how he thinks he is solving the problem in India.

'I know that going to a village and training 100 people might look more impactful than what Aspiring Minds is doing. Our market is dysfunctional, where people are not getting jobs based on what they know but by the virtue of the colleges they went to. To break in and say that we will get people jobs based on their skills makes more impact in my opinion. Let me argue how—if people are getting trained but not the benefit of training, then (a) that training is useless and (b) the whole ecosystem collapses because when there is no benefit, people stop doing the training. I remember visiting colleges where not a single person is getting the job. It cannot be true that none of these people have the requisite skills. And what happens is that when the brightest student is not getting the job, others have no incentive to study. So the problem trickles down. The same problem is with MOOCs you know. There is no point of doing a course if you cannot get a job based on that.'

Varun pauses and cites multiple studies which talk about market inefficiency and that we need a testing mechanism.

'We are trying to bring some governance and discipline around this training and employment ecosystem. My assertion is that if you can get this matching right, you will make both your trainings efficient and employment efficient. Whenever we talk of our Indian economy, people say that create more jobs and get more people in job-oriented courses. But unless you get the matching done, it won't solve the problem. My argument on why people don't talk about matching is that it is a harder problem to solve. It is easier for the government to say that we will put 100 million in training or job creation, but matching needs to happen first in my opinion.'

Himanshu and Varun Aggarwal (left to right)

The passion is palpable. So are the results reported by Aspiring Minds. As per their reports, the number of tier-2 and tier-3 college students who get offers via AMCAT are much higher than what they get in open job market (79 per cent vs 58 per cent). Twenty-two per cent of the students who were hired via AMCAT had a GPA lower than what hiring company preferred in open market. The number of students who have changed their study schedule based on their AMCAT scores is 70+ per cent.

Key Takeaways

Person

- *Knowing his own shortcomings:* His awareness that he doesn't understand business or sales made Varun ready to learning those quickly.
- *Intellectual curiosity and driven by social causes:* Leans towards solving the problems that very few people care to.
- *MIT network and connections:* Getting easy accessibility to advisors and mentors, and credibility when approaching the corporate customers.

Product

- *Solving harder-to-solve problems:* Combining science of adaptive testing with his study of education psychology positioned Varun uniquely to address very tough problems in a way that is not easy to replicate, thereby creating high barriers to entry.
- *Timely validation:* First 800 paid test takers provided validation as well as data for creating real adaptive tests in version 2.0.
- *Focus on usability and Indian market realities:* Building features around network security, working without the Internet, etc., for adapting to colleges' infrastructure helped in faster and wider adoption. It also provided a competitive edge.

- *Using the AMCAT test for internal hiring:* Helped generate feedback and improve the product based on the company's own experience.

Sales

- *Selling from day one:* Combatting the bad infrastructure, lack of professionalism and sloth attitude of Indian college staff, the founders tirelessly visited campuses, learnt their language and succeeded in getting meetings with the students.
- *Breaking the chicken and egg problem of a marketplace model:* By administering tests for free when recession hit helped in solving one side of the hiring marketplace.
- *Product diversification:* Building specialized tests for a few companies that were hiring during recession kept the company afloat in a tough market.
- *Making cold emails work:* Founders succeeded in getting top level meetings through cold emails.
- *Thoughtful expansion overseas:* Doing trials and adapting the product for the market before scaling the salesforce and spending too much helped in successfully increasing their global presence.

People

- *Basis for hiring:* Figured that learning ability matters more than experience in case of start-ups. Employees who already felt motivated by what Aspiring Minds was doing fared better.
- *Sales hiring:* Varun fine-tuned his interviewing process to allow a sales candidate to ask questions at the end. The nature of questions he asked about product and market became a good indicator of his potential to sell.

Always deliver more than expected.

—Larry Page

13 Deepak Syal and Chakshu Kalra: GreyB

How did three small-town engineers learn sales, marketing and hiring to build one of the fastest growing services start-ups in India?

Patent Research Consulting and Service
#sales #marketing #hiring #bootstrapped #intellectual_property

Deepak Syal, Chakshu Kalra and Avneet Bansal started GreyB in 2007 to improve the quality of patent services work in India. When his previous employer Evalueserve was reluctant to integrate the improvements he was suggesting in patent analytics, Deepak quit to build his own IP services company and started with charging ₹5,000 for a project. Little did he know that starting a company was the easiest part of the journey. Frustrated with failure to scale beyond initial clients, Chakshu took over the sales and developed a framework which he calls 'friendship sales process' that helped them charge US$75,000 a project and reach US$1 million in revenue in three years with a profitability of 50 per cent.

Many *aha!* moments were to present themselves as the founders built the team—employee by employee—after getting horrible reviews on Glassdoor. Very often comic but nonetheless insightful, Deepak's recounting strikes at the root of any founder's biggest dilemmas. A services company needs a well-oiled machinery to grow, and the founders did not relent until they figured out the lessons in marketing and hiring—lessons that had been put into theory so often by others but are hard to understand until you live them out. Scaling from 20 to 200 clients (including the likes of Apple and Samsung) and adding another million in revenues by 2016, GreyB has grown without any external funding.

GreyB is the only pure services company featured in this book. Deepak shares how the challenges and lessons differ from those of the product start-ups.

'In a services company, the revenue is directly proportional to the number of employees as your revenue is directly linked with the number of billable hours. For us, it was easier to grow to 10–15 employees, but growth stagnated after that. If I look back now, I believe it's because the skills that are required for you to get started are very different from the skills that are required to scale the business. Getting from 1 to 10 clients was pretty easy. We had worked in similar domain with bigger companies before. So getting initial projects was not a big problem. And we thought the same strategies will also help us grow bigger, but we were so wrong.'

Developing the Domain Expertise

Deepak spent his initial years in the R&D team of Quark in Chandigarh. It is a product-based company that develops software for the publication houses to design newspaper and magazines. The R&D team would spend weeks to make sure every pixel in the letter 'S' is displayed correctly on the screen and in print. 'After a couple of months, I realized that this is not what I like. I like working on new technologies, something that is futuristic. So after a year, I ended up switching to Evalueserve in Gurgaon.' This is also where he met his future business partner, Chakshu.

Evalueserve is a services company, and Deepak worked in its patent research and analytics section.

'In the initial training period, I was made to study 10 different inventions in my first week itself—it was crazy but I loved it! These projects were generally one to four weeks long. Today you are working on gaming, next week on satellite communication, third week on driverless automobiles and the fourth week I was working on what material inside a chewable gum can help in improving teeth strength for pets!'

Deepak was thinking of a lot of new ideas on how the patent work could be improved. 'I was thinking of using fractals in analysis or an intelligent dashboard to help a patent analyst find better insights in a landscape analysis.' He offered to try out these ideas for his company but his suggestions were falling on deaf ears.

'That is when I thought that if they don't want to do it, maybe I should do it. Back in the days (2006–2007), Orkut was very popular. I saw a post from Avneet on one of the forums in which he talked about starting a business. I reached out to him and started discussing a few ideas in the patent industry. He liked those, and we started building a website where I started putting interesting information about patents but quickly realized that people in the patent industry were not very Internet savvy. So we both kept experimenting different things. Then one day I discussed this with Chakshu who was working at a start-up in Noida, and since he was also enthusiastic to moonlight and work on new ideas after office hours, we three started to talk about starting a business together.'

The initial idea was to build a patent research company that provides high-quality output by using the benefits that are possible through technology. So they resigned and incorporated a company called Echo Mirror.

'Chakshu told us that he will try contacting some people he knows from his alum network and see if we can source some work. He also tried to contact some attorneys in the USA but that did not work. However, we started getting work from one lawyer he knew in Chandigarh.'

These projects were for ₹4,000 or ₹5,000 but the team delivered high-quality work. They used to work 18 hours a day and were sustaining in ₹20,000 per month. 'At that point of time, *zyada paiso ki zarurat nahi thi. Hum khush the* because we were doing good work,' Deepak reminisces with a smile.

Initial Hiring Nightmares

Their first employee left in a couple of months to join Airtel. Deepak hired his next employee from his alma mater, SGSITS in Indore.

'I floated a nice email in our college group and somehow got one candidate from the electronics department. However, when he came in and saw that we were working from a house, he was shocked. I told him, "Don't worry. We are doing very interesting work and it is going to be all good as you start working" and all of that stuff to boost his morale. But the next morning, he came and said, "I don't want to continue. I want to go to IBM, because I had an offer from IBM". He just went away without resigning *ki koi farak hi nahi padta resign karne se.* One thing I figured out is that you should not hire from the colleges where students don't have the start-up exposure.

At one point of time, we went to Big Bazaar and stacked our fridge with a lot of juice packages, chocolates and snacks. I had this idea from my Quark days, *ki vahan ye sab cheeze free milti thi.* So maybe that's what is required. *Uske baad pata chala logo ne paani peena hi band kar diya, they are drinking only juice....* We also kept a trained chef for cooking lunch but nothing worked.'

Then they faced the severe electricity crisis of Gurgaon when power cuts were so long that even the inverters died. Deepak adds sardonically, 'If it rained, Gurgaon roads turned into a river. So we decided to shift to Chandigarh.'

There is a special provision in the engineering colleges of Punjab where they have six months of mandatory industrial training in their last semester. Deepak grabbed the opportunity to select five to six interns who were now committed to work with them for six months. At that time getting six additional computers was a huge investment and the team did not even have that much money.

'So we had to request them to bring their own laptops. I was clear with them that they would get the best learning in these six months and they can take their computer back after they complete their training. I was sure *ki agle din koi vapis nahi aayega*. However, we had no other option. A lot of people did not return the next day. To be honest, I will not advise someone else to do these things. Those were the moments when the desire for success was driving me to think out of the box and sometimes even cross the line.'

But it worked! And that turned the corner for them. Two to three interns stayed and continued their training.

'I spent a lot of time with these guys to teach them the minute aspect of patent research. Since we genuinely wanted them to join us full time, I was personally involved in their training to ensure that they learn fast and get the best in return. After that day, I developed an immense respect for people who have done training with us. Shikhar who leads our whole patent research team right now is from the same training batch. He has seen everything. I have noticed that some of the best people at GreyB came out of this six-month apprentice programme. In these six months, we groom them very well and by the time they join full time, they are already trained in the type of work we want them to do. We never faced a shortage because we always had people who were ready to join us.'

The Birth of GreyB: From ₹5,000 to US$5,000

The founders felt that the real business opportunity lies in working directly with global clients. To start afresh, they incorporated GreyB in 2007. They sent automated emails to attorneys in the USA.

'I remember MS Word *mein ek feature hota tha*—mail merge. We used to press a button and send emails. Out of the blue, we got one project this way.

Slowly some clients started calling us directly, "I have two projects. But I can only give you US$5,000 for one". That is when we started growing.'

The next three to four years constituted a rapid growth phase where the company grew 100 per cent year over year to 50 employees. They learnt the finer tricks of selling to the global audience.

'Now, we had also started travelling to the USA to attend different conferences, meeting new people. I specifically remember when we were debating whether *hume Blackberry lena chahiye ya nahi* because that would cost us extra ₹500 per month. But then Chakshu insisted that we have to be quick in replying. *Agar email raat ke 3 baje aayega toh* you are not going to open the laptop but you can do it from the Blackberry itself. If you send me an email and I reply quickly, you will not feel that I am in another country. We made it a point to be quick in our replies to the clients.'

The next dilemma they faced was where to position themselves in the market.

'If we go to the low-end consumers, there can be a lot of projects but it will consume all our energy for little profit. If we work with a client who is giving us US$5,000 a month in one go, we can peacefully work and give him what he wants. At one point, we decided that we would do only high-cost and high-quality work. When Samsung faces a lawsuit, they have to either pay US$500 million to Apple or the fee to us to save themselves from that lawsuit. We realized these are the people who actually can understand the worth of our work. It is funny how we had read "product market fit" and all these jargons but we had no idea what it meant until we reached this stage. So we stopped working on the low-cost projects and only focused on those who needed high-quality work.'

Deepak shares an example to clarify the difference between high-cost and low-cost work in services.

'I am not talking about beefing up the prices (so you become costly). The high-cost work I am referring to means the high-value delivered to the client. This is a zone where you become agnostic to standard business metrics like hours spent, resource utilization, etc. Let's say someone already owns a patent. He wants to find out if other companies are illegally using this patent. So he hires someone like us to find that out. Companies in our domain would invest 40 hours of research and in 40 hours they will give you whatever they can find. On the other hand, our aim is to find the result whether it takes us 40 hours or more. We had to spend longer in the start, but gradually we became smarter, faster and better. Phase 1: we started finding results at 60–70 hour mark. Phase 2: we started hitting results at the 50-hour mark and then, the phase we love, Phase 3, when we automatically started finding results at the 40-hour mark—Bingo! With this attitude, we could attract companies like Apple who will hire us for the premium work. The root of all high-value work is culture, mindset, etc.'

As they grew, the three founders took up different responsibilities. Avneet started looking after finance and banking. Chakshu handled sales. HR, marketing and operations fell under Deepak's portfolio.

Marketing and Branding

Deepak started his marketing efforts from content marketing. But when freelance content writers produced dismal quality work, Deepak started thinking of ways to use his in-house talent.

'I read somewhere that one should never outsource content marketing. What they mean is that another person can never convey the context as well as you can. We had to write for a US audience and our domain was something that only few experts can write about. What struck me was that our people had great knowledge on what we were doing. But the problem was how do we get engineers to write something and that too in middle of the work day. In our office, we have a culture of doing 10-minute activities every day. It can be a puzzle, an art to make on paintbrush, an interesting treasure hunt on Google, etc.'

Deepak decided to create a new experiment. He divided the employees in three teams and asked them to search for the word 'patent' on Quora and answer questions to the best of their knowledge in the first five minutes. After five minutes, they had to read all other answers written by their colleagues and upvote the ones they liked.

'Imagine 100 people writing about patents on Quora and then getting votes on them. And people wanted to win, so they were writing great answers so that they can get maximum votes. So answers started getting boosted as well. Slowly, when people were searching for patent related word on Google, these answers started coming on the first page.'

But ranking on Google did not take them any further since people were not trying to find patent services on a search engine.

'I had also read somewhere that one should concentrate on one channel only. So we started with Twitter—we followed everyone related to patents and increased our following. At some point, we were not able to get more than 1,000 followers no matter what we did. But that I think is a B2B problem. It is again related to your target audience behaviour. What we had to think is *hamari target audience hang out kahan karti hai? Agar Twitter pe bhi nahi hai, Google pe bhi nahi search kar rahe, to hain kahan?* We saw that every client of ours had a profile on LinkedIn and it seemed they were very active also. So we tried next on LinkedIn and that worked! This was the time I really understood the meaning of "You should be where your target audience hangs out".'

As soon as they started posting on LinkedIn, people started liking and commenting. On their sales calls, people said, 'I have already heard about GreyB.' Deepak remembers how the type of questions completely changed on the sales calls.

'Earlier, people would ask us that there are other companies cheaper than you and why should I pay an Indian company such a high price. We started doubting our service/product and our pricing. After our consistent branding efforts started taking shape, we found that on the first call itself, people were already half convinced that we will be able to solve their problem. The objective of these calls that were earlier focused on sharing why we are better, why you should work with us, etc. suddenly changed just into relationship calls. Now our name started coming up, we were getting awards like "Best Entrepreneur in Singapore", "IAM Top 300 IP Strategist of the World", etc. Once you become known, more people start writing about you and so on.'

Deepak makes an interesting comment on the psychology of consumers.

'What I have learnt (and it took us a long time to get it) is that a buyer already knows what he is going to buy. The decision is made long before the transaction actually happens. You already know that you want an iPhone and then you just justify your buying decision with the specs or design. That is the power of a brand.'

Scaling the Team and Retaining Talent

GreyB's Glassdoor reviews could not have started more miserably. Deepak recounts how people posted the picture of a sleeping dog outside the office and said that this is what the company is about. It is a tough business to keep employees happy.

'I would not lie, our retention rate is very low in the first two years. Some people leave for higher studies or higher salaries, but once a guy crosses the two-year mark, he understands the vision and works with us for longer period.'

It took some time for Deepak to understand what culture meant.

'At other places, employees would work for a specific number of hours, and create a report at the end and send that. At our place, we worked for the results. It could mean working nights at times. And looking back, we had done that since our earliest days in Gurgaon. So that was our culture—that we will not send the report until we have something useful for the client. I realized that it was our culture that was enabling people to deliver that way. This is how we trained people since the moment they joined. When these people go to a company with a different culture, which is not pushing them, the output is different. And of course, there will be few who would come and complain that we were not told that we had to work so much. They would badmouth you also, but I figured out later it is simply that they do not fit the culture. They slowly leave on their own.'

Accepting that only a certain kind of people would work well for them, Deepak refined his hiring process accordingly.

'When I am interviewing a fresh grad for my team, checking his tech skill is a lower priority in comparison to checking if he has the right mindset for us. Our work is primarily text mining. It is an open-ended skill. For example, for invalidating a patent on iPod, you have to find a music player like iPod which came before 2001. When you are working on such projects, it needs a certain mindset. I have worked with people who did countless mistakes even after one month of training, and I know people who learnt everything on their own in one week and produced amazing output. It has nothing to do with marks.'

Gradually, he also improved on retaining people. He shares few key strategies that he uses.

'I often ask our employees, "I don't want to remain the head of this company always. I want somebody else to take it over. Do you think you can do that?" Most of the times, the answer is YES! Then, I tell him, "If it is yes, you have to do a lot of things that are not asked for and every decision of yours should be as if you own this company". I believe in motivating everyone to grow. Also, when you see people working sincerely for your company, you should reward them. We don't believe in promoting everyone after one year only. If someone is growing faster, we promote him more quickly.'

From Services to Product

One wonders how to innovate in the services space. In case of GreyB, Deepak has been exploring artificial intelligence and a machine-learning-based product that can help them in patent research.

'We built it in collaboration with our existing clients and called it Neo. During testing, I noticed a few interesting suggestions from it, and these were the suggestions that an analyst cannot think on its own. That is when I felt that it will work. But what is more amazing is that it has become a great differentiator for us in front of the clients. Six to seven months back, we created a video on what Neo can do and shared it with patent community for marketing.'

The initial response has been promising.

'People wanted to license and pay money for it. I believe a bad product and good marketing can work, but a good product and bad marketing never yields results. I mean people have not even seen Neo and they wanted to pay such prices for it. That is what marketing is. So basically, what I have learnt is that business is marketing plus innovation. If you can keep doing something or the other in these two areas, you will continue growing.'

Friendly Human Sales Model

At one point, GreyB was finding it impossible to scale beyond 50 employees. Their salesperson alleged that their price has become a bottleneck and the product is too expensive to sell.

Chakshu shares how he overtook the sales process and built his own model.

'Honestly, I was very uncomfortable thinking that pricing is the only reason why we are not able to grow. I believe that there always will be someone who is cheaper than you; how long can you lower your price? That was the time I started getting into sales, learning about it. First we thought that by describing the features well, we will get the buyer interested, but we noticed that buyer always came up with one or another excuse. For example, the buyer would ask for a client reference and we would give them the names of our bigger clients. We thought that would impress the prospective buyer but then also the buyer would find some fault. The breakthrough for us happened when I started approaching the sales in a more human fashion.'

So in the earlier example, Chakshu started to respond differently.

'See I can give you the reference of my best clients but they will never tell you if we have done something wrong. I will still give you the reference but the fact is we have made errors and we learn from it. As a result, we have constantly improved ourselves.'

This openness and vulnerability, according to Chakshu, hits the nerve and establishes a credibility.

Chakshu further elaborates his friendly sales approach.

'I was thinking that I get along so well with my friends, so why can't I do the same with our clients? The more I thought, the more I realized that we are genuine with our friends but we are afraid that the client would think we are weak if we talk to them genuinely. But what I believe is that business does not happen between companies, it happens between real people. I do not work with Apple, I work with someone named John at Apple. It is personal and relationship based. What I now do is train our salespeople on their language, way of talking and making sure that they convey what needs to be conveyed.'

Chakshu applied this even on the Contact page of GreyB's website. He shows the old and new content:

OLD TEXT

'Thank you for your interest in GreyB's services. Our Engineers, Project Managers are among the best in their respective fields. Let one of GreyB's experienced sales staff assist you with your particular requirements. Please provide the following information about your business needs to help us serve you better. You should receive a response within 24 hours.'

NEW TEXT

'Behind this lovely website are people and we know the secret sauce—people love to talk with people. I am playing the role of "Chief Helper" at GreyB and if there is a project for which you need help—directly message me at Chakshu@GreyB.com (yes, that's my real email) and I will get you the help from Team-GreyB. BTW, just in case, you prefer to leave a message in the enquiry form below—great! It goes directly to founders and trust me, we love listening to your suggestions, comments, feedback, questions or your story.'

'And one thing is good about us—we don't suck in responding—try us!'

Many companies struggle when dealing with Western clients because of the language and culture differences.

Chakshu turned it around to his advantage.

'I tell the clients before the meeting formally starts that we are new to selling to the American audience and what I might be assuming that you are looking for may not be correct. Indians are instruction-oriented people, so if you give very clear instructions, I may do my job in a much better manner. Despite the traditional advice, I feel the best way to do business with Americans and Europeans is to be vulnerable in front of them. One of our large oil and gas clients was based in Houston. I called our contact there to say that I am in the area and would love to meet for a working lunch. In that lunch, I did not try to sell to him at all. I asked him for advice as an entrepreneur. I told him that we have developed an intelligent functionality of deriving key business inferences from technology documents. I asked him how we can pitch this feature to pharmaceutical companies. This person enjoyed giving me advice and continued to talk of some of his own problems that he was facing with his current vendor. In the end, I told him that there are things that we can do to solve his problems and eventually we converted him for a large project. We were amazed at what we had just done! He would not have shared his problem with me if I was just selling to him all the time. Don't sell with sneaky strategies, don't hide your intentions. Be genuine to people, and I have seen that works better than a rehearsed sales call. This is what I mean by treating sales as a relationships thing.'

Chakshu experiments constantly. Sometimes, he has sent handwritten responses to a client who is no longer responding. At other times, he has tried turning down a client softly. He shares an example.

'I told the client, "We are unable to process this at US$1,500 and we know there are other companies who will do it at that price point, but we would rather give you more value than cheaper price because six months down the line, you will not remember the price but you will remember that GreyB did or did not deliver". This was again the human approach and it was working. Prices became less relevant when we were connecting at a human level. I have so many stories because I just kept experimenting and seeing the client's reaction. Sales is such a different game than what most people think it is.

Deepak Syal, Avneet Bansal, Chakshu Kalra (left to right) in Chandigarh. Since the founders had no money, the furniture behind was given by someone as a gesture of kindness

Once again, people work with people. Establish the connection! Try to get them to share the truth with you. Why are they not responding or what problems are they facing—these are things that a person only shares when he trusts you and feels comfortable. Once you reach that point, doing business is much easier.'

What Helps Deepak Learn?

Deepak confesses that while he reads a ton of books, he was not able to relate to those stories because he had not experienced those problems. 'But now I know what many of those things meant. The learning has come from experiments and experiencing things ourselves.' He recommends:

- *Traction* by Gino Wickman (Measurement)
- *Tribe* by Seth Godin (Marketing)
- *Good to Great* by Jim Collins (Moving to next level when you are stuck)
- *Blue Ocean Strategy* by W. Chan Kim (Strategy)

- Rather than sharing a fifth book, I believe the person will be able to derive more value, in the same time, by watching *Shark Tank*

Key Takeaways

Person

- *Initiative:* Co-founders Deepak and Chakshu took ownership of new functions whenever needed despite lack of any formal backgrounds or natural talent.
- *Relentless hustle:* Organically found a way out of every problem and stagnation.

Sales

- *Developing a human-centric approach:* Leveraging his personal communication skills, Chakshu organically figured strategies that worked well for him.
- *Understanding the client:* Instead of feigning resemblance to Western clients, Chakshu understood where the difference lies and found a way to work around that by showing vulnerability.
- *Targeting right segment instead of competing on price:* Being audacious to experiment with higher prices and finding a strong fit with price insensitive corporations whose focus is on quality.

People

- *Focus on mindset instead of academic excellence:* Vetting candidates that fit well for the rigour of patent research instead of resume-based hiring.
- *Building a culture that conditioned people to perform:* The culture of 'finding the results no matter what it takes' prepped the employees to the company's expectations and weeded out non-performers.

- *Keeping supply of freshers ready:* Training 15 new freshers each year kept the risk of running low on human resources at bay.

Marketing

- *Innovate ways to generate content:* Using employees to generate quality answers on Quora paved the way for high search-engine rankings.
- *Finding right channel:* Visibility on LinkedIn had the highest returns, for that is where the patent audience was hanging out.

PART 5

People, Operations and Customer Service

We were looking for six to seven guys who would do everything like running operations, running supply chain. There were only two conditions—one, you cannot be from food industry because we were frustrated with those people. Two, you cannot send us the CV.
—Jaydeep Barman (Faasos)

Many a times, start-ups grow from 5 to 500 in no time and there is no time to build the culture.
—Sameer Guglani (Madhouse)

We are here talking about start-ups that are meant to excite millions of users or thousands of enterprises. Getting there is a function of the impact you are able to create, and unless you are Nelson Mandela, Mother Teresa or Charlie Chaplin, it means building a solid team that can propagate your vision and mission with the same enthusiasm —that is what 'culture' is.

Jaydeep Barman's ability to scale Faasos to 15 cities would have been impossible if not for his innovative hiring through an entrepreneur-in-residence programme. In fact, his story shows how hiring industry veterans had nearly killed Faasos in its early days. Sameer Guglani's laser focus on keeping both the employees and the users happy translated into a service that people loved to use and work for. His comments on hiring, culture and customer service show that, in the end, it is all about people.

Interesting hiring and retention strategies are also discussed by Deepak at GreyB, Varun at Aspiring Minds, Amit at SlideShare and Girish at Freshworks.

You can do anything you want to do. What is rare is this actual wanting to do a certain thing; wanting it so much that you are practically blind to all other things, that nothing else will satisfy you. The real work of art is the result of a magnificent struggle.

—Robert Henri

14   Jaydeep Barman: Faasos

From selling Kolkata rolls to finding new ways to recruit talent and create buzz about his company, Faasos, Jaydeep Barman is building a food company that users and investors love alike. The craziness began in the name itself!

End-to-End Delivery Focused Food-on-Demand App
#hiring #culture #operations #food

Faasos started as a Kolkata roll store chain in Pune in 2004, and it took seven years for the founders Jaydeep Barman (INSEAD, McKinsey) and Kallol Banerjee (INSEAD, Bosch) to return to it with full-time commitment. Pivoting to an end-to-end delivery focused food-on-demand company, Faasos takes the order, prepares the food fresh and delivers it to the customer's doorstep. A management consultant at heart, Jaydeep focused on running the business frugally and keeping fixed costs low—strategies that attracted the attention of Sequoia Capital early on in the journey. Having no background in food business, his intuitive decisions have served him well so far. He thinks it was his lack of food and beverages experience that enabled him to disrupt a centuries-old industry.

Scaling to Mumbai presented the first major hiccup as the company struggled to hire the right people and understand the food business laws and regulations. With innovative hiring and operating decisions, Faasos got back on track and has expanded to 150 locations in 15 major cities by the year 2017. A culture of ownership driven by a few early recruits and the ability of the team to learn from mistakes has served the company well time and again. Leveraging technology wherever possible, experimenting with food menus and creative marketing are integrated in the Faasos DNA as it combats the growing competition in the food apps category. Faasos has raised US$50 million till July 2017 from prominent investors including Sequoia and Lightbox.

The Side Hustle Starts with 'Ghar Ka Khana'

Jaydeep hails from Calcutta, and the Bengalis' love for food had found its way into his DNA too. One fine morning in 2003, when he was working in Pune, his craving for good old Calcutta rolls got the better of him. He convinced his partner in crime, Kallol, and they brought down a cook from Calcutta to start a 200 sq. ft store in Pune. This was the first Faasos kitchen. The first financing came from a ₹400,000 loan from the father of his friend from college, Anand.

'Kallol and I had been to IIM Lucknow before this. But we didn't study at all there. As soon as we opened the first store, we were struggling with everything. We had never stepped in a kitchen and we did not know how to run a business. Like, first month's electricity bill was more than our sales. We were going to run out of money in two to three months, but we were learning and that motivated us to keep going. We would not even use the AC the next month to keep the electricity cost low. It was scary.'

Wisened-up with the experience from first store, the second store was opened in a back alley and that became the DNA of Faasos. The bet paid off. 'You have to worry about too much fixed costs. Delivery costs are okay because they come only when you have an order. So our overall focus has been to reduce the fixed costs and create an efficient operations around the variable costs.'

Remember, this was the early 2000s. Domino's had opened, but was still struggling in India. There was barely anyone delivering rolls at that time.

'We did not have any marketing budget and relied on word of mouth marketing. Whenever we did the delivery, we would drop fliers in the neighbouring apartments and leaflets in door knobs. That used to work. We took orders on phone and cash on delivery. It was just me and Kallol in the core team, and then we had delivery boys.'

Wait a minute, what does Faasos even mean?

'I don't think you can print it in the book. It's a drunken night story,' he chuckles. 'I and Kallol were trying to come up with a name. We started checking out names of all the countries on Google. There was something called Burkina Faso and according to Wikipedia, the name meant "the land of the incorruptible".'

Don't worry if you have never heard of this country. Jaydeep hadn't either, but he is good at connecting the dots in hindsight.

'It sounded nice and we thought we can tell people about this exotic country. The connection was that we never used artificial colours or ingredients in our food, so we were incorruptible in that sense. We kept telling this story for a couple of years until we met a guy who had actually been to Burkina Faso! He told us, "Don't give this bullshit to me, I have seen this place and it is most corrupt country in the whole world".'

Unfortunately they had to drop using that story, but they retained the name. So they went back to the drawing board and reverse engineered a full form for Faasos—Fanatic Activism Against Sub-standard Occidental Shit.

Broadening Worldview from INSEAD and McKinsey

After breaking even in 2005, Jaydeep headed for an MBA at INSEAD.

'I was getting bored at my job and I wanted to see the world and work abroad for some time. INSEAD was the only good one-year MBA option, plus it was in France. There is this romanticism about that country among Bengalis. It was the first time I actually studied in my life because I had taken a big loan. The whole thing cost me about ₹75 lakh and all of it was borrowed from banks who mortgaged my father's property in Calcutta. I could not NOT end up without a job after that. INSEAD has two intakes—one from July and one from January. Six months into it, Kallol also joined.'

Jaydeep definitely burnt the midnight oil this time and got placed at McKinsey London in 2006. At McKinsey, his first project was with the CEO of a Fortune 100 pharmaceutical company. He went on to work with four to five other bigshot CEOs in his stint there. 'I think I was fairly good at consulting. I became an associate principal in the London office in four years, which was one of the fastest ever.'

Consulting trained him on how to see through the clutter and find an insight from a data/information perspective.

'You get to see things that you cannot when you are caught up in day-to-day running of the business. Once in a while, I try to do that in Faasos too where I sit and try to think things from a distance. And I have found answers more often than not. The bad part is that everything is done on a PowerPoint presentation. I used to truly hate that. There was a joke running in the company that we are changing the world one slide at a time.'

Meanwhile, Kallol went to work at Bosch in Singapore. And Faasos was handed over to Siddharth Joshi and Vishwanath for the day-to-day operations in return for 50 per cent stake. This was their livelihood, so they were fully invested into the success of these stores. Jaydeep would go to India once or twice a year and see how things were going.

Start-Up Itch Returns: A New Faasos Is Born

Fast forward to 2010. Faasos had four stores now in Pune. Jaydeep was father to a 2.5-year-old daughter. He had just become an associate partner in McKinsey. This is the time when a lot of people take some months off from McKinsey and decide whether they want to get into the partner game or want to do something else. To mull it over, Jaydeep had taken a sabbatical and was back in India for six months. For a couple of months, he got involved into running the actual business at Faasos and thought that he could grow it bigger.

'It was of course very tiny and I could not even afford the lifestyle I had in London. It also meant putting my family through a tough time. So I talked to my wife, and although she wasn't happy, she was surprisingly okay with it.'

Plus, her daughter would be closer to his extended family and that felt the right thing to do. With just a few months left off his sabbatical, Jaydeep decided not to go back and give Faasos a serious try.

'I have been fortunate enough to travel a lot across continents. But I had never seen any Indian food business at scale anywhere in the world. Like, there was this *kathi* rolls place in the village area in New York but there is no chain. There are pizzas and burgers but nothing Indian. And the economics were quite nice because it was devoid of any fixed costs. It was 75–90 per cent delivery. So it felt like something that would not take too much money to scale.'

And this was the birth of Faasos as we know it today.

The food businesses are generally considered to be low margins and risky because of perishability.

'Of course, there are challenges, but that is true for any business. I felt that it was not an insurmountable issue if we could use our data and analysis well.

On the up side, you have the opportunity to build a brand and become a global player. While I rely heavily on data and analytics, inherently, I am a very impulsive kind of guy. So although I didn't have and probably still don't have all the answers, I felt it was worth risking my and my family's livelihood.'

The tough moments that he has seen are reduced to a pause in the narration. He moves on, 'I am quite fortunate. My wife had left her job in the UK and decided not to take a new one in India because we figured that I would be away most of the time and someone was needed at home.'

Kallol, like a true partner in crime, found his way back too. 'We later on realized that our wives went to the same school! There must be some cosmic connection I think,' Jaydeep chuckles. 'We incorporated a new company and created a franchisee agreement for our older stores. So Siddharth and Vishwanath were going to run those stores as the franchisee and I would start the new business from scratch. Now, they operate under the name Eatsome.'

Learning from the Past and Sticking to Their Gut

Jaydeep was very clear on keeping the focus on delivery. He wanted to establish a model that consumes small capital and runs from a small place but has a large catchment. What that means is the ability to serve a larger place from a small store through an efficient delivery mechanism. One wonders if the management consultant background gives an edge.

'See, that's the difference. When you are a management consultant and you are working on a problem, you are looking at things from outside in an impersonal way. But building a business is very personal. Shit happens almost on a daily basis and all the method goes out of the window. At least in the beginning, until you have the key business, you are involved in the daily grind and you don't get the time to look at the big picture. So I would say between 2010 and 2012, I hardly had any chance to sit back and methodically analyse the business. I was too much drawn into it.'

The first outlet was very small and they took orders on phone. 70–80 per cent of the orders were wraps and it started better than the older stores. They added two more outlets in Pune and then expanded to Mumbai. In the beginning of 2012, Sequoia invested—adding to the validation of Faasos's completely different economics as opposed to any other food business.

'Everybody wanted to have a coffee shop and beautiful facade because it is a reflection of where they themselves want to go. But we were doing it differently and Sequoia understood that. In end of 2012, we entered Bangalore. Soon after, another inflection point came in the business. We started our website. We were one of the first to go online for the orders and we completely closed the phone ordering side. This freed people from taking the calls and it was another win in terms of economics. Now people were either producing or delivering. Around 2015 is when we closed out physical stores and actually started putting dark stores. This means putting stores that are not visible to the public. They could order only through web or the app. So out of the 150 stores that we have now, only about 30 are visible.'

First Big Scare: Almost Calling It Quits

But let's not jump ahead. Pune had been a familiar territory for the founders but shit started hitting the fan the moment they ventured into Mumbai in 2011.

'I considered Bangalore and other options, but given the proximity to Pune, it made sense to open the next Faasos in Mumbai. We tried the same concept—small stores with everything prepared in the store. In Pune, we had an established network of suppliers, which was non-existent in Mumbai. Plus, rentals in Mumbai are so high that we had to go even smaller. It meant we were more back-heavy. First, fixed costs were much higher, second, supplier networks were not there. Third, you need five to six licences to operate a food venture and we had figured that out in Pune, but in Mumbai, it was a complete mess.'

Jaydeep tried to get kitchen-cum-warehouses in Mumbai. It was daunting because all he had managed so far was these small stores in Pune. They had raised the money by this time and Kallol had joined too. This was the first time he hired food industry veterans to run these warehouses.

'That was probably our biggest mistake. We thought these people would easily run the central kitchen in Mumbai. But then, we didn't realize that if one is in food and beverages industry for 20–30 years, one doesn't have much fresh thinking left. Second, we were a bunch of inexperienced guys and we wanted to do things that felt right to us.'

For example, Jaydeep didn't want to put preservatives in the food and that was unheard of in the industry. The veterans were not getting it.

'In hindsight, these veterans were not high-calibre people but probably some rejected candidates from big foodchains. Because, come to think of it, if you were having fun or if you were successful in food industry for decades, why would you leave that to join a company which had no background in food! And we were paying a lot to them. So things started turning for the worse in the beginning of 2012.'

What exactly was going wrong in the Mumbai stores?

'Services were not up to the mark, we were not scaling well. I was not seeing results, and when I would have a chat with them about why something is not happening, a bunch of excuses would come. They had figured out quickly that I knew jackshit, and always tried to fleece the business right from submitting 20 mineral water bottle vouchers for a single day to making money on the side for a property deal. See, I was just expecting that stores should be operating nicely, revenues should increase. From revenues to property maintenance to customer service, everything was in a deep shit.'

The animation in Jaydeep's voice is telling. '2011 in its entirety was a big struggle and that was the only time, when I had thought of quitting. I had a very young family and I was 20–30 days away from home at a stretch. It was a tough time.'

A little respite came from having his confidante on board. At least, he had Kallol to talk to on a daily basis now. He reminds me again, 'Anyone who wants to start a company should find a partner. I know there are companies where founders end up fighting, but Kallol and I have been very lucky.'

Out of Box Hiring: Finding the Perfect Employees

I have not talked to Kallol for this book but his presence is very much felt.

'I and Kallol have this habit of just taking a break and going off somewhere to discuss things once in a while. In one such session, we thought why don't we hire people like us? Because we were looking for a sense of ownership. That is when FER (Faasos Entrepreneurs-in-Residence) programme was conceptualized. The idea was to get people who are one or two years out of college (either MBA or engineering). We didn't have the money to go to campuses, and anyway, people attending campus placements are thinking of McKinsey and Goldman Sachs, and not companies like us. But it is only after one or two years that you realize how you are not doing the stuff you thought you would be doing. You are either selling some stuff in a remote village or you are doing a PowerPoint presentation. That is the time you start thinking "is this what I am going to do rest of my life?" We wanted to catch on that. We were looking for six to seven guys who would do everything like running operations, managing supply chain, etc.

We kept two conditions for the applicants—one, you cannot be from food industry because we were frustrated with those people; two, we said that you will be rejected if you sent a CV. Everyone glorifies things on their CV, I might have done too. The job had no structure and pay was not the best in the industry. Instead, we wanted people to realize what they really wanted from this journey, we wanted to see entrepreneurial side of the people. We wrote all that down and floated a blog post that went viral.'[1]

Jaydeep sent the blog post link to IIM Lucknow, the INSEAD alumni list and a couple of friends. People started forwarding it. Soon, they had 1,000 applications. It took them a lot of time, but they did the shortlisting diligently because the need for good people was a desperation at this point. Finally, they interviewed 50 of them on telephone, 20 in person and recruited around eight people.

'When these guys joined, that's what turned the corner for us. Out of the eight people we hired, six have been with us for five years now. These people had zero experience in food but a tremendous sense of ownership. We worked seven days a week. We would not think of anything else but how to make this work. That is exactly what we wanted. They basically ended up running the company.'

FER is a crowning example of Jaydeep's creative management. He shares how he implemented it.

'It was not at all structured. I will give you an example. Four people joined at first and four more came after two to three months. At that time, our Mumbai office was very small. I, Kallol and one other guy were the only people in there. So when this first FER came, he asked us, "Okay where do I do my joining and HR formalities?" and I pointed to this other guy and said, "He is our HR". Then this FER asked us, "I am relocating from Delhi, so I need to sort out my finances". So I pointed to the same guy and said, "He is also our finance guy". The point is it was just us and we were doing everything. There were no departments.

    I wanted to tackle four areas as soon as possible. First was operations and running the stores. Second was the finance-cum-systems role because we were spending money and I was just tracking everything on an Excel. Third was marketing and fourth was technology. I could sense even back then that if

[1] See http://brownianmusings.blogspot.in/2011/11/entrepreneurs-wanted.html, accessed on 8 August 2018.

we want to keep our cost low and focus on delivery primarily, we need to have a solid tech backbone. I was correct and this became a big reason of our success so far. So I asked these four people, who wants to do marketing and who wants to do this and that. Someone took up one area and the other person picked another. We had one guy who started looking at our Mumbai operations. And one guy who took up both tech and marketing. One person ended up doing business development, running the other stores, licensing and everything else. So this is how we started.'

Handling Venture Capital

Faasos was started with ₹50 lakh from friends and family before 2011. The Pune stores were breaking even in two to three months. It was not consuming extra money and that is the reason Sequoia invested US$5 million in 2012, but in tranches.

'Sequoia has been the most wonderful VC for us. It never came to a point when they pressurized us or made us do something that we did not want. We used to have quarterly board meetings in which we would share the updates, brainstorm, and come up with more plans. It was always a discussion and we would debate at times. It may not always be friendly because we are trying to solve a problem, but it is never finger pointing or doubting our intentions. I know there are other companies where things have not gone well with their investors. I always felt that more than the company, person matters. I am extremely fond of G. V. (Ravishankar G. V.). I cannot comment on other people at Sequoia but G. V. was a tremendous support for us.'

There was a panic moment in 2013 when Jaydeep wondered if he will be able to pay the salaries or not. Once that happened, he became extra cautious.

'But Sequoia was very supportive, especially in downturns. Besides, we did not burn money unnecessarily, and people appreciated that. In our six years, we have been spendthrift only once and that was in 2015. It was a mistake and I quickly realized that you can pump in a lot of money into marketing and your growth will come. But if it is not coming with two other things—customer experience and profitability—then it will not sustain. I guess it's important that you make such mistakes because you learn from it. That was the only point in time, otherwise we have never spent money on high-profile advertising. Even till date, I cannot tell you what kind of salaries I and my top management draw. We have been extremely frugal in terms of hiring, PR and so on. It may take more time that ways, but if your team is committed for long term, you will reach there.'

Many entrepreneurs are not good at managing money. Jaydeep advises to always have a grip over cash balance you have and track it diligently.

'Sometimes, people keep meeting the revenue targets but do not realize if they have enough cash or not. You might have a CFO and he says, "The accounts payable has decreased significantly, but our profitability is intact. However, cash is low". You need to understand what that means. Cash is different from profits and payables and receivables. You need to understand the technicality.'

Different CEOs use different metrics to evaluate the health of their businesses. After some deliberation, Jaydeep tells that he believes in CAC—customer acquisition cost—versus LTV—customer lifetime value.

'So if it takes you ₹100 to acquire a customer and he gives you ₹100 profit, the LTV/CAC ratio is 1. If he stays back and orders five times, your LTV/CAC is 5. Less than 1 ratio means you are overspending and not making enough profit. It is important to keep it growing.'

Building the Faasos Culture

Having survived the Mumbai crisis, Jaydeep grew restless and wanted to start another city. By this time, four other FERs had also joined. One of them opted to start out Bangalore office. So he took one other person from their Mumbai office and drove down to Bangalore. The first time Jaydeep visited Bangalore was when this was starting a second store there. All this happened within a gap of a few months. No wonder Jaydeep calls them 'as much the founder of Faasos as I am.'

In times when employees have barely any loyalty, how did Jaydeep manage such smart people and kept them motivated?

'If you look at the background of all these people, they were mostly engineers and/or MBAs. They had worked with Deloitte, Vodafone, Cognizant and so on. They were a version of me 10 years ago. And from my experience of working with a start-up in 2002–2003, what I hated the most was when somebody micromanaged me. What I loved the most was when I was given a freehand with a target. So that's what I decided to do when I hired these people. You will never find me telling people what to do and how to do. I give them broader objectives and give them whatever they need. Maybe it is delegation, maybe it is my laziness. I don't have time or energy to track what they are doing, and in some ways, that helped me.'

What worked for these people was the fact that they were being given important responsibilities. The person in charge of Bangalore knew that for next two to three years, he had to take care of the entire operations there and he had to do it himself, build his team and do whatever is required. He was barely 24 or 25 when he joined. That is big responsibility for someone that young.

Plus, they were given equity.

'At the beginning itself, we created a 10 per cent pool marked for people like them. These guys got quite a bit of the equity. And they could see over the time that their net worth was growing. But I think freedom and respon-sibility are the bigger things. For example, I had equity at the start-up I was working but I left it so early that it's not even in my CV. So equity works as a top-up but it's not the only thing that matters. Interestingly, when these people hired other people, they also followed same instincts. That became the culture of Faasos that if you are coming on board, you will be given an objective and you have to find your own way. And while at times some people are not able to adapt to that, overall, we have one of the lowest attrition rates. One of the reasons is that we are very choosy. Even today, especially for P&L roles, we ask them to not submit any CV. People sort of caught on from my first email that we used for FER and that has become the cultural underpinning of the company. Another mistake I see start-ups making is trying to hire industry veterans whenever they raise a large round; we never did that. We had to hire a finance guy only because it involves technicalities.'

Today, Faasos has around 1,500 people including the store staff.

How to Keep the Menu Exciting?

In the end, Faasos is all about food and what makes their users tick. Getting the right menu involves creativity. Faasos has found a way to manage creativity at an organizational level.

'We use our UMD test which stands for "unique, memorable and delightful". There is a panel where each member tastes the product, looks at the packaging and decides whether it meets our UMD criterion or not. Then they vote. So if any product doesn't meet our UMD criterion, we don't launch it.'

Another unique feather in Faasos's cap would be the *desi* chai in its menu. Do people really order chai?
    'A lot,' he chuckles.

'It had to clear the UMD test, of course. If you think about it, the product is not unique. So how do we make it unique? I don't know if you have tried our chai but it comes up in a disposable thermos flask which is an extremely unique way of delivering chai. So the way chai fits into our pitch is that the packaging is completely unique and once you have it, people were delighted. Many people actually Instagrammed their experience of having Faasos chai. Then, we launched a collection of wraps this month where each wrap had at least two cuisines. Like one was dal *makhni* and falafel wrap. Another was burnt salsa and falafel. So something has to be unique. That has been the cornerstone of our product development. May be we didn't have enough background in food, so we tried to experiment around. Another thing we do is that we launch a product in one or two locations first. We don't spend any marketing money either. Once we have feedback about this product and it looks positive, then only we make it available at other locations.'

By trying it internally and in a few locations first, Faasos keeps its experimental losses low. When McDonald's and Pizza Hut launch a new product, they have to change their menu, print fliers and spend marketing budget. Even before they know whether the product can be successful, they have to spend money.

'We just send a notification to hundred customers in one location that we have launched this new product. And we are very quickly able to gather good feedback. So we don't spend any money before knowing enough about the potential of any product.

What we have done is standardized innovation. For example, creating this process where we have to present five new dishes every Wednesday. Then out of those five products, one may see the light of the day based on internal panel and UMD test.'

In terms of organization, Faasos R&D centres are located in Mumbai where menu experiments and tasting happens. Once an approved recipe is sent to the stores, they come back with some tweaks and a simplified recipe based on that. 'By the time, a dish is rolled out to the entire country, this back and forth has happened and recipe has been fine tuned.'

Can you guess the most popular menu item in terms of sales?— 'Still wraps. 45 per cent of our orders come for wraps,' Jaydeep smiles.

Competition

'Our competition exists at several layers. There are QSR (quick service restaurant) companies like McDonald's. The second category is local players like your local Chinese and tandoori guys. Third would be the cloud kitchen players which have come up very recently like Freshmenu, Holachef and all. We root for competition. The first two are primarily brick and mortar or offline ventures. Delivery is only 10 per cent for them apart for Domino's. They don't invest as much on technology and efficient delivery as we have. We have streamlined the entire process. I believe we are several steps ahead in that at least from these first two categories. We have been eating into their share for some time now. The third group is interesting because they operate at the same level and focus on customer experience from technology to food to delivery like us. We have gotten some head start over them. For example, we are in 150 locations as of today. There is nobody else which is doing more than 20 locations in India. However, we have to keep innovating and stay ahead of the game all the time. But at least, from a distribution standpoint, we have some lead.'

Keeping an Experimental Mindset

FER is not the only experiment that Jaydeep tried. He came up with another experiment called 'ordering through Twitter' that allowed anyone to place an order using twitter alone. It never constituted a large portion of their revenue but it generated enough PR and buzz. Jaydeep reflects on his most impactful decisions.

'If I have to list three big things that worked for us, one would be the FER programme, and second would be our decision to focus entirely on technology-based delivery rather than a QSR. The third one would be our ability to assemble a team of people at back end who are extremely passionate about food. Culture was built through FER, technology was built as a backbone for our business and what ties it all is this passion for food.'

Jaydeep is too grounded to call himself innovative or creative.

'But one thing is there. Whenever I face a problem, I am able to think out of the box. Our focus on technology to improve operational efficiency or our customer experience is an example of that. Similarly, the FER programme for me is an innovation. Traditional wisdom said hire someone experienced, but we did something different. In our teams, if someone comes to me with a problem, I tell them to figure it out for themselves. When one is pushed out of their comfort and starts trying out things, I think innovation happens. That has been in our DNA.'

Reliance on technology is not immediately evident—but everything in Faasos works on their tech backbone called Dash.

'Every time we faced a problem, we try to first solve it through technology. For example, if a customer orders online someone would pick that order on the call centre side and pass it on to the nearest store. That is how Domino's operated, that is how we operated until 2013. But then we made an architectural change so that the order directly goes to a centre located closest to the customer and a print out is generated at the store. Two to three years back, we were the first one to do this.'

Jaydeep's excitement translates into a rising speech tempo.

'Another thing is our real-time delivery estimate. If you look at Faasos app, you see a promised delivery time. It is based on the real traffic situation, distance, load of the kitchen and preparation time of the dish. I think this architecture is unique to us. Other places give you a standard wait time of 45 minutes or so, ours is totally dynamic and real time. The third case is my favourite. If a customer has a problem with an order or wants to make some changes, we again route it to the store and kitchen directly. And we make the kitchen directly accountable for each complaint. It is their duty to resolve it fast. So each morning, I look at the number of complaints, resolution time, etc. It has helped eliminate the entire call centre for this purpose. So I feel we are probably the only company doing this.'

Has Faasos gone on the data science and machine-learning bandwagon too? You bet!

'I will give you an example of how we use it. Around our kitchens, we have a radius of 2–3 km on which we draw virtual polygons on Google Maps. When we get a new order, we trace which polygon it belongs to and then route to the corresponding kitchen. Now, businesses usually struggle to determine where to open a new location. What we do is, we add a virtual polygon to our proposed location and see whether there is enough demand in that polygon or not. We open a kitchen only if we see enough demand. Second, we know our customer very well—what does she order, is she a non-vegetarian turned vegetarian on Tuesdays, does she observe fasts, is she a *navratri* customer? We are also coming up with personal recommendation engines similar to Netflix. So we are data driven and we have around 50 people in our engineering team.'

On a Lighter Note

'For every kitchen of ours, we need five licences and they are so arcane that you will laugh. For example, there is a law that comes from 1910 or something that says each kitchen should come up with a drinking water provision for horses! This is because the guest might be coming on a horse. I have gone through municipality documents on this and it is incredible. I have heard of cases when a BMC official came to a restaurant kitchen in Mumbai and asked for their horse drinking water. What is funnier is that their manager showed him the swimming pool!'

Jaydeep feels that licenses just create hassle for businessmen and encourage the culture of bribe.

'Initially, we did not even know what licences are required. Now we know, and we are able to start a new kitchen in about 1–1.5 months. It is tough to start in India in non-tech industries. But if you can make it work and stick to five years, you can create an advantage and it's harder for someone else to enter.'

Today, Faasos is present in 150 locations across 15 major cities in India. It continues to grow at a significant rate, and Jaydeep is confident that it will double its turnover again in the 2017–2018 financial year, while turning profitable towards the end of the financial year.

Jaydeep's Book Recommendations

Being an avid reader, Jaydeep shares his favourite books:

- *High Output Management* by Andy Grove
- *Good to Great* by James Collins
- *First, Break All the Rules* by Curt Coffman and Marcus Buckingham
- *Hard Things About Hard Things* by Ben Horowitz
- *Made in America* by Sam Walton
- *Onward* by Howard Schultz

In life, he has looked up to Sam Walton and Swami Vivekananda.

Kallol Banerjee and Jaydeep Barman (left to right)

Key Takeaways

Person

- *Creative thinking:* Whenever faced with a problem, the founders were able to think out of the box—dark stores, FER, leveraging technology, etc.
- *Choosing passion over experience:* Learning what is required.
- *Thinking big from the start:* Helped in aggressive expansion.

People

- *Innovative hiring:* Instead of competing on salaries, FER managed to attract the right kind of people without bleeding money.
- *Creating the culture of 'ownership':* By preferring driven people with no experience over industry veterans, and letting

these people hire forward using the same strategy, the culture of 'ownership' sustained and thrived.

- *Empowering the team through right incentives:* Freedom, responsibility and equity.

Operations

- *Creating a viable operating model:* Faasos grew with a brutal focus on reducing fixed costs and, thereby, created an efficient operations around delivery. Their stores consume small capital and run from a small place that has a large catchment area. Introducing dark stores is an example of rethinking existing food space trends to empower the business.
- *Innovation management:* Processes such as weekly tasting and UMD tests make it possible to capture new opportunities with a systematic approach to creativity.

Product

- *Leveraging technology:* To minimize the marketing and operating costs, and experimental losses, Faasos aggressively uses technology.

When you look back on your life, it looks as though it were a plot, but when you are into it, it's a mess: just one surprise after another. Then, later, you see it was perfect.

—Schopenhauer

15   Sameer Guglani: Madhouse

Attempting to build the Netflix of India, Sameer found his calling in start-ups when the word 'start-up' was not even used in mainstream language at all. How did Sameer carry over the unconventional lessons from one of India's first start-ups to build an entrepreneur-friendly start-up accelerator, Morpheus? The best part—none of it was intentional.

Netflix for India
#hiring #culture #customer_service #fundraising #acquired

Sameer Guglani is an entrepreneur turned investor turned yogi. He co-founded Madhouse Media, which was acquired by SeventyMM, and continued with co-founding India's one of the first start-up accelerators 'The Morpheus' in 2008. Morpheus incubated more than 80 companies that include leading names in the start-up space such as CommonFloor, Practo, Airwoot, HackerRank, iimjobs.com, Tapzo and Plivo before it ended its accelerator operations in 2014.

Madhouse was a Netflix-inspired Indian movie-rental business founded by Sameer Guglani and Nandini Hirianniah in 2004. Trying to replicate the Silicon Valley model of Netflix, the husband–wife duo soon realized the challenges of nascence of the Indian market. They set their resourcefulness to solve every piece of the puzzle—be it call centres, logistics or payment—while keeping customer satisfaction as their topmost priority. As funding dried up with the entry of bigger, globally funded players, Madhouse was acquired by SeventyMM in 2007, but not before leaving an indelible impression on the users, early employees and, most importantly, the founders. Considered as one of the earliest Indian start-ups to successfully exit, Madhouse served 4,000+ users and employed 40 people at its peak in its brief stint.

The Nudge of Destiny

Sameer had wanted to take up fashion designing but his parents did not agree. So he became an engineer instead! Graduating from Thapar University in 1998, he worked with multiple companies including a struggling stint at ATL. 'The company had stopped paying salaries. It was a tough time for me, and I remember giving home tuitions after office hours, living a super frugal life and surviving on two meals a day.' Things finally smoothened when he joined a wireless telecom start-up called Sonim.

'At Sonim, we partnered with a lot of big companies—Ericsson, Siemens, Samsung, Symbian, LG, TI, Motorola, etc. The interesting thing was that we would be two to three people on our side working with 15–20 people teams on the other end. That is where I learnt about the power of start-ups, small teams and moving very fast.'

Somewhere in mid-2002, he wanted to leave technology and start moonlighting as a film-maker. On a short-film project, he met Nandini. 'We had common interests and aspirations for life. We gelled well and decided to get married.' The couple moved to the USA in 2003, when Sameer was still working in tech start-ups and Nandini was doing film courses and other things on the side. The plan was to save money and start film-making. During this period, they used to watch a lot of films on Netflix.

Towards the end of August 2004, they came to India for Sameer's brother's wedding.

'But when I went for the H-1B visa interview, it was turned down. I tried one more time and was rejected again. So that was the nudge of destiny that made us stay in India instead of going back to the job in the USA.'

Starting the Netflix of India

'Our logical mind told us that we should start looking for another job in India because we need to keep earning money. But I started getting calls from people I had worked for before saying that if you are back, we would be happy to hire you any day. A similar thing happened with Nandini as well. This gave us the confidence that we can experiment for three months and find a job later.'

They initially tried to start a book café, but soon realized the complexities involved in setting it up. Although the idea to start something stayed, the idea itself morphed into Netflix because whenever they tried to rent movies in India, the selection and quality was pathetic. 'The VCD could stop anytime, most of them were pirated.'

By December, they registered a company for running this venture—Madhouse.

Sameer laughs,

'The name was inspired from Gabriel García Márquez's *One Hundred Years of Solitude*. When we applied to the Company Registrar office in Jalandhar, they rejected us because they thought that Madhouse was an obscene name!

We were shocked and we went back to the registrar with dictionary definitions of the word "Madhouse" (it is basically a symbol of great creativity and chaos). They were interpreting it as an asylum. We heard comments like *"Aap log America se aa jaate ho aur Bharat ka culture kharaab karte ho"*.

We finally got it done by a CA in Delhi and he laughed while listening to our story. That is the journey of an entrepreneur, these small small things stay with you.'

Netflix USA was a DVD-in-mail service with an effective recommendation app which helped the user discover movies that he otherwise did not know. To compete with them, Sameer was thinking of raising ₹1 crore. Since there was no start-up ecosystem in 2004, Sameer reached out to friends and relatives, especially in Mumbai, while trying to get rental licences and permissions to rent the movies.

'One of them was B. S. Nagesh, who was the founding CEO of Shoppers Stop. He was also Nandini's second cousin. He introduced us to a bunch of people, but somehow no one was investing. Then, one day, he asked, how is it going? I said that we have met so many people but it seems that no money is coming up. He asked us how much can you invest? And it is funny because that had not even crossed my mind. There was somehow this ingrained feeling that money will come from someone else. So we did some calculations and figured out that we can arrange ₹8 lakh (400,000–500,000 in savings and borrowing upto ₹4 lakh from our parents). When we told this to Nagesh, he recommended that we go back to Chandigarh and create a pilot in ₹8 lakh. He said, "Create a mini business, and if you build a great business, money will find you". I somehow never forgot that advice.'

Creating the Pilot

Back in Chandigarh, the work seemed never ending. There were movie licences to be arranged, an office to be rented and so on.

'One day, we had an insight that we need to pick a hard launch date and then work backwards to make it happen. So we decided that we will launch on 23 May 2005 no matter what and we did. We realized that unless we decide a date, work will never finish.'

Another key decision was to do the business in an Indian style.

'First, you need a warehouse where DVDs would be stored. Then there were shipping challenges, but the biggest was the marketing. In India, retail chain was a new concept on the rise. I remember CCD going national; Reliance was the first telecom company to launch their own stores. When people walk into the store, there is a certain trust in brand and visibility. So we came up with this "call and visit" model. Also, call centres were big in India at that time. The idea was that a customer would discover us through the retail, sign up and buy the membership there. Afterwards, he wouldn't need to visit anymore and can call to order. We set up a call centre process with one number and five different phones. We built a nice process using Excel, listing our member information and their preferences.'

Being a software engineer, Sameer could handle software more easily but he did not get swayed. Together with Nandini, he printed beautiful catalogues and put a delivery team in place which used to deliver movies two times a day.

'We did not have a website for a year and a half because the Internet was not still a big thing. We did not expect housewives to go online and order. And whenever we would add new movies to our collection each month, we sent new pages that the customer could attach to their existing catalogues.

We kept the pricing along the line of Netflix. A user could go for a two-DVD or three-DVD per month plan, which costed ₹399 and ₹499, respectively. It was a monthly subscription model and people could get discounts by signing up for whole year.'

Initial customers came from their stalls at the Chandigarh Mall, newspaper ads and discounted memberships in corporate offices. 'There was no understanding of start-ups. Towards the end of 2005 was when I first went to a Tiecon in Delhi and learnt about the start-up world and ecosystem.'

Team Building and Customer Service

If you build a good product, not only funding but co-founders also come in! Sameer shares how they got their CTO from one of their customers.

'One day we received a call from a customer who wanted to talk to the founders. My first thought was that he must be upset with our services. I called back expecting a complaint but on the other side, it was this gentleman named Ankur. He was an IIT Delhi graduate and was working in Chandigarh, and he was aware of Netflix. He said that he was also thinking of starting a Netflix-type model in India. He said, "I thought I could join you guys instead of building something new". So we met and he was a perfect addition for CTO. None of us had been building the technology. First thing he said was, "Man, this is too much of a mess, Excel and all. For the first two weeks of my part in the company, I would just sit at home and build a system that we can use". So that is what happened. For the first two weeks, he built an internal software to run our back end.'

One reason why Ankur trusted the service enough to join them was a simple plum cake! Sameer recounts how they had a process whereby if they could not deliver a movie on time or missed out on something from their side, they used to send a handwritten apology along with a plum cake to the customer. 'Ankur's close friend had received our plum cake. He heard the story and the plum cake stayed with him. I strongly believe that if you put your heart and soul into something, then *khushboo phail jaati hai.*'

Sameer today runs a community called Oneness. Previously, he built the Morpheus community of entrepreneurs. He has always been a people person. Some of those skills go back to his Madhouse days.

'We needed call centre executives, delivery boys and lot of skill-driven operational staff who can learn on the go and repeat stuff. They were not the brains, they were the hands and legs of the company which are equally important. We read books, experimented, and it took a lot of trial and error.'

As the first delivery associate, they hired an enthusiastic English-speaking guy who had just finished his 10+2 and came from a good family.

'Soon, we realized that he was not open to learning new things at all. Our protocol was to greet the customer with Sir or Madam. He would go and say *bhaiya ji, bhabhi ji*, and wouldn't take our feedback. He had pocket money from home and he was not struggling or anything. So we had to fire him and it was my first time firing anybody. I was pretty nervous. It took me couple of days and searching things to say on the Internet. I had a script with me when I talked to him. What I conveyed was that it's our mistake, we were not clear on what we wanted. You are as you are but it is not fitting with our team.'

Sameer shares an advice he received on hiring and followed since—you should hire somebody whose house depends on your salary and then you will get the sincerity. 'Another thing we did was poaching actually,' he admits with a smile.

'Whenever we went to Barista or CCD and if we liked a worker, we would chat with him. Once, we chatted with someone at McDonald's. He didn't join but sent a friend who joined. The thing with these people was that they were from lower income families, so they were more serious. Many of them had worked as courier boys before and got no respect in their organizations. They were treated like machines. At Madhouse, there was no hierarchy and everybody was equally respected. Everybody was called on a first name basis. We had this aspiration that employees should want to work with us and tell their friends about us. I think we achieved that. By the time we sold Madhouse, we had 10 delivery boys in Chandigarh and everybody had come from a reference.'

A major hurdle for Sameer was to convince not only the employees but their families.

'When someone told at their home that they are leaving Airtel to join Madhouse, their parents used to object. So we created a PowerPoint that they could show to their parents. All of this has come from facing real problems. I feel that one has to try hiring and make the mistakes. Am I looking for the wrong quality, is my interview process wrong, am I not able to articulate the vision of the company?'

Developing the Culture

Sameer shares the threefold secret to having productive and happy employees: empowering them, making the process clear and giving them the tools to let them do their jobs well.

'For example, whenever our delivery staff went to pick up the payments, we used to give them exact change. And we could see it because I and Nandini had done all these chores ourselves. So we knew the problems. Then, we documented various scenarios that can occur when the delivery team goes to a customer's house and how to respond to those. A dog may come, a servant may come or you may not get any response. We built the process and then they took over. We had this bubbling of ideas from the bottom. Once we were designing the sleeve to carry the DVDs and it had certain things written on top. One of our field executives suggested to Nandini, *"Madam, ispe aisa kuch likho ki log isko ganda na karein"*. So Nandini added something like, "Please don't dirty me".'

To build the middle-level layer of team leaders, Sameer recommends looking for that one guy who has the potential to lead that team.

'You can usually spot them. I recommend growing the culture organically. Many a times, start-ups grow from 5 to 500 in no time and there is no time to build the culture. The initial team has the skin and passion because they have put everything in the efforts. Once you hire people and many people are coming in just for the salary, then there is no real connection and soul left. Initially, we focused on quality and never rushed into hiring. When we hired fast in the second half because of fundraising pressure, it hit us back really hard. We simply did not have the DNA to build the company that fast. We hired people whose resume looked impressive from an investor's point of view and we had to pay much higher salaries. While the guys were genuine, they couldn't do the work because of bottlenecks in our system, and I have seen the same in many other Morpheus companies as well. The best people to hire for a leadership role in a start-up are the people who have been entrepreneurs themselves. They know how to take initiatives and manage things independently. They have an innate sense of responsibility.'

The Trap of Fundraising and Fast Hiring

Sameer sees the three-year lifespan of Madhouse as two distinct chapters—the first 1.5 years were what he calls a 'period of desireless action'.

'During the first phase, we were totally unexposed to start-up culture and actively learning. Both of us, in our own ways, had an innate commitment to excellence. If we are doing something, we wanted to do it well. All the good work happened in this period. At a basic level, a good business is one that can (a) sell something which customer wants, (b) deliver in a manner that customer is willing to pay for and keeps him happy and (c) the cost of delivery should be lower than what you spend. We were frugal and very good with simple and unit economics. Our payment collection rate was very good. Our customers were very happy because we paid a lot of attention to detail. By the end of 1.5 years, we had four people in the call centre, four to five delivery boys or field agents, and a few marketing folks. Our culture was really good —first name basis, eat together, go out together.'

Sameer's dad had a friend whose son was living in □he USA and knew Netflix. He started talking frequently to Sameer and became the first investor.

'Along with his friend, he put in ₹25 lakh. That was sort of the first money coming in by itself, and then one of Ankur's friends from IIT days put in another ₹10 lakh. After that, we basically got distracted by the desire to raise more money.'

Sameer went to a TIE conference, and somewhere after that, the focus shifted to fundraising.

'The already good work that we had done helped us in raising an angel round of ₹1.5 crore from Mumbai Angels, Indian Angel network and some other individual investors. There was a misconception that a good business needs to be big and have money. It is not enough to run a company from Chandigarh but that I should expand. This was not out of greed but an incorrect understanding, I would say. The logical progression of business seemed that way. Going into TIEcons, listening to VCs talks about money, they would say that we are not ready yet—this kind of stuff. We were talking to many VCs, and whatever impressions we carried made us believe that to be worth getting an investment, we had to be a certain way—big numbers, faster growth, team working under us, etc. So we launched in Delhi around the beginning of 2006 to follow this advice. Our Chandigarh office rent when we started was ₹6,000 and our first Delhi office was ₹35,000. So our burn rate was increasing. We were renting more places, hiring more people on much higher salaries so that we look right to the VCs. We hired an operations head and a marketing head—each one was on ₹10 lakh annual package. Instead of Nandini running marketing directly, it would happen through the marketing head who was not a start-up guy. So things slowed down and we were spending more money on marketing too.'

All this hustle brought them to a partner-level meeting with Sequoia and Canaan. However, since their angel round, SeventyMM had entered the Indian market with US$2 million in funding. Second, Reliance got into the field with BIGFlix. Investors could see that Madhouse will be competing against massively funded competitors.

'Plus, we were a husband–wife team with non-media background. Whatever the reason was, maybe we weren't good enough, but in the end we did not get the venture capital. Nexus and Matrix were new. We met them too. Now there was nowhere to go and with a higher burn rate, we had just ₹25 lakh of cash left. SeventyMM had launched in Bangalore and were very savvy in creating an image. Matrix ended up putting in US$7–8 million in them. So they were plush with money. We knew that in four months, we are going to run out.'

The Hasty Exit and Acquisition Realities

Sameer recounts the options they considered. They could either trim down the operations and try to be profitable again, or shut down and return the leftover money to the investors. The third option was to look for acquisition since they were already getting interest from BIGFlix and SeventyMM. 'We called our meeting of investors and asked their opinions. Investors favoured the acquisition exit. It was agreed that the existing money should be used in increasing our numbers so that we can get better valuation in the exit.'

Finally, the SeventyMM exit materialized.

'It was not big money and only a fraction of what we had raised. Whatever we got, we distributed back in pro-rata form to our investors. I and Nandini joined SeventyMM, and a part of our team was also absorbed there. Our Delhi team got absorbed into SeventyMM Delhi office and we joined at VP level in the Bangalore office.'

Sameer's voice hardly wavers. The memories have been distilled into wisdom in hindsight.

He responds objectively,

'See, I have never been an emotional or ambitious person. I don't get too attached to the past or future. When the acquisition happened, there was no time to think. There was stress around partners, competitions, etc.—normal things that happen at any start-up. Even when we sold to SeventyMM, we were not doing that with an idea of getting rich. We genuinely wanted to provide a service as good as Netflix and we felt we could do that at SeventyMM too. They had US$10 million in funding. Madhouse was very well executed in its tiny scale. The first year was tremendous. When we did not have money, we had to really understand everything carefully. So we had developed a very good understanding of the system. BIGFlix and SeventyMM were inspired by us in many aspects, for example, the way we designed the movie delivery envelopes, etc. BIGFlix had their software designed from the same company who was our software vendor. Lot of discussions had happened when acquisition talks were going and we shared a lot of information because we knew we had to find the buyer. But the offer never came from them, and they might be just waiting for us to shut down so that they could hire us.'

Soon, they realized that SeventyMM's CEO is living in Seattle and had minimal day-to-day involvement with the team in India. The culture was focused not around excellence but to grow the valuation via showing growth in numbers and sales.

'Even when the customers left, they did not pay attention to it or record it. They just wanted to be more valuable and keep raising the money. The founder had already sold a company in the USA; for this venture he has raised US$2 million from DFJ in the USA before starting out in India. He used the money to build an impressive-looking senior team. It was this team on which the next round VCs agreed to put in another US$7 million. They had general managers for big areas and there were 5–10 VPs and AVPs in marketing, HR, etc. Then we came. I joined as VP in strategy and Nandini in marketing.

We never knew this game—show numbers, raise money. We had operational experience on the ground and we could have given a lot of suggestions, but the way they were doing things was not sensitive to it. And the moment we said that hey guys, let's make the changes, the whole management started pushing back on us. After six months, we realized that nothing is going to change. So we met the CEO and told him that we would like to leave. He was okay with that and said that we can leave after finishing 12 months of contract. The whole aspiration of building Netflix was still a possibility when we joined SeventyMM, but it faded away as we saw things from inside.'

One can rue it, but Sameer looks at it as a tremendous transformation phase for the entrepreneur in him. At Madhouse, they had learnt doing business from scratch. In the USA, Netflix was started when people were already comfortable ordering online. All payments happened on credit cards and delivery happened through robust postal services. But Madhouse had to set call centres, figure out couriers and logistic teams, and figure out how to pick cash from homes which Sameer calls 'nothing but cash on delivery'. In the USA, movie-rental industry agreements were already figured out because Blockbuster rental service was there. Netflix picked up on that. But in India, no one had a clue about movie-rental business. 'So in a way I feel that we were building four companies in one. Call centre, content, payment and logistics.'

But when they saw SeventyMM, funded by top VCs but struggling so badly to execute, their confidence in their own abilities and quality of work shot up.

'If we were to consciously evaluate Madhouse, it might be called a failure in terms of financial success and return to investors. We still had credit card debts after the exit, hardly 4,000 customers, no larger impact. But over the time, I have realized that we had become very good because of it. One of the outcome of any start-up is to create better people and resources for the world. All of us are doing well, so that is a success for me.'

Mistakes That Could Have Been Avoided

Sameer thinks looking for investors too early was a mistake. Second, getting into a second round of fundraising when they had just raised one round was another mistake.

'We could have grown slow and built our business bit by bit rather than increasing our burn rate in a race to raise more money when our feet were shaky. Hiring wrong people, looking for wrong things. One more thing—we worked too hard. For three years, we did not take any holiday. Now I know that when you burn yourself so much, it is not good. But then, failure is nature's beautiful tool. One who has not failed has not learnt. In the journey of Madhouse, I think we created more value in ₹8 lakh than after raising ₹1.5 crore.'

From Entrepreneur to Investor: Morpheus Accelerator

Soon after resigning, Sameer and Nandini found themselves meeting entrepreneurs and sharing their thoughts openly with them.

'It was clear to us that this work makes us happy. So we thought we will try to work with young entrepreneurs for a small portion of the equity. We had savings of ₹15–20 lakh and that we felt could help us sustain for couple of years, and if some of these companies did well economically, that would make things take off. So that was the crude idea.'

It became more concrete when Sameer was attending a start-up event as a start-up advisor. He met Instablogs team, Ankit and Arjun Maheshwari, who were struggling to create a PowerPoint for the pitch event.

'They had a wonderful product and good traction. We stayed back and started helping them, and before we knew, we were there for five hours working with them. Later on, Ankit asked us to become their advisors and we said yes. He insisted that we should take some form of payment. So we thought of a model. A rough calculation was, for six months, he wanted 10 hours a week of our time. Based on our previous salaries, which was, I think, ₹26 lakh per annum, we came to a number. Since this is equity arrangement, so we took risk into consideration and multiplied that amount by three to four times. Roughly we saw what the valuation of the company is and calculated that the worth of our time came to 1 per cent. So we did a six-month advisory arrangement for this much equity. But we added the clause that if any party is unhappy with the other, they could walk out with a 15-day notice and we would prorate the equity. This is how our first engagement started.'

The next start-up which they agreed to advise was CommonFloor, and soon thereafter, they had four such engagements while they were still at SeventyMM. It was just an experiment, and they named it Morpheus after the Greek god of dreams—'that fit in with what we were doing.'

Sameer and Nandini had blogs and their own followings. They created a blog post to announce the launch of Morpheus programme, which was featured by the leading start-up blogs of those days.

'We had very basic website at that time. The application form was created in MS Word. People had to download it and then fill it out and send to us to apply. Some young founders started contacting us and we would do an initial call with them. It was all about how comfortable they were feeling in that call.'

While they had researched how YC and Techstars worked in the USA, they went for a lot of deviations in their own venture. During the first year, they operated from Bangalore, and then moved to Chandigarh.

'We worked with start-ups across Mumbai, Chennai, Delhi and Bangalore. Almost every month, we travelled to these cities, and the community meet-ups and face-to-face interactions happened; the rest of the interactions took place over email, chats and voice calls. Our Batch 2 announcement attracted over 100 applications. We invited the shortlisted teams to work with us for two weeks without any commitment from either side. As we were now full time on this path, we looked at the economics more closely and realized that 1 per cent doesn't work out very well. We looked at some other data and probability of the success, and other factors. So we raised the stake to 4–6 per cent. Companies were essentially paying us equity for 10-hours-per-week time; there was no money being invested at this point.'

Instead of demo days, they started Morpheus Yatra where they took their graduated batch to different cities and booked half a day with each VC firm. 'The whole group went and spent time in VC offices. The wisdom of doing things in an Indian context had come from Madhouse,' Sameer adds.

Over six years, Morpheus incubated 80+ start-ups including Practo, CommonFloor, HackerRank and iimjobs.com.

As innovative entrepreneurs became a part of Morpheus, Sameer decided to create a mailing list or community for the whole group where anyone could email their problems or whatever they wanted to share. This is how Morpheus Gang as a community was born.

'We were able to assimilate some very diverse entrepreneurial start-up situations and cross-apply them. We worked with all kind of sectors and ideas—healthcare, retail, HR, everything. It was fantastic to get a view across the ecosystem. With this community, the point is that engagement never really ended. For me, personally, that was more gratifying than the accelerator programme. That is my biggest takeaway because whatever I am doing now, my approach is community based.'

What Is Success?

Sameer has seen both the sides of a start-up. He believes that people who do start-ups are very high-quality people who can get highly paid jobs.

'Statistically speaking, the probability of financial success is much higher if you are on a traditional career path. So money is not the thing an entrepreneur seeks. Social narrative of success talks about money, power and influence, but a few individuals may not find it in line with his innate nature, leading to an emptiness. And a genuine individual might feel the need to fill that void via entrepreneurship. And if you do what aligns with your inner self, you can achieve personal growth/success and also create a company which is successful in the social context. I personally would call that journey a success which leads to tremendous personal growth in line with a person's inner nature and creates an organization that stands for its excellence.'

To achieve this excellence, one first needs to have his own definition and understanding of success.

'As my understanding progressed, I realized that everyone first needs to find themselves, and then their true path will become clear to them and they will have their own definition of success. But the social definition of business success is based on rigid metrics—How much money have you raised? What is your valuation? Now, when I would meet start-ups in Morpheus, I would tell them that what they are thinking may not be the success they want. I wanted to help them in finding their own understanding of success, but I realized that the people coming to Morpheus did not want that. They wanted what the popular narrative is—help to become a successful start-up. At this point, I felt we cannot continue Morpheus because our understanding and intention was now divergent than that of the start-ups coming to us. I was at a different stage of life than them, so no hard feelings, but it was clear that we cannot help each other because we are talking different languages.'

From Investor to Student of Yoga: Oneness Community

Starting in early 2012, Sameer committed himself to understanding and studying the vast Indian tradition of yoga and spirituality. After closing down Morpheus Accelerator in 2014 (Morpheus Gang still continues), Sameer led two to three years of an almost secluded life before curating a community of 'seekers' who live actively in the contemporary society but see spirituality as a necessary ingredient of a complete life. The community currently, as of early 2018, has 270+ members living in different parts of India and the world. An offshoot of this is the Morpheus One, a community of entrepreneurs who are building conscious business organizations.

Wait a minute, what is a conscious business?

'It is hard to define. One quality, of course, is excellence. It should maximize the impact for everyone and not just profits for shareholders. An entrepreneur doesn't merely replicate something that is already there. A pure entrepreneur is someone who is so connected to reality, nature and oneself that they are able to become a channel for manifesting a new way of doing things on earth. An obvious example is iPhone and Steve Jobs. Nothing like it existed. All things which are waiting to manifest on earth are on a higher plane of consciousness, and it takes some effort to reach there and bring it down. When someone is able to do that, he enriches entire humanity. I would say that is a good way to think about it.'

What Gets Sameer Going?

Sameer has been researching on mind and intuition for past five years.

'I was reflecting upon the success of Morpheus portfolio start-ups, and comparing the journeys of 50 per cent which took off and other 50 per cent which did not take off. I was trying to spot the levers or factors that helped some founders take off the way they did. As I looked carefully some patterns became visible—founders that received and followed the intuitive insights during the process of critical problem solving were finding the required solutions way more often than the other group. On the other hand, founders who operated from a logical mindset were unable to come up with good solutions and hence did not make a lot of progress.

It all made sense—if you are doing something familiar all the time, then logic helps but start-ups are about dealing with unknown problems, and logic fails over there. These guys who were succeeding had been able to find those solutions mysteriously. I studied folks like Ford, Steve Jobs, Richard Branson and many others, and I saw the same pattern. So my question stayed—why were some people intuitive?'

Over the next one to two years, he read voraciously. Neither books nor academic papers nor scientific research could give him a satisfactory explanation. Around the same time, while looking for a good school for his daughter, he happened to visit a learning community called Coveda in Chandigarh.

'When I went there, they asked me some fundamental questions. One of them was—"You want your child to be more free in her education and upbringing. But are you free yourself?" The thing is that if you are living in a certain limitation in your mindset, you will pass that onto your child also; so if you are committed to your child's freedom, you have to be committed to your freedom as well. After that conversation, I started exploring processes via which I can know myself and learn about my limitations, and work on them so that I don't pass them to the child.'

His exploration, henceforth, continued from Jiddu Krishnamurti to a book called *Integral Education* written by Partho (who is also one of the founders of the learning community) based on the teachings of Sri Aurobindo and Mother. 'I decided to take one year for an experiential journey during which I tried to live what I was reading, I attended workshops/retreats, travelled and met people on similar journeys.'

In a year, he developed an experiential understanding of what intuition is. He elaborates that humans can operate from three different states of consciousness.

'The first and basic state is the surface consciousness where we believe that we are an individual entity that is separate from the rest of the nature. All our learning happens from what we perceive via sense organs and process via the brain. This is a very limiting existence and every person of logical mindset works within this limitation. This can be compared to a computer that is not connected to any network, hence the only information it has is the stuff which has been directly stored on its hard disk.

The next stage of consciousness can be called interconnected consciousness, in which we feel an inner connect with everything and every person around us, and we can perceive things via this inner channel without any sensory contact. For example, a start-up investor knows within five minutes of meeting the founder whether he is going to invest or not. Where is that coming from? Or you might go to a library looking for a specific book and spot another book that you have never seen before and feel a significant pull towards it. And you pick it up and find that it is exactly the book you

NO SHORTCUTS

need to read. So you can receive these signals from people and things. This is more like a computer that is connected via a network to other computers and devices around it and has a wider access to information beyond its own hard disk.

Sameer at his home in Chandigarh

The last stage is universal consciousness, where you realize that the whole universe is a single, continuous consciousness and you are that same consciousness. This is where everything becomes obvious and known to you. So the process of intuition that I was looking for is a part of these higher levels of consciousness. And yoga is the process via which an individual consciousness can expand into levels of interconnected and universal consciousness. After stopping the Morpheus programme, I wanted to dedicate my life to this journey of yoga, and after spending a couple of years, I have realized a few things. First, this journey of consciousness is a long one and it's a lifetime commitment. Second, this journey does not need to happen outside the social/personal/professional life—in fact, it needs to take place right in the middle of everything so that more people and processes can be affected by it. So the journey continues...'

Key Takeaways

Person

- Focus on learning and original thinking instead of chasing a popular definition of success led to a more fulfilling journey.
- Putting people first created a strong kinship with employees.
- Translating mistakes into lessons for subsequent ventures.

People

- *Channels of hiring:* Understanding that the right people to hire are those who are dependent on the salary led to building a good on-field workforce.
- *Creating the culture of 'respect and equality':* By creating a respectful environment in the early days, employees felt happier and driven to refer their friends.

Product

- *Understanding Indian audience:* Madhouse knew that the only way to succeed in Indian market was to translate the American online model of Netflix to an offline/call-based model for India.

Customer Service

- *Translating happy customer experience to marketing and hiring:* With policies such as plum cake, exact change, etc. and a laser focus on customer happiness, Madhouse attracted new customers and employees alike.

Fundraising

- Raising too much and too soon can put growth pressure and hamper good decision-making.
- Burning money to attract or please investors perpetuates bad decision-making and being more dependent on the investors.

About the Author

Nistha Tripathi is the author of a spiritual novel, *Seven Conversations*, and a popular reference book, *Smart Engineer's Guide to MS in USA*. She is the founder of Scholar Strategy which prides itself in guiding hundreds of young professionals into MIT, Harvard and other top international engineering and business schools and leading more fulfilling careers.

With 38,000 followers and 6 million views on her answers on the popular Q&A-based website Quora, Nistha writes extensively on careers, entrepreneurship and pursuing one's passion. Her articles have appeared in *Entrepreneur*, *The Times*, *DailyO*, *DNA*, *The Tribune* and other leading media outlets.

Previously, she studied computer science at the University of Illinois at Urbana-Champaign, and dropped out of the MBA programme at NYU Stern School of Business where she organized Stern's first entrepreneurship summit inviting the likes of Seth Godin and Chris Dixon. She worked on Wall Street and with fast-growing Manhattan start-ups before returning to India. Apart from running Scholar Strategy, she conducts aspirational talks for students and writing workshops for bloggers.

She is currently known for her travelling-six-months-a-year lifestyle, working from Southeast Asia. You can reach her on http://nisthaonweb.com.

Don't forget to check out our companion website. Sign up to download extra resources from the book on http://startupbookindia.com.

All feedbacks and suggestions are welcomed, and you can tweet the same to @NisthaTripathi.

Gratitude

If you find this project to be akin to *Founders at Work* by Jessica Livingston, then you are not far from the truth. The initial inspiration indeed came from reading that book and wondering why such a book does not exist in the context of Indian start-ups. So I am grateful to Jessica for writing a book like that.

When I started writing this book, I never thought I would get so many insightful interviews done, and yet here it is. All I can say is that the book was meant to be written and chose me as its medium of creation. And for that, I am grateful. Writing this book has enlightened me so much that I desire to reap no more reward from it—it has been a reward in itself.

They say you should surround yourself with people who inspire you and empower you to do things you never could have imagined. This book is a result of having those mentors, friends and well-wishers. If not for Sameer Guglani, Umesh Rangasamy and Kavita Devgan, this book will not exist. Thanks to Aditya Babbar, Jayesh Gopalan, Vivek Yaratapalli and Disha Chhabra for reading a few ridiculously long drafts. There were many other friends who supported me emotionally through this journey and while it is not possible to enlist them all, they know what a special place they hold in my heart.

Thanks to my parents and my family for letting me be foolishly myself. Thanks to Dad and my late grandfather for surrounding me with books in my childhood. Thanks to Ma for supporting me like no one can.

Thanks to Neel Chatterjee and Kanagaraj for aiding in the painful process of transcription. Thanks to Vikram Rastogi, Trilok Hebbur, Rabi Gupta, Shreyas Tirunagari, Vishal Bhargava, Srix, Balaji Viswanathan, Aashish Gupta, and Saurabh Raj for providing their candid thoughts on Indian start-ups. I also got invaluable inputs from Rehan Yar Khan, Prashant Mehta and Vijay Anand for which I am grateful.

A big thanks to Madhava Vasantha for letting me stay at his place in the heart of Bangalore during the interviews. He has saved me at least 50 hours of commute. Thanks to Dr Sushil whose wonderful remote cottage in Satoli, Uttarakhand, and Uma, whose guesthouse in Auroville provided me the perfect silent places to contemplate.

My deepest gratitude to my editor, Manisha Mathews, for understanding my vision and truly making this book more readable and perceptive. You made it easy for me to share any concern day or night, thanks! I must also thank my literary agent, Anuj Bahri, whose insights are unparalleled.

Last but not the least, the founders and experts featured in this book were humble and wonderful to talk to. I thank them and their teams who cooperated with my exacting requests.